Also by Walt Prothero

Stalking Big Game, Stackpole
Stalking Trophy Mule Deer, Horizon
Me & Joe, Safari Press
Safari: A Dangerous Affair, Safari Press
Mule Deer Strategies, Lyons Press
Mule Deer Quest, Safari Press
The Dangerous Game, Safari Press

The

Fair Chase
Chronicles

WALT PROTHERO

Fulton Books
Meadville, PA

Published by Fulton Books 2022

ISBN 978-1-63985-099-0 (paperback)
ISBN 978-1-63985-101-0 (hardcover)
ISBN 978-1-63985-100-3 (digital)

Printed in the United States of America

Dedicated to John Wamback, Namibian professional hunter, who died of Covid in July of 2021.

I'll always remember those safari camps in the Namib, Kalahari, Caprivi, and Cuneneland.

Dedicated to Nikki and Rick Lovell for half a century of friendship and tolerance.

PROLOGUE

We hunters often see the term "fair chase," most often in the form of "fair chase hunting," in magazine advertisements for high fence hunting in South Africa and elsewhere, we hear it in hunting videos purchased at conventions, are bombarded with it in seminars and hunting books. Every modern hunter has heard it, but few agree on its meaning.

The term "fair chase" isn't an absolute, it's a matter of degree. No specific and comfortable definition exists. This hunt, say a boar hunt in Anatolia by moonlight, might be more fair chase than another hunt, like a pronghorn antelope hunt in Wyoming, or the other way around. (If you must have a concrete, concise definition, *Wikipedia* does as good a job as anyone and better than most.) So I'm not trying to define "fair chase" in this tome. Instead, I've written a variety of hunting narratives, essays and stories with varying degrees of fair chase and it's up to you to decide; it's not even important that you do. You can simply read the hunting tale for the enjoyment.

We can say, however, that some hunts are definitely *not* fair-chase, in my and many other opinions. I'm thinking specifically of those hunts where the game animal is restrained by high fences. Nearly any high fence hunt is not fair chase, because ultimately, the animal can't escape. The hunt conclusion and kill are a given, and that is not "hunting," another term that should be defined (Ortega y Gasset's *Meditations on Hunting* defines it very well, though not simply). Hunting must always contain an element of doubt, not a surety of kill. High fences that restrain game animals eliminate the chance that the animal can escape. Without that doubt, you have a trip to the market.

High fence hunting is becoming more common at least partly because wild lands and game are becoming more and more scarce (some texts aver 70% of large mammals in Africa have disappeared within the last half century; the figures are nearly as dismal elsewhere on the planet). Much of European hunting occurs behind escape-proof fences, and nearly all hunting within the Republic of South Africa is behind high fences though the area fenced is often tremendous, giving the illusion of fair-chase. Texas contains exotic species from other continents on high-fence ranches including sheep from the Middle-East, goat and antelope from India and Africa and other beasts. High fence deer and elk hunts are common on private lands throughout the U.S; indeed, the animals are bred on the game farm, inoculated and fed antibiotics and hormones, handled in corrals, and the "hunter" often selects the "trophy" beforehand by computer. I've heard the argument that a standard cattle fence in Texas isn't "high-fence," and that's true if the game animal isn't hindered by that fence, a deer or elk, for example. But a diminutive Middle-East *moufloni-form* sheep is hindered and is effectively restrained by that fence, so the fence is high enough.

Probably the second great danger to fair-chase hunting is the over-use of technology. Humans evolved to create new tools and weapons, and it started on the savanna of East Africa 1.5 million years ago when *Homo erectus* (*Homo sapiens'* direct ancestor), the first hominid to make serious wood and stone tools, evolved into eating meat and hunting game, and it hasn't slowed. When modern man began the Agricultural Revolution in the Tigris-Euphrates valleys and what is now the eastern Balkans 11,000 years ago, he gradually gave up the hunter-gatherer lifestyle. Growing crops and raising livestock increased the security of existence; humans no longer had to wander far and wide to find berries and gourds in the territory of an aggressive neighboring tribe, or risk drownings, snake bite and becoming "hors" for lions or leopards, or stomped into strawberry goo by a buffalo that resented having a spear stuck into it. Modern man post-Agricultural Revolution seldom must feed himself from hunting, so hunting evolved into "sport."

Humans couldn't give up technology, therefore they restrained themselves in its application when hunting became a "sport' (for lack of a better term). The word most likely comes from the Spanish *deporte*, meaning "to be in port." When a sailor is *de porte*, he is free to eat, drink, gamble, whore—sport.

As weapons became more sophisticated (bow, crossbow, gunpowder), man had to impose more and more restrictions on himself in the form of limited hunting seasons, bag limits, game laws, and today to rid himself of the technological gadgetry that reduces the chance of the game to practice its evolved wiles that allow for escape. Without those self-imposed technological restraints, the game hasn't a chance. Increased technology in whatever form reduces the chance the game has of escape because it makes the hunter and prey too unequal. What modern hunting humans must do in today's hunting climate is to reduce technology to the bare minimum to maintain any semblance of fair chase. I've seen too many hunters loaded with so much technology, including tech that baffles me, they mimic a grunt in Afghanistan. This is perhaps the toughest thing hunters must do to keep hunting as fair chase as it is, because we're technological beasts. I started hunting with a binocular, belt knife and rifle half a century ago. I added a riflescope in that time because my boyhood heroes like Russell Annabel, Ted Trueblood and Jack O'Conner used them. I couldn't discard them and go back, either, but I refuse to use any more technology than I started with. I want to struggle for the animal trophy, to strive, and to doubt. Every true hunter battles most the beast's absence and scarcity, and these give we hunters the struggle of fair chase hunting. Reduce that struggle, reduce the game's absence and scarcity, reduce the doubt of a successful kill, and you reduce the degree of fair chase.

In today's morphing hunting world, restraint is the most powerful weapon in preserving fair chase. Without that restraint in the overuse of technology, hunting is most endangered from within hunter ranks. Anti-hunting sentiments are merely expressions of what we hunters would see if we looked in the mirror.

Non-hunter sentiments are complicated. First, we hunters must face those non-hunting citizens sitting on the fence, who have made no decision on whether or not hunting should exist in the 21st century. They are the hunters' single most important hope, because there are millions of them and ultimately, those millions will decide if hunting will continue in the 21st century.

I've taught in the university for decades, and I'm familiar with passive anti-hunters, the second category, and many of my colleagues are; they dislike the idea of killing game for enjoyment, the disappearance of game animals around the world though largely sport hunting plays little or no part in that, but they are not rabid about it. Many of my best friends are passive anti-hunters and have ogled the several hundred game trophies in my house and still bend an elbow with me. Indeed, I've had civil and enjoyable hunting conversations with them over a single-malt Scotch whiskey.

Then there's the anti-hunting activist. They are absolutely certain about something where certainty is impossible. These are the people picketing and vandalizing hunters' homes, that intimidate those entering various hunter conventions (such as the Safari Club International's last convention in Reno). Several years ago, those activists protesting the pending auction of a black rhinoceros hunting tag in Dallas (including some of the press that made it into a media spectacle) entertained no doubts about their righteousness. No matter that the individual bull rhino targeted by wildlife biologists and that the wealthy and successfully bidding sportsman would bag was long past its prime, would die of natural causes soon anyway, had killed several other very endangered rhinos in its senile rages (it would have been destroyed by biologists even without the auction), and that funds generated from the auction would funnel into black rhinoceros conservation in Namibia. The Namibian game biologists and Dallas Safari Club honchos hoped for a million dollar bid; what they got was a third that. What the activists had accomplished in their self-righteous zeal and intimidation was far less funds going to highly endangered black rhinoceros research and conservation. None of the activists had any idea of the ramifications of the auction, or of their threatening protests, nor wanted to know.

The brutal surety of anti-hunting activism in the guise of tender concern for all species, is a form of barbarism similar to Hitler's certainty of Arian superiority and fed by a virulent form of ignorance. I have no patience with the anti-hunting activist or any other fool so sure in his own sanctity that he (and perhaps more often "she"; use of the third person "he" here refers to the human species itself, not to gender) can't listen to the other side of any argument. That conviction means that the activist is incapable of learning (A wise man changes his mind many times, a fool never). Fortunately, in more than four decades of university teaching, I have taught very, very few such bigots, which gives me hope in our future leaders. They will, with any luck, govern with that same classroom rationality.

*****

The first chapters of this book contain the more overt "fair chase" or ethics essays. Later narrative essays or stories are tales of the hunt, but deal with the metaphor of fair chase. The fair chase theme is always present, but the narratives are entertainment enough, I hope.

Those hunters that aren't so philosophically inclined, will find hunting action in all stories or essays, but the hunting story itself is strongest later in the book. In these stories, one need not concern himself with the metaphor behind the death of a trophy buck or ram, unless he's so inclined. There's nothing wrong with reading a story simply for entertainment. I do it all the time.

For those that skip around when reading an apt book, my favorite stories are: "Rite of Passage," "Saga of the One-Eyed Bull" (this was published first in *Field & Stream* and later in the anthology *The Best of Field & Stream—100 Years of Great Writing)*," "Joe Everyman," and "Hunter, Look in the Mirror."

Many of the stories or essays in this book have appeared in magazines, especially *Field & Stream, Outdoor Life, Gray's Sporting Journal, Sports Afield, Wild Sheep* and others. I was an editor and appeared on the masthead of all of those mentioned except *GSJ*.

EXPEDITIONS

More than half a century ago Jack O'Connor bemoaned the passing of extended pack hunts into wild North America. The modern sportsman of the mid-twentieth century no longer owned the commitment, time, or will to bivouac in sodden wall tents in wilderness for two months merely to collect a ram, goat or grizzly. They wouldn't leave the old salt mine, the wife or civilized comforts that long, it seemed.

Modern nimrods haven't improved, and big wilderness continues to vaporize, further morphing expedition-type hunts into historical curiosities. Why make that kind of commitment when you can Cessna to a hunt camp in 40 minutes, stalk a ram the guides had pegged just for you, hook a mess of grayling, wing back to civilization and catch the first Series game at the sports bar in days? If you're like the modern shooters I know, you wouldn't. The goal these days is tacking another head on the wall in the least possible time. The total experience—ogling John Huston sunsets, slogging snow drifts, finger-and-toeing scree, enduring blisters and soggy boots day after day—is to be avoided. That's modern hunt philosophy and outfitters know it. Namibian outfitter John Wamback told me that he did whatever the client wanted, period, so he shielded clients from mosquitos, dust, physical exertion meaning hiking, and any unpleasantness. Wamback was one of the more fair-chase professional hunters, too, and later specialized in back-packing safaris for those few nimrods that desired them.

I don't mean to editorialize here or point fingers. Heck, I admit it, I've booked hunts merely because they fit a three-day gap in my schedule. But in the decades, in 300 North American hunts, in more than a dozen real (meaning *wild* and unfenced) African safaris and at least that many shebangs in Europe, and in two dozen shikars in Asia, I got lucky and made a handful of those historical curiosities I mentioned, the hunt expedition.

*****

Mongolia, 2007: Speak of accidents. We'd journeyed to the Gobi Desert the previous December in temps that seldom climbed above twenty below zero and sand gales that would pluck a capercaillie, just to score an argali. Perhaps because the outfitter failed to secure a tag, a typo on the gun permit and other oddities that remain murky, we didn't, though we bagged a stunning Gobi ibex. But when you fail at argali sheep, everything else is mere consolation. Baasanhu Jantzen felt badly enough about it to offer us the argali hunt again the next spring, he'd even throw in an Altai ibex, and after agreeing on price, I left my pet .300 Winchester magnum with him to avoid the hassle of getting it back into the States.

It's May, and we catch the morning flight out of Seoul and make Ulan Bator in afternoon. Baasanhu and famed guide Zorig grab our gear, this time Delta Airlines doesn't lose it in 'Frisco, and sardine it into the Russian *Uaz* jeep. Zorig's wife Erdensetsag, Erka for short, hunkers buried in gear enough for five people to last 3000 kilometers of cross-country argosy into the most remote geography in Central Asia.

We're so pumped we aim straight out of Ulan Bator, leave Mongolia's few miles of decaying pavement and not-so-arguably the dirtiest coal-fouled atmosphere on the planet behind, and take a compass heading southwest toward the Hanghai Mountains. Zorig (rural nomads own only one name) drives like he's leading the Baja 500 on the odd dirt road but mostly roadless gravel desert. I chomp and bloody my lip when he caroms a gully. I envy his kidney belt, too. We make Luya's ger (the Mongol *yurt*) camp in the night, and we stagger from that jeep beating. In the dawn we're glassing from a Gobi scarp. No one wastes time. Cheri eyeballs eight rams trotting out of the eastern gravel wastes as they lope across the drainage that's become the so-called official east boundary between Gobi and Hanghai argali terrain. They disappear into on-end geography. We trek from scarp to crag and glass, and after two hours, Cheri ogles them again. She doesn't come on these expeditions to be ornamental; she's owns game eyes with the best.

To shorten a long story, we blow the stalk, find the rams again, stalk and fail again, I miss a gimme shot because of unholy overconfidence, and in late afternoon eventually catch them. I slap the big ram on the gravel and fully relax for the first time since December. I don't even care about that ibex that's still on the docket, I'm so high—if I score the ibex, fine, and if not, also fine. For those into stats, the ram tapes 50 x 19 inches, and might be the most stunning thing I've ever seen. Chinese wine with argali stew that evening top off what is one of those handful of glorious days afield I'll remember 'til I die. Hold on, though, this is just the first day.

We're in no hurry and it's my habit to take a day off after scoring one of those trophies of your life, and just absorb. Two dawns later we jeep westerly cross-country again and lunch at Orog Lake, a verdant oasis in the gravel wastes. White *gers* pock the emerald grass like so many magnum hail stones, and sheep, camels and horses graze the green. The *Uaz* then probes west toward the south Altai, loses its way until a wandering nomad draws us a map in the sand, and drops onto another endless gravel plain. Our eye sockets are ghostly white against grey dust-layered faces when we remove sunglasses, and surreal five-inch dust devils whirl about inside the jeep. In the afternoon we consult another nomad and his sand map at a *ger* encampment in a trailless canyon choked with winter overflow ice. I don't care if we're lost, those argali horns are tucked in back and I chuckle each time I think of them. No road maps, GPS, road signs and very few dirt roads exist in these wastes, but the nomad points us in the right direction. The Mongol trail leads into the Edren scarps and Zorig says that very big ibex wander the geography because no western hunter has been there and nomads don't care about big horns, only meat. As we descend a bluffed canyon into setting sun, we spy a village far out on the gravel plain.

"There we sleep," Basaan says, and Erka grins. We find a dirt road and motor to a decrepit adobe USAID midwifery. "Here the nomads have babies."

Before the guys unload the gear, Erka shoves into Cheri's and my room with steaming supper cooked on a Coleman. The building owns no toilets so we're pointed to the overflowing village outhouse. We use an alley like everyone else. A woman tells us with glee that a nomad died of bubonic plague in our room last summer. We flee next dawn, and I pray what I hope are voracious bedbug bites aren't from plague-toting fleas.

We're still aiming southwest toward the south Altai Range and grand ibex. We spot foxes and jolt down the creek bed of another bouldered canyon and onto gravel desert and gasp at a long mountain reclining on the plain.

"*Eej Khairkhan*," Zorig tells us. I ask the meaning, but he feigns ignorance. Khairkhan has a sense of the sacred to it, and the term is used to avoid its real name. The gods anger if anyone speaks the real name.

"The Sacred Mountain," Baasan lies. "Women pilgrimage and circle the mountain to get pregnant." Later, I learn that part of the story is true.

We motor into another canyon and across overflow ice that if it collapses would plunge us eight feet to the creek bed below. We survive the ice, thank the Red Gods, and lunch with a nomad family. I'm always awed by Mongol hospitality; though poor as Gobi gravel, they share whatever they have without expectation of payment. It's the nomad way. After sipping fermented mare's milk, I slip them a twenty out of guilt and slightly alcoholic good will, and they discuss it with baffled curiosity. They've never seen one. We're off after lunch and the jeep grinds up-canyon always southwest, and three hours later onto an alpine plateau with 15-foot snow drifts on the lee of the 11,000 foot ridges of the south Altai Mountains.

Zorig sighs audibly when we spy two *gers* between distant snow-fields. Apparently, the nomads erected them for us by previous agreement. The jeep isn't big enough to tote a *ger*, either. We stow gear and again Erka serves another of those short-notice wonder dinners. Cheri and I get one *ger*, and the guys the other. We scope ibex that evening, and in sand-hazy distance gaze into Chinese Mongolia.

Great 60-inch argali and ancient ibex skulls litter the high plateau. *"Dzug,"* a years-long drought followed by an extended 60-below zero cold, Zorig explains. The *Dzug* wiped out the argali for good, since they no longer exist in that geography.

We're glassing next sunup. "There!" Cheri says. "Standing in the sun across the gorge." She's found King Kong again. The ibex would measure 45 inches or more. He beds while the other billies feed. "He's a Methuselah."

We make a three-hour stalk and late that afternoon, I drop him with a single shot at 290 meters. The billy owns 14 annular horn rings and four teeth and wouldn't have survived the year. You like to get them like that. It doesn't beat the argali, but it gives elation enough for anyone, and I punch a fist into the cerulean Mongol sky as we grunt the meat and trophy out of the gorge.

We take a day off and hike the scarps next day, glass ibex and a lynx, sup on ibex so tough you have to swallow chunks whole, and that Chinese wine, and revel in the unhurried hunting. No one is pushed on an extended expedition, and we all have time to enjoy the pace. We do little the following day, either, but savor the geography and camaraderie. The time to relax is an added benefit to an expedition. Those undergraduate compositions I haven't graded or the neighbor's barking dog haven't crossed my mind since I stepped off the plane in Ulan.

Days later we work the jeep northwest through bouldered trailless canyons and around tremendous snowfields and finally down onto the Altai foothills. We glass from dramatic sandstone phalluses and spot gazelle, too, but none we can stalk, and then we motor out onto the western Gobi, not even dirt roads now, and north toward the town of Altay and maybe a flight back to the capital. The plane doesn't show up that day or the one after in spite of the official schedule scrawled on a small blackboard, no surprise in Mongolia, but we've still got time so we motor back into the Gobi, score a magnum

17

black-tailed goitered gazelle, exchange ibex blood Baasan collected in plastic pop bottles for camel's milk chilled in a spring, and sleep in very decrepit roadhouses on the dirt "highway" back east to Ulan. Then it's north toward the Siberian border, and in a week I score a Mongolian roe buck with a 14-inch beam.

After 3000 kilometers of dirt, part of me longs for crisp white sheets and a scalding bath, but the other part doesn't want to end what I know will become one of the grandest expeditions of my life. I'll miss the sweat streaks in the dust on our faces, the filthy hair, and Zorig's snoring in the next *ger*.

TANZANIA, 1993: It didn't start well. Delta Airlines left the big hard case and my .375 and 7mm/08 back in Salt Lake City or New York, the KLM officials explained. It never got onto the KLM flight to Amsterdam. We hung around Arusha baggage claim until long after everyone had left, though, hoping against hopes.

After a night in a hotel adapted from a colonial coffee *shamba*, we began a month *shauri* in East Africa. We climbed into a circa 1970 polychrome VW van and aimed toward a colonial hotel on the rim of *Ngoro Ngoro* Crater. Thirteen hours of washboard and potholed roads hub-deep in dust battered us into quivering lumps, and we staggered into the cinder block rondavel that became our home. No better place to view the Big Five and scores of other beasts exists in Africa, and we spent the best part of a week photographing them. Then we caromed across the 4WD trails that pass for roads to *Olduvai* Gorge, home of Leakey's earliest *hominid* fossils and the cradle of modern human evolution. We inadvertently began to follow Hemingway's expedition that produced his book *Green Hills of Africa* across the high plateau and through native *shambas* scattered across the verdant green before the van dropped down the Rift Escarpment on a red-dirt trail to the dry-dusty lowlands and Lake Manyara. We photographed hippo, wildebeest and crocodile where Hemingway hunted rhino, too.

By the time we made Arusha again, dust-coated and weary, my guns had turned up, to my immense relief. Next day we bush-planed west over wildebeest herds flattened with altitude and buffalo bedded in the *mopane* scrub to Inyonga village, and from there we motored into the tangled savannas five hours to the safari camp on the Msima River. The camp tents scattered between gun barrel straight palms and dreadlocks papyrus beside marabou storks and snowy-white egrets hunting the green of the bog seemed out of an old Stuart Granger flick.

Next dawn we're hunting antelope and anything else we can score for cat baits. I really made the safari to bag a hairy lion, with leopard, buffalo, lesser kudu, fringe-eared oryx, roan and other antelope as gravy. Though I'd bagged buff in Botswana and elsewhere, they're always adrenaline-pumping hunting and I have three on my license. We score two topi antelope for cat baits and impala for camp meat that first day, but find only old lion spoor. We spot scores of common and *bohor* reedbuck, a dozen warthogs, and cow roan antelope. We revel in the hunting, no hurry in those early days of the safari, hunting whatever might turn up. We just know we'll score a lion.

Days turn into weeks, and we hear no lions roaring in the night, see no fresh lion spoor, spot no vultures dropping to kills. We put a grand roan antelope in the salt, bag two good buffalo, a trophy topi, Defassa waterbuck, and we've got male leopards working baits. But through it all, no lions. The early unhurried hunting turns a little desperate.

After six afternoons and evenings in a blind, we bag a grand Spots in the last light. The skinners, trackers and camp staff chant and carry me on shoulders in camp that night. All cats are a big deal. In later weeks, we bag more antelope of various species, but can't find *Simba*.

And then it's days journeying east to South Maasailand and the Maasai Steppe.

"You'll get a lion there," PH Larry Richards assures. I've become tense, but it's the best of tension when it's hunting something you want so badly it wakes you in the night and causes headaches you can only cure with a double Scotch.

That first night in the Maasailand camp with the initials "EH" carved ten feet up a fever tree that we like to believe belonged to Ernest Hemingway (his safari in *Green Hills of Africa* happened very near this place), lions roaring and grunting in the predawn wake us not far up the stream that's the only water within 30 kilometers. We don't score them the next dawn, or the next, but another evening a Maasai runner trots into camp and tells us the big pride is hunting buffalo in the Two-Mile Thicket, and that surely they made a kill and we'll find them there in the dawn.

The Land Cruiser grinds out of camp in the predawn black, passes the Maasai village and slips down the sandy track as black fades to gray.

Just before sunup Gabreli, the head tracker, hisses, "*Simba!*" Vultures hunch in the big acacia trees, and we know lions are on a buffalo kill. To shorten a long and adrenalin-pumping story, I shoot, score a hit I'm sure is fatal but nobody else is, and we track the hairy lion into thorn scrub so thick we have to belly through it, all the while expecting the charge no one will be able to do anything about, and find a quarter ton of cat stone dead with 300 grains of copper and lead through the heart. The hairy lion is a famed cattle killer, and the local Maasai assure us it has mauled herders, and that night they and we throw a grand and ecstatic *ngoma* with antediluvian chanting and dancing and spears glinting in the firelight and the hissing lanterns, I'm carried on shoulders again, this time to the *simis*—a native dagger—slapping buffalo hide shields to a rhythm that touches a genetic memory, and the grand dry-bloody lion skull rests on the dining table as we sup on kudu chops and quaff too much Lion Lager and I never felt finer, ever.

Everything else in anticlimax, but anticlimax I wouldn't miss for anything. I collect my other buff after it gets up again from looking as dead as anything can and I blast it again so close it sprays my chukkas with gore. The government game scout asks us to deal with two buffalo that are killing Maasai cattle at a distant waterhole, and we do. I score a grand battler of a lesser kudu, a very good fringe-eared oryx, Grant's gazelle, and what everyone believes is a world record East African greater kudu. I consult Hemingway's *Green Hills of Africa*, and find that except for the Msima terrain, we've largely traced the country he'd hunted. Perhaps that "EH" on the camp fever tree is genuine.

In spite of an atrocious Texan outfitter we'll call "S & S" that I am told has been sued out of the business, the camp staff—trackers, skinners, cooks and others—couldn't have been grander. You can't experience the country and the hunting and the people in any other way than taking time, and an expedition is the way to do it.

*****

Lucky me—I've made other extended hunting expeditions. In the decade from 1981 to 1990, I, and then later "we" when Cheri joined up, made annual five to nine-week expeditions into true Arctic wilderness 300 miles from the nearest pavement and hospital. The drill: Arctic bush pilots Roger Dowding or Joe Firmin flew us to the upper Sheenjek or Coleen River drainages, landed the Cessna 185 or 206 on a river bar or dry lake bed, and then Cheri and I would trek into and out of the sheep scarps for weeks at a time, and then eventually float-hunt out, either to the bush village of Fort Yukon or a river bar on the Porcupine River many weeks later, where we'd meet up with the bush pilots again and they'd fly us to my log cabin up the Yukon River. Neither of us were in any hurry to travel out to our second house at Harding Lake near Fairbanks for more civilized comforts, like pizza, phones, and hot showers.

All this in those golden years before the cell phone, and we didn't carry radios because of the weight, I told myself, but really because we cherished the true solitude that even the presence of a radio would destroy. We relied totally on ourselves, lived off the land and the meat we'd bag and what little canned and dehydrated grub we could sardine into the 185. On any given year we could bag Dall sheep, moose, caribou, grizzly, and we had the best ptarmigan shooting ever, and as many 2 lb. grayling as we cared to hook on smoke-colored dry flies. We both plan to scatter our ashes in that magic place—we think of it as our Nirvana. I wrote about it in one of my books, *The Dangerous Game*, and in *Field & Stream*, *Outdoor Life* and other magazines, and I'm now putting together a book devoted solely to those wine and roses years.

And a bit farther back into history, I solo expeditioned into the Beartooth-Absaroka Wilderness north of Yellowstone Park with a Montana combo license in my pocket and hunted bighorns, elk, deer, black bear and fished. I led a packhorse afoot, backpacked, and waited out days-long blizzards and a lighting-caused forest fire and wished I'd been conceived a century earlier.

*****

I've survived long enough and the Red Gods smiled enough that I've made other expeditions, too. Like I said, you can't fully experience the terrain, the wildlife, the solitude, the people, the hunting, or yourself in any other way. I know sports that own trophy rooms with 200 mounts that haven't made a single extended expedition-style hunt. Hunting's focus has changed over the decades, and not many modern hunters have any desire to aim out into the remote bush for a month or two at a time. The young hunters coming up stand only a slim chance of making a true expedition. I pity them all.

HUNTER, LOOK IN THE MIRROR

O n a bad day, after a suicide bombing in Iraq, say, or another psycho runs amok with an assault rifle, I take faith. In American young people, that is.

I'm lucky because I occasionally talk to college students about hunting. I teach in university zoology and English departments, but in addition I'm often the token guest hunter in seminars or courses on topics ranging from the "Human Omnivore," a Weber State University honors class, to conservation biology courses at the University of Utah, to panels discussing hunting often composed of non-hunters. Nearly all of my audiences are non-hunters, and most of them are open-minded. These are the audiences we hunters must reach if hunting is to continue in our western culture, since we can no longer claim to hunt for food.

Statistics are only part of the question, too. Sure, we hunters foot much of the bill for conserving species, we spend millions on guzzlers and wildlife acreage and we feed starving wildlife in Mongolia, but those stats count zero when non-hunters are concerned about ethics, morality and what many hunters dismiss as "tree-hugging" sentimentality. We can't answer those subjective concerns with a bushel-basket of objective statistics.

Yes, I begin my lectures with those statistics, since on a per capita basis we hunters spend more than nearly any conservation group. Students accept those stats with raised eyebrows, and one University of Utah senior ran the numbers I gave the group through a computer to check my math. "You're dead-on," he said with surprise. After the stats, though, most of my sessions drift into student questions on hunting ethics and morality, and not because these students have already made up their minds, but because they want to decide. It's up to we hunters to help, and dismissing their beliefs as "tree-hugging" won't do it. That too common hunter arrogance is a fast track to losing the audience that will determine the future of hunting, our future. That's not to say objective data and logic haven't a place here, because in any argument, logic takes the fore. It is to say, though, that we must consider all of their concerns with respect.

Selected student Questions and my Answers:

Q: "Do you eat what you shoot?"

A: "Yes. Any red meat and most fowl I eat is game meat. I also hunt overseas, and you can't import game meat into this country, however I eat some there and nearly all of it goes to local peoples that are often protein-starved." [At this point, I show old-fashioned 35mm Kodachrome slides of 60 Caprivi natives butchering a rogue bull elephant I bagged and carting off the bloody meat; the elephant destroyed crops the starving people relied upon for the year, and the occasional farmer that got in its way].

Q: "Americans don't have to kill game to eat. Why do you do it?"

A: "It's healthier than domestic meat. Studies say 70% of all antibiotics are given to the livestock we eat, thus contributing to the world crisis of antibiotic-resistant pathogens. We scarf various livestock hormones with our T-bones and burgers, and domestic red meat is higher in saturated fats and LDLs, contributing to a western epidemic of colon cancer and cardiovascular disease. I've had students ask where they can get game meat, because of health concerns. We've all heard the horror stories of feedlot and chicken factory cruelty, so I'm not going to regurgitate them. Hunting is more humane, it's healthier, and I'd do it anyway because I love it. I plan one or two deer hunts a year simply to fill the freezer. Most hunters eat at least part of the animal they bag.

"I also hunt overseas, it's costly, and remember that cost goes largely to conserving the species, so I don't do it for food; however, I'll always eat some of what I shoot, be it a rogue elephant or man-eating crocodile. Yes it's symbolic, but we can't ignore those stats; hunters largely pay for those animals and in many cases worldwide, those animals wouldn't exist without hunters. Ironic, I know, that hunting and killing wildlife actually preserves its existence." [Here, I detail how this works in places like Tajikistan and Tanzania, usually accompanied with more slides that include dead and often bloody game animals; sanitizing hunting photos won't fool students].

The state of Utah auctioned off a mule deer tag for nearly a quarter million dollars on Antelope Island in the Great Salt Lake. That tag was featured in local newspapers and TV, and it bothered people.

Q: (This from the class professor) "Has hunting become the realm of the wealthy?"

A: "To a large extent, yes. But with 8 billion hominids on the planet, wildlife habitat is disappearing and wild game along with it (something like 70% of all megafauna species have disappeared in the last half century). It is, unfortunately, a matter of supply and demand. That deer tag is an extreme, but a recent Montana governor's bighorn sheep tag auctioned at double that figure. If there's a good side, most of those dollars go directly to conserving the species hunted and many non-hunted species. Most of us can't afford those game tags, but some exist that we can afford. That said, I don't justify those extreme auctions because they give the wrong message to the public, yet I haven't an alternative that would put so much money in conservation coffers, either." [I then compare and contrast safaris and shikars I've made decades ago in places like Botswana and Mongolia using my slides again, with current prices for those same hunts. In many cases, those hunt prices have tripled or even quadrupled. I also ask the group if they've got a viable alternative.]

Q: "What about 30-shot pistol clips, assault rifles, and the NRA?"

A: "Hunters don't use 30-round clips and none I know use assault rifles. You're talking now of the gun rights question, and that's different than hunting. Let's head this off—yes, the NRA is a PAC; no, I don't belong but I used to and only a few hunters

I know do; yes, I own handguns, but no 30-round clips; yes, I own a dozen firearms. Now, let's get back to hunting."

Q: "Why do you hunt?"

A: "This is the toughest question I face, and I'm not trying to blow it off here.

It sounds trite, I know, but I must. Human nature is still inseparable from hunting and killing, and it's genetic. We would not have evolved iPods or any modern technology without it, and it perhaps started with *Homo erectus* improving upon the latest stone or wood hunting implement.

Second, I'm more involved at all levels—intellectual, physical, emotional—than in anything I've done. Few of us must hunt for meat, and I no longer do it to tack another trophy animal head on the wall, which leaves only the total experience—the nicker of a pack horse in a Canadian Rockies camp, lions roaring in the night on the Maasai Steppe, and campfire smoke in my eyes. I know this is a non-answer, but it's the best I can do. I hear this question once a month, and it always troubles me."

Q: "How ethical is hunting fenced game, and the people you hear of that order a Texas farm deer by computer and have it executed?"

A: "You're making me work. I know people that have hunted in high-fence situations where the animals can't escape, ultimately, and a few say it's no slam-dunk. Most if not all Republic of South Africa plains safaris are high-fence, and sadly desert bighorn sheep hunting in Mexico has morphed into largely fenced propositions, not to mention hunts for exotic species that may no longer exist in their native habitats in India or elsewhere. Any fenced hunt largely eliminates the chance of not bagging the game, thus eliminating the "hunting" part of the whole enterprise. I won't do or condone it, but if others want to, let them. Democracy can't exist without tolerance for the other guy, even if he disagrees with you. With the burgeoning human population, we may have no choice anyway.

"I've heard about the Texas deer thing, and I'm not sure if this is an urban myth like the crocodiles in the sewers of New York, or not. If it isn't, it doesn't bear the slightest resemblance to any hunting most hunters do. If it exists, it's an extreme. I do know you can order freaky-huge, hormone-pumped farmed whitetail deer or elk off the computer, and then "hunt" them behind a fence. I do not approve, it horrifies non-hunters and ethical hunters, but I won't go so far as to say it should be unlawful. Who knows? With the increasing human population, all so-called future "hunting" may become that controlled. Happily, I'll be dead then."

Q: "And you don't think hunting is cruel?"

A: "Many hunters I know won't take a shot unless they're reasonably certain they can make a clean kill. If they wound an animal, they beat themselves up over it. Hunters work at marksmanship so wounding doesn't occur. Hunting is more humane than any cattle feedlot or chicken farm I've seen and I've known people that owned them, and it's more humane than most slaughter-houses—I worked in one as an undergrad [Here, I throw in an anecdote or two]. In a real sense, anytime we order a Big Mac, we're practicing animal cruelty; we may not throw the switch that shocks the beasts senseless on the kill floor, or personally condemn cattle to living hock-deep in manure, but we pay the people that do. On the flip side, many hunters treat bird dogs as part of the family, get involved in community philanthropy such as volunteering at homeless shelters, and I capture any spider I find in the house and turn it loose outdoors. I go through $2,000 worth of wild birdseed and nearly that in deer feed mix each year and bird watching is an almost daily part of my life, and I plant flowers that attract butterflies. We hunters are not cave-dwelling ogres. That's ironic to many."

Q: "You see hunters in their camo outfits roaring around the back roads on ATVs with rifles across the handlebars. How is this sporting?"

A: Hunting is a life philosophy; see, for example, Jose Ortega y Gasset's *Meditations on Hunting*. Calling hunting a sport is possibly trivializing it and that life a hunter takes.

"Second, yes, we use too much technology in hunting, but humans have evolved to make things easier, to improve technology, and I don't know that there's a thing we can do about it. It started with wood and stone tools early hominids used to make it easier and safer to kill big beasts on African savannas at least a million years ago, and it hasn't stopped. The more technology anyone uses in hunting, from simple range finders to lasers and digital riflescopes and gadgetry I no longer understand, the more we remove ourselves from those things we go afield for in the first place—physical challenge, pitting yourself against the game in its native habitat, patience, knowledge of bush lore, and the sting of snow pelting you in the face. Some good men of my acquaintance tote so much gadgetry afield they look like they are going to war. I carry a rifle, folding knife and compact binocular, period. Yes, it's gadgetry, but it's what I learned with and it's tough to go back to an earlier time and hunt with, say, a spear. Still, simpler is better. Remember Thoreau's 'simplify, simplify?'"

Q: "How do you feel when you kill an animal?"

A: "'Every good hunter is uneasy in the depths of his conscience when faced with the death he is about to inflict on the enchanting animal.' So says Ortega y Gasset.

"I think about what I've done. It always bothers me at some level. I try to honor the animal, whatever that means. Once I walked off and sat on a termite mound in Botswana while the trackers skinned a buffalo I'd shot, and tried to think of the bull's life. Sounds corny, I know. Europeans place a plant sprig in the quarry's mouth, and may give the hunter another sprig if the hunt was honorable. A Shuswap Indian guide smeared blood of the buck I'd shot on my face as a hunter's rite of passage; of course I was a youngster then. I've seen mountain sheep hunters shed tears at a trophy animal's death, and not tears of relief because sheep hunts are expensive. When I shot my first pronghorn as a 17-year-old college freshman, I walked off into the sagebrush because I couldn't speak for the lump in my throat. I could go on and on, but any ethical, concerned hunter ponders his killing to some degree. After all, he has just taken a consciousness. Ortega y Gasset again: '...the greatest and most moral homage we can pay to certain animals is to kill them with certain means and rituals.'

"I cringe when I see videos of camo-clad troglodytes hooting and hollering and dramatizing an animal they've blasted; unfortunately, these are too often the images the public sees. Like anyone else, hunters aren't perfect."

I've had scores of students ask how they could start hunting. Of course, I try to help. One woman student wanted me to take her along. The hunting topic fascinates young non-hunters, I'm talking about anyone under 35 here, including those that have no intention of ever hunting. We hunters own an incredible opportunity now— an open-minded and largely sympathetic audience.

We're lucky, but only for the moment. Young people are still as broad-minded as we hunters should be. They can still change their minds and form new opinions. They are tomorrow's voters, CEOs, government decision-makers, and PAC directors. What decisions will they form when we hunters in our smug arrogance dismiss their concerns as tree-hugging sentimentality?

ETHICAL CHASE?

Hunting mountain game is still largely an ethical proposition. I'll teeter on a crag here, and say that North American sheep hunters are the most ethical nimrods on the planet. After all, wild sheep and goat hunters must be fanatically devoted (demented?) to hunt a beast that might require weeks grunting a backpack heavy enough to fuse vertebrae through dog-hair blowdowns or chest-deep glacial torrents, or finger-and-toe vertical, pucker-class geography for 38 days as I've done. In other words, it's tougher to cheat on sheep and goat hunts.

Sure, we're all ethical hunters, right? But what does it mean? The Boone and Crockett Club has overseen hunter ethics for over a century—its publication is entitled *Fair Chase*. Their position statement defines fair chase as, "the ethical, sportsmanlike, and lawful pursuit and taking of any free-ranging wild, native North American big game animal in a manner that does not give the hunter an improper advantage over such animals." Sounds good, but many of the terms used in the definition should themselves be defined. Are your ethical standards the same as a suicide bomber in a Kabul market; is end zone dancing sportsmanlike; and is hunting in a many-square mile enclosure free-range? It's sometimes tough deciding, and therein lies the need for more objective definition.

The B & C Club recognizes the limitation, and in another paragraph states, "…ethics in hunting ultimately rest with the individual…" So we're back to the original question—what, exactly, is ethical or fair chase hunting?

The Boone and Crockett Club's influence is planet-wide; when I try to pin Europeans and Africans down on hunting ethics, I'm invariably referred to the Club's position statements. Definitions vary widely between hunters and countries, and I've had heated discussions in Austria, Botswana, Russia and elsewhere over those definitions.

*****

I began forming my own ideas of hunt ethics nearly half-a-century ago when I bagged my first Coues deer in Mexico as a precocial ten-year-old. Those were the days of mule pack trains, roadless Sierra Madre wilderness, and Jack O'Connor. In high school I spent months listing "Hunting Commandments."

Let's deal with those commandments, somewhat refined and polished over the decades because hunters and hunting continue to evolve.

The first commandment—the quarry shall be native to the place hunted. Otherwise, doesn't hunting become a bit like shooting in a safari park zoo? I've tried to adhere to this through half a century, and so far, I believe I have. I've zero interest in hunting Old World ibex in New Mexico or any of the various beasts including sheep from the Middle East and elsewhere roaming U.S. ranches and foreign estates. Utah owns hunt-able populations of mountain goats in places where they never existed. If you want to hunt them, since they're already there, go ahead, but not me. I've been called an elitist and worse on this, too. I've good pals that have hunted these animals, though, and we still bend an elbow together. If you can't agree with me, remember democracy requires tolerance.

Other game animals are more confusing. Take European mouflon, for example. Biologists disagree on mouflon evolution—some say it's native to Sardinia and Corsica, others swear it's ancestor to domestic sheep, and still others believe it's a feral descendant of domestic sheep. Some evidence says they've migrated into Europe millennia ago from the Middle-East; for proof, I've seen paleolithic (long before animal domestication) sheep glyphs in the limestone scarps in Bosnia, and the Hotel Biokovo in Makarska, Croatia, owns a heroic ram as its logo; the concierge assures me it's a depiction of rock art from a nearby cave. I'm not absolutely sold, so my free-range mouflon ram from the fenceless Peljesac Peninsula in Croatia hangs in a distant, dark corner of one of my trophy rooms. Another concern—some European mouflon are bagged behind fences and over grain baits, and that's unethical to many. Of course those mouflon outside of the Mediterranean region are not native (defining native is subject enough for another essay).

And what about alpine ibex in Europe? Good historical evidence says they were wiped out throughout their range except on one reserve in Italy, where ultimately all modern alpine ibex originate. Some biologists argue they now roam places where they've never been historically. Should we cut this impressive trophy out of our collections?

Let's discuss the second commandment. Thou shalt not hunt high-fenced game. Game movement shouldn't be hampered by fences or even natural obstructions, such as water surrounding an island. A December 2014 hunt for Austrian red stag made me reexamine this one; indeed, it motivated me to write this essay.

I'd labored under the impression we'd hunt free-range (another of those terms that must be defined) stag, and in the pre-hunt briefing I heard from the outfitter that stags can "…come in and they can go out" over low fences and broken high fences. To me, that meant free-range, at least in Europe; heck, we see low cattle fences throughout the U.S. and they hamper deer or elk not one whit. The outfitter drew a rough diagram of the large property on the Hungarian border, and he sketched in open gates, too. I'd hunted Europe enough to know hunting is often very controlled, so I didn't expect the kind of fair chase we'd see in Tajikistan's Pamirs, Tanzania's Maasai Steppe, or America's Rockies.

Now, I'm not blaming anyone. I picked up on what I wanted to hear—game could, "come in and they could go out,"—and perhaps ignored other clues as to the degree of free-range ethics, so it's my own fault. I admit it.

Well, I shot a grand stag, and we crossed into and out of fenced areas. I believed the high fences kept deer out of sensitive agricultural or re-seeded areas. The stag hunt wasn't a slam dunk, and a grand stag rocketed away from us through dreadlocks timber, and though we trailed it, we didn't catch it. The stag I bagged nearly made its get-away, too, so the hunt wasn't a given. The lease was so large I didn't see fences hamper deer movement in the least. So was this fair chase? Free-range? I doubt it, though it was entirely legal; fenced game hunting is popular in Europe, especially Austria. In dozens of com-munications with game managers, guides, outfitters, and guys like Andreas Duscher, CEO of the hunters' organization of Burgenland at the time, where I shot the stag, I've come to the conclusion that the fences kept game in, not out of sensitive areas. I'm also thinking that fair chase in the 21st century is a matter of degree ("How wild is our wildlife?" Duscher asks; and hunting should be "…as close as *possible* to a fair chase," according to Klaus Hacklaender). One hunter in Austria shot a very drugged stag; the guides told him it could barely stand because it was exhausted from rutting.

I like what Simon Gould in a *High Peak* newsletter (New Zealand) says: "If you don't ask…you risk being sold something that you didn't sign up for," and "…that trophy could be on your wall for many years to come."

A concern that's no doubt got fair chase patron saint Jack O'Connor whirling like a dervish in his grave is Mexican desert big-horn ranch hunts. The bighorns are shipped in cattle trucks from ranch to ranch, often simply to satisfy a hunter flying in from the States next week, and I've seen photos of rams sporting plastic ear tags crammed into enclosures like cattle. Wild?

Onto the third commandment. We hunters shall not eliminate any chance the quarry can detect us. Humans with our overwhelm-ing mental advantage must control our technological tendencies in hunting. Are heat-seeking bullets and drone hunting in our future? We're shoving along in that direction with techno geeks that can shoot half a mile plus, laser gadgetry, and robo riflescopes, and those guys kill beasts that have no possible way to detect them. Whatever happened to stalking and bush skills? The farther we remove ourselves from the travails of hunting—bellying through *chollal*, hunkering in a ten-below zero whiteout, spooring hours and miles across endless tundra—the less we hunt.

I once witnessed two corpulent "hunters" in northern Utah glass a very distant buck, unload a bench rest from the pickup bed, and start shooting. The buck had no inkling what was happening.

One fellow touched off. "Four feet left," the other guy said. The shooter made adjustments and fired again. The fellow watching through the spotting scope said, "Two feet high, two left." The buck danced between bullets powdering rock maybe a mile across the gorge.

They eventually scored a hit, and the buck dragged itself into the bottom and out of sight. They offered me a C note to retrieve the head, back when a Franklin was worth something. As a kid, I was tempted enough to do it. The shootists each scaling maybe 300 pounds couldn't waddle a block, let alone a mile straight into a gorge and back out. (To paraphrase Gretchen Stark's priceless quip, "…if you're too old and too fat, stay home.")

Sure, this is an extreme, but how many videos have we seen with the nimrod blasting a ram or billy at 500 yards plus? It takes far more skill to belly close. Heck, my wife Cheri bagged a 375-point bull elk a few seasons back with a single shot from her muzzle loader at 25 yards. It took hours to stalk the last quarter mile. Yes, I've shot bucks, rams and billies at 300 yards, but only if I could see no way to close the gap. Over the years I've put maybe 20 native wild sheep and that many native wild goats in the salt on three continents, and the average range in open alpine country worked out to 135 yards, and that's because I slaved to get intimate. I bagged a 40-inch Yakutsk snow sheep from 24 yards, and two 160-class Dall rams at just over that. What fun! I'm less thrilled about those long range shots I had to take.

The fourth commandment says to kill clean. And quick. It's related to the third, but it means closing the gap using bush skills and not a motor vehicle, to reduce any chance of wounding game. Most sheep hunters I know work at the rifle range so wounding doesn't occur, because they know they might be forced to shoot at longer ranges. That's a given in open sheep country, but if remotely possible, even sheep hunters must struggle to get close. Never shoot too far for your abilities. It's our responsibility to kill quick and clean, and we *should* agonize if we don't. In Europe and elsewhere, you pay for the beast you wound even if it escapes.

The above anecdote of the two obese deer hunters is just one example of what happens when we don't get close. Sure, if we hunt long enough, we wound an animal that we may or may not be able to retrieve. As a kid I spent 13 hours over two days tracking down a buck I wounded, (and later wrote an article about it for *Field & Stream*), and vowed never to take an "iffy" shot again.

To the fifth commandment, dear hunter. The quarry must be wild—that is, not born in captivity then years later turned out for the shoot. Here, good examples include whitetail and elk farms in the U.S. Shooters order heads over the internet, those hormone-pumped beasts are loosed in an enclosure, and shootists execute the buck or bull. Hard to believe, isn't it? What do you suppose the billions of non-hunters think? Remember, the non-hunting majority will determine the ultimate future of our passion, hunting, so appearance is critical. After all, majority rules.

"Sure," you say, "but these are deer. It can't happen with sheep or goats." Remember those Mexican ranch bighorn hunts, and what about exotic sheep on ranches and estates?

In Bosnia we couldn't score a chamois, a diminutive wild mountain "goat" more closely related to Asian goral and serow than true goats. "Ve cahn fix zees," the guide said. Seems he could arrange for chamois from a nearby estate to be turned loose in the crags. I declined.

The sixth commandment—hunters should not increase the mental, physical and philosophical distance between the quarry and the hunter. More technology always does it, and ditto anything that makes hunting too easy.

Half a dozen African professional hunters have assured me that many clients never leave the vehicle and bag all their trophies from the Land Cruiser high seat.

"We do what the client wants," that Namibian PH and pal said.

This is most true on plains game safaris on high fence farms in southern African countries. Botswana PH Willie Phillips asserted that even on wild safaris where no fences exist, 80-90% of African game is killed from the motor vehicle, often because shooters are too obese too leave it. I nearly came to blows with one Tanzanian PH because he insisted I shoot a magnum bushbuck from the Toyota. I know of European chamois and mouflon taken from motor vehicles, and exotic sheep on U.S. ranches, and at least one wild argali in fenceless Mongolia.

Another way to put it: The more we remove those things we went afield for in the first place—campfire smoke in our eyes, mosquitos and gnats, blisters and simplicity—the farther we step away from ethical hunting.

I'm not in the class of these guys, but I know men that quit centerfire hunting and took up the long bow.

The seventh commandment, that hunters should honor the ethics, customs, and habits of the place he is hunting, can be tough. The problem is that those customs or ethics may conflict with our own.

My first Zimbabwe leopard safari nearly four decades ago is a case in point. I'd read the old stories and seen the videos, and they shot leopards in the daylight. I never asked, but I assumed we'd hunt in daylight. Using spotlights to kill any game, even if it is legal, at night when it's more difficult to call your shot and avoid wounding is simply, black and white, breaking several of my ethical hunting commandments. What could I do? Go home and eat the deposit, or give it a try?

We set up three baits. The greatest distance from blind to bait measured 49 yards. We tried out one shooting set-up after dark; using the spotlight and resting the .270 with four-power scope over a rest built into the blind, I vaporized a beer can on the bait branch. That seemed to take care of the fourth commandment—make sure of your shot.

That first night in the leopard blind, I learned the odds were all in favor of the leopard. A wise man changes his mind many times, a fool never. Zimbabwe leopards had been poisoned, trapped and killed any way possible for over a century and those cats that showed themselves in daylight no longer existed. Those that survived were wizards at staying alive. Commandment six satisfied.

It took PH Russell Tarr, Cheri and me six night vigils over maggoty impala and reedbuck carcasses before we finally scored a stunning Spots with one shot through the neck. I've baited leopards in other places since, and it's always been as ethical as I could hope for.

Early in my Asian hunting, before many guides and outfitters understood foreign hunter ethics—think the early 1990s—a Russian guide urged me to shoot a grand Okhotsk snow sheep on the helicopter ride to camp. I refused, of course, but many if not most foreign hunters in those days did not. Guides and outfitters were therefore rightly confused about our ethics. When Vladimir Plaschenko learned our habits, he morphed into a grand guide and companion, and I hunted with him many times in later years. Another time, the U.S. hunt broker's man Anatoli urged me to shoot a bear from the copter flying us to the Kamchatka camp, apparently standard practice. I refused this one, too. Sometimes, we know our ethics are right regardless of what local hunting custom says.

Not least is the eighth commandment, obey the laws. This seems obvious, but we all wonder at times what this reg or that one means, right? If you're confused, do your best to learn, and it may require a lawyer and a trip to the game department office. Decades ago I wrangled over residency with Alaskan fish and game cops. I met all the requirements for residence—owned two houses, banked, voted, licensed vehicles and resided in the state for nine years, but since I could prove I'd spent only 346 consecutive days in the state in any given year and not the 365 one zealous trooper said I must do (this reg wasn't printed anywhere), we went to court. After some expense and a plea bargain, I came out OK. The cop fed the newspapers pre-trial info and got the publicity headlines he wanted—about an outdoor writer breaking laws (in those days I was a *Field & Stream* editor; later executive editor David Petzal concluded that I'd been "rail-roaded," and my name returned to the masthead.). The fish cop Joe Campbell also fed the papers some post-trial info that was largely incorrect, and of course, favorable to him. Though I didn't have to pay a penny in fines (I wrote articles as community service for honcho Rick Lovell of the Utah Ducks Unlimited chapter), the article said I paid $4000.

No one hunting much doesn't break some law, minor or not, usually through misinterpretation or just bad luck. Are you wearing the proper number of square inches of hunter orange? A hunting pal dropped a 6x6 Coues buck in Arizona's Huachuca Mountains, but as he approached the trophy, it got up and he shot it a second time. When he got there, he had not one but two bucks on the ground. What to do? He went home and agonized, and the next day returned to gut the second buck and do his duty, but it was gone. A black bear had carted it off.

I'm not sure about this one—baiting. Possibly it should be our ninth commandment, if I could figure all the ramifications. It's obvious that baiting can be fair and ethical, as in the case of the leopard hunt above, or an African lion baiting where hunt broker Charlie Goldenberg lucked out and survived, but it's equally obvious that many baiting setups are definitely unethical. This one was told me by one of the participants, maybe: Seems the South African PH bought a leopard from a menagerie, shot it in the ear with a .22, froze it, then placed it on an acacia branch with a chum hidden in the bush with a line attached to the stiff cat. When the PH got the client into the blind that night and shined the spotlight on it, the client fired, and the guy hidden in brush pulled the cat out of the tree. It backfired because the client could see the leopard on the ground, and insisted on approaching and not waiting for morning when the cat would have thawed. Honest, I'm not sure if this is myth, like the crocodiles in the sewers of New York, but it's a good story. If you're concerned about hunting ethics, though, you'll recognize what is ethical and what isn't, perhaps.

Those black bear hunts where the bear reaches into a hole cut into a garbage-filled oil drum chained to a poplar tree are not ethical. The drums are kept stuffed with rotting road kills, out-of-date Eskimo Pies, and things too foul to identify so bears can depend on a meal. This changes wildlife behavior, in effect making wild animals into something else. The practice pretty much eliminates any chance of the hunter not scoring his quarry, and outfitters allow two-bear kills, and that's not ethical hunting, even if it is legal. Who wants to score a trophy over a jelly-donut bait anyway? (*Outdoor Life's* top two editors lost their jobs largely over taking a stand against bear baiting back in the '90s. I know because they'd just hired me as field editor.)

"Okay," you say, "you're talking leopards and bears, but what about mountain game?"

After a barely successful western tur hunt in Karachai-Cherkessia in the western Caucasus Mountains years ago, the guides offered me a sure-fire chamois hunt at a gravel pit filled with 20 chamois slurping rock salt the outfitters used to keep them there.

"Forget it," I said.

At a recent hunting convention, a member complimenting one of my books said, "It's great to read what hunting was like in the old days and to talk to old timers." It took a day, but if finally sunk in—I was the "old timer!" I hate epiphanies like that.

Well, as an old timer, I can say it—hunting was more ethical in the "old days," probably because today it may take a quarter century accumulating bonus points just to draw one sheep tag, you have to mortgage the manse to afford a guided sheep shebang in BC or Mongolia, and tag numbers and places to hunt are vaporizing (think Turkmenistan and China, for examples).

Who can blame the hunter, man or woman? They've made such a tremendous investment in time and/or money, why wouldn't he or she strive to make sure they've got something to show for that once-in-a-lifetime tag? Why not get fifteen pals to scour the canyons from an RV and tent city and equip them with the latest communications and optical technology (as in an Arizona desert bighorn video I watched recently), buy the best technology and longest range shooting gear they can (as in at least two Mongolia argali videos I own), shoot across a car hood, or take an iffy shot? Truth is, more and more, they would, and who can blame them? They may never get another chance at that tag, beast or hunt. Yes, things change and we "old timers" often bemoan those changes. And therein lies the need for a concrete definition of ethical chase.

We hunters and clients pay the bills. First, we must decide what is and is not ethical, then say "no" to questionable practices, and unethical hunting will disappear like *Archaeopteryx*. It's true, the fair chase and ethics concepts can get awfully gray, and the Boone and Crockett Club and others do what they can to keep hunting as ethical as it is, but we hunters must burnish our tarnished images or hunting will disappear, because there's more non-hunters than hunters, and most non-hunters haven't yet made up their minds. When they do, look out.

My "Hunt Ethics Commandments" is a work in progress. I don't have all the answers, the Red Gods know, so forgive me if I trod on your toes. Perhaps some nimrod saint insensitive to epithets should start the *Hunt Ethics Club* and define fair chase, free-range, ethical and other terms, and give us a concrete, crystalline standard to follow. Anyone out there feel the calling?

The Tenth Commandment

"Hence the confrontation between man and animal has a precise boundary beyond which hunting ceases to become hunting, just at the point where man unleashes his immense technical superiority…" *Meditations on Hunting*, Jose Ortega y Gasset.

"What about those battery-powered quads?" the guy sitting across from me asks. We're at the last high school reunion. Don't ask me which one. "You can drive right up to the deer and blast it, they're so quiet. How's that fair?"

"I just wrote an article about hunting ethics," I tell him, hoping to gain leverage in the looming discussion (I'm referring to "Hunt Ethics?" in the summer 2015 issue of *Wild Sheep*.). The guy isn't an "Anti," but he wants to know. He's like the vast majority of non-hunters, on the fence about hunting and its existence, and he could go either way.

"And all that techno crap that doesn't give the game a chance?" Seems he watches those late night techy hunt programs when he can't sleep. He's right, though. It's tough half-defending something I don't believe in, so I don't. After another Chivas-on-the-rocks, fortunately, the talk degenerates into something less cerebral—Dixie's sweaters in Miss Callahan's civics class and Shorty puking his very first beer at the Brown Jug football game.

Over the past five years, I've had similar discussions in universities, at conventions, in hunting camps, and in bars on four continents—discussions on technology in hunting, that is, not Dixie's sweaters. Those discussions involved hunters and even more non-hunters; none involved Antis since they're less rational than a presidential candidate or a stump. No reasonable person would waste breath on one.

My essay "Hunt Ethics?" also listed only nine commandments, and that's an odd number. Moses knew enough to come down from the mount with an even ten. Some of my nine made reference to hunting technology and how it removes us from the act of hunting, but it left a gap in the document. So let's get concrete here. *Though shalt not use too much hunting technology!* Now, we've got an even ten commandments.

First, let's defend human technological tendencies. Techno geeks evolved into their predispositions, and it started more than a million years ago when *Homo erectus* fire-hardened wooden points on staffs to more effectively slay big beasts and indulge their evolving meat passion, and it accelerated when modern humans appeared on the savannas of Africa 300,000 years ago. Those that didn't use the new projectile points disappeared; they spent too much time just surviving instead of passing on those genes that aimed them toward inventing and using new technology and thriving like their techno geek cousins—Darwin's Natural Selection in action. But keep in mind we modern humans seldom hunt to survive, and that's the critical difference.

Quads aren't much use in the high peaks, I like to believe. Technology adds weight, too, and we don't need more of it while clawing up the crags. I'm atypical, but I won't own those robo riflescopes, don't shoot any farther than necessary, and slave to close the gap—indeed I shredded the knees of one of those four-figure, high-tech designer camo outfits a dealer made me a gift of on one of those stalks—and never used any laser and don't own a range finder. I learned with an Enfield .303 war surplus bolt-action rifle at the advanced age of 10, eventually upgraded to a series of Winchesters and Remingtons and gave in to a riflescope (if Jack O'Connor did it, why not? Vision doesn't improve with age, either.), and I toted a compact binocular and folding knife. Same today. So what if I'm a Paleolithic relic, but I've got pals that feel the same, in spite of scores of hunt magazines that look more like technology catalogs. After all, we don't hunt to survive, and we won't starve if we fail to score, either, so how much hunting technology do we need?

Trouble is, you can buy a Porsche for the cost of a mountain sheep hunt. That's not a fly in the ointment, it's a dinosaur. Think Mongolia, for example, where Altai argali tags can exceed a hundred grand. Drawing out on a bighorn tag in a western state may take a lifetime—and how many octogenarians cavort the peaks? Auctions for high-end ram tags push half-a-million bucks, too, while most hunters choke at the bottom line of a once-in-a-lifetime Dall sheep shebang. If you slave thirty years for that ram tag or draw out on a bighorn ticket before they wheel you into the home, you're going to take every advantage to make sure you put that ram in the salt. It's human nature. And that includes technology overkill (I'm not perfect, either, and bought a $2000 Swarovski binocular for my first desert bighorn shindig). I sympathize with the techno geeks, too, especially since I'm old enough to have bagged 20 or so world sheep over the decades when they were more affordable (heck, I bought a BC goat hunt for $350 in the '60s as a teenager, a Stone sheep hunt for $8100 and a BC bighorn for $9000 in the '80s, and sheep hunting pioneer Vance Corrigan spent $800 for an Alberta ram and stalked Mongolian argali back in the '60s for a pittance!), so I'm not pointing fingers here. I'm commiserating, in my way. I'm also glad I did it when I wasn't on the downside of the decades. I bemoan those missed opportunities, too—like the $3900 argali and ibex combo in Mongolia three decades ago; I backed out when they raised the price $500.

Of course we're talking about "sport" (I don't really agree with the implications of the term, but can't think of a better one) hunting here, not subsistence hunting. Good info says "sport" came from the Spanish (or French, depending on which volume you read) *deport*, "in port" or "leisure," referring to sailors in port with nothing to do but drink, gamble, whore—"sport." Sport hunting isn't obligatory, and was a way to get us back to a simpler and happier existence. Since modern man freed himself from the need to hunt to survive, hunting became a sport. As a result, he imposed more and more limitations on himself and his technology in the form of game laws and encumbrances to keep the hunter from becoming too superior. But new hunting toys are outpacing and weakening those imposed limitations, and game departments intent on pleasing everyone widen the gap, (for example, Utah moved muzzleloader scope magnification from a legal 1x to a higher magnification to satisfy techno-geek demand) and that gap between hunter and quarry continues to expand. Hunting is on the verge of becoming a push-button affair, like a virtual reality video game with real blood, unless we do something about it.

More and more, modern man hauls the trappings of work and civilization with him—smart phones and other electronica that keep him in constant contact with the travails he is presumably trying to escape; tents so weatherproof and comfy they're like home; gourmet backpack food that weighs mere ounces and contains as much salt as a restaurant meal; *ad nauseam*. Again, this is human evolution, but we've gotten so efficient our technology nearly obliterates the hunt act itself and killing becomes the high point.

Our technology strives to make the total experience easier, to remove sodden boots, foggy rifle scopes, learning to judge distance; to invent absolutely weather-proof tents if we use them at all, to eliminate exertion at every level, to remove pack trips and to quickly get us back to the comforts of civilization without ever having truly left them. Too often, the only goal of a hunting trip is to nail another trophy on the wall. When I pin pals down on their latest hunt, they brag up trophy sizes—that 160-point ram, that 370 elk, 180 buck—or how quickly they bagged the quarry, not about clinging to frozen scree, the sizzle of elk chops on spruce coals, blisters from those high-end boots, or playing match-stick poker in the cook tent. The hunt act itself is something one must endure to get the trophy. How long before the hunt becomes only the kill, as it has already done in many high-fence "hunts" throughout the planet? What happened? I ask myself that question once a month, anyhow.

What can we do? I ask myself that question, too. Years ago I prohibited electronic technology in my university classes. Soon I got inundated, so I limited the use of electronics, and that didn't work, either. Now my syllabi say technology may be used for classroom purposes only, but how am I to know? Today, in this age of the Pandemic, I am teaching online courses via technology. I hate it.

Another example: As director on my last university study abroad trip to China, our chartered bus motored through a five-thousand-year-old scene—a verdant valley with peasants tilling rice paddies with water buffalo and wooden plows that hadn't changed in millennia. Anything that happened on the trip could be part of the final exams for the upper division zoology, literature and writing classes they were getting credit for. As director of the shebang, I stood up to draw attention to the incredible scene. All but one student was engrossed in their mobile device. I thought, *to hell with it*. I chided them about it in our nightly class meeting, though, and questions about the scene showed up on the exams.

I sometimes escorted hunters abroad, and earlier I refused to go if they toted mobile devices. After all, the hunt was mine, too, and I didn't want it diluted. But as those devices became more universal, "my" hunters snuck off into the bush to use them.

On a Namibian elephant and croc safari a few years ago, we collected our Kung! Bushman trackers in dirt-floored, mud-and-wattle huts *sans* electricity, plumbing, or central heating. They both produced cell phones the moment I bagged the jumbo and within an hour 60 Natives also armed with cell phones misted out of thick bush and began hacking up the beast. It's universal. Today, the "bush telegraph" is a mobile device. In the old days, mobile devices weren't even a dream; you occupied yourself with what went on around you—hence, the "experience."

"We just dial 'em in, and we kill 'em. That's all." The promoter and hunter bragged up a robo riflescope for his Mongolian sheep hunt video sponsor. In fairness, the fellow stalked and toted ram heads, but the quote too often epitomizes modern hunter attitudes. The guy was loaded down with technology—gadgets hanging from his cap bill, range finders at finger tips—neat toys, but those toys take attention away from what we're paying for, the hunt act itself. Again, what happened?

Then we had the safari hunter whose angle was extreme range shooting. He produced the most professional videos I'd seen, owned a riveting personality, he gifted me his latest videos, and even I admit lusting after his long-range rifles. Trouble was, the emphasis was on technology and what you could do with it, not on hunting—he killed beasts that had no inkling they were being hunted 500 yards away. That's not hunting, it's technology.

I just thumbed through a 160-page hunting magazine. Technology ads or articles owned 49 of those pages, and that's typical. There's gadgets that enhance our hearing so we can sense noises humans never could; they've got up to eight channels and a dozen digital bands. Scratch one more game animal advantage. There's a binocular with a "...super-light polycarbonate frame...," multi-coated lenses, and "center-click diopter adjustments." Not to mention that it's "nitrogen-purged, fog proof and 100% waterproof." And a riflescope with brightness settings, LED reticle illumination, adjustable windage and elevation controls. I see a long range shooting "system," too, that calculates windage and bullet drop based upon muzzle velocity, sight height and zero range; the ad is fond of acronyms—MOA, MRAD, BDC. The system even makes adjustments for altitude and ambient temperature. These selections were random, honest, and scores more pages exist in that magazine.

Humans evolved to invent and use technology, originally to make it easier and safer to bag big and dangerous beasts. It's in our genes. But with that first crude spear, man began a thing human biologists call cultural evolution. It sent us from those first crude hunting tools to modern technology humans even half a century ago couldn't fathom. It also led us to printing, languages, sanitation, nutrition, and to medicine, religion, art, philosophy and ethics. If civilization can produce the *Arabian Nights* and antibiotics, we can control our over indulgences in hunting, especially those involved with technology. We shouldn't eliminate technology or its development, and we couldn't even if we should. But we must control its use in hunting because nearly all of it insulates us from the hunt act itself. Today, some sports don't hunt, they "collect." If we don't control ourselves, hunting will be better named "killing." If we won't control ourselves, what will the billions of fence-sitters decide? One way or another, the majority will rule.

I've got my fingers crossed.

What is "Fair Chase?"

The good news is the term "fair chase" is tougher to find in hunting ads by a margin of two to one than it was 15 years ago, at least in the two publications I browsed. Back then, you'd find the term in advertisements for high-fence hunting in the Republic of South Africa, Europe, Texas, and other places few would consider "fair chase" or "free-range" hunting. Since "fair-chase" ads seem to be declining, and no "fair-chase" police exist, brokers and outfitters must be policing themselves. Or nimrods are getting more skeptical and outfitters don't want to get caught out.

The not-so-good news—few of us have any but a vague understanding of the term. I've made hunts that I thought were fair enough chase at the time, that in retrospect these decades later, I'm not so sure of. I'm unsure of them because I'm unsure of the term.

The Boone and Crockett Club's publication is entitled *Fair Chase*. If anyone knows the definition, they would, right? B & C's definition is, "The ethical, sportsmanlike, and lawful pursuit and taking of any free-ranging, wild, native North American big game animal in a manner that does not give the hunter an improper advantage over such animals."

Yes, it sounds grand, like those cotton candy campaign speeches that make us feel warm and fuzzy but when we bite into them, there's nothing there. Or maybe one of those valedictorian lectures at graduation, or an old fashioned fire-and-brimstone sermon. Yes, it's easy to critique the definition, but Mongol, Tanzanian, Croat and Canadian hunters still refer to B & C's definition in lively fireside discussions.

Hats off to the B & C Club, though, because they recognized their definition's short-comings and added a caveat—"…ethics in hunting ultimately rest with the individual…"

The U.S. government owns a system of checks and balances because our founding fathers wisely wouldn't trust the ethics of the individual(s), be they the president (this essay was written long before the Trump debacle), the congress, or the court(s), when left to their own devices. Can we really trust individual ethics? Turn on the news on any given day and you'll find we can't. So what's next? Can we hunters formulate a concrete definition of "fair chase"? I've already issued a challenge to fellow nimrods to help out in my published essay "Ethical Chase." So far, no serious takers, so let's again struggle toward that will-o'-the-wisp definition. Defining "fair chase" is defining hunting "ethics," or trying to cage fog.

Often enough, concepts and objects we otherwise have a tough time getting our heads around, and "fair chase" is one of these, are defined by telling what they are not. I've taught university creative *non*-fiction writing classes for decades. This most popular of the creative writing genres is defined by what it is not—fiction. Sleep biologists often define stages 1, 2, 3, and 5 sleep as non-Rapid Eye-Movement (REM) sleep, or NREM sleep. We could go on and on.

*****

Many nimrods agree with me on this one—high fence hunting. The problem often comes with the term "high-fence." I've had arguments with outfitters that claim that since the fence is a standard cattle fence, maybe four feet high, it isn't "high." Fair enough if the quarry is an elk or deer or even North American sheep that can easily vault it and go about its business without hindrance. But if it's a diminutive Middle-East *Moufloniformes* on a Texas ranch, it's kept restricted, so the fence is "high" enough.

It seems that high-fence hunting is clearly not fair chase hunting, but that's not always the case, maybe. I'm still not sure of this one, so help me out. Three years back, we safaried in Mozambique. Cheri and I have hunted Africa for over three decades now, we've avoided any high fence canned hunting which is far too common, and I've long since bagged everything I wanted, so we now mainly safari for fun. This safari, I bagged another magnum fair chase croc, ditto a bush pig, a Methuselah of a cape buffalo—my 7th, all absolutely fair chase. I scored a grand nyala, too, and didn't see a high-fence anywhere, but in mulling the hunt over in later days, I began to wonder.

We hunted a few hectares of the combo eco-tourist and lumbering property, always the same relatively small area on the two days we hunted nyala. We saw bulls and cows, and odd, the bulls were all trophy-sized. The moment I slapped my bull in the salt, we saw no more bull nyala though we hunted wart hogs for two more days in the same geography. They vaporized. Were they turned out of an enclosure for the hunt and did they then return after the hunt because of bait in the enclosure? Or am I too suspicious? Nobody admitted anything, nor did they deny it. What can you do? If it was a high-fence deal, I want to know about it. High fences aren't illegal, and it's popular in the RSA, Europe, and North America. It's just that it's unethical in my and many other books.

Now I'd hunted with this Austrian outfitter before, and scored an absolutely fair chase and grand chamois in four days of skidding about the snowy alps, and another time a cull red stag (the only tag he had available at that time) in the very tops of the alps without a fence within miles. No question fair chase, and we had a grand time, so I booked another hunt after those big stags we spotted when I'd scored my small one.

Originally, the hunt was to be in the same geography, but somehow the tag vaporized, as I understood it, so we ended hunting in the lowlands. I didn't learn about this until late, and the hunt would take place on a large private property and adjoining "common areas" open to Hans Everyman. The stags "could go in and they could go out," through broken fences, the outfitter told me, which meant "free-range" as far as I understood the term.

We saw plenty of fences that first morning, also roe deer, fallow deer, boars and a handful of smaller stags. I'd hunted in Hungary and elsewhere with fences, and I was assured they were to keep game out of sensitive reseeded or crop areas, not keep them in for shooters. And that's what I'd gleaned from the outfitter as we drove around looking for big tracks.

Eventually we let off our two drivers and then motored a few kilometers away and the guys hiked toward us with the idea they'd spook game our way. And they did—roe deer, boars, fallow deer, a mouflon, and one grand stag. I tried hard to get a shot as it sprinted through the close-growing pines, but couldn't and it vaporized toward Hungary. We drove around more the second day, stalked a jack-pine tangle and flushed small stags and hinds, returned for lunch at the moldering lodge in the dank woods and then in late afternoon trekked through a gloomy oak forest and settled into a rickety blind ten feet off the forest floor. Peter, our main man, would again hike through the woods with hopes of flushing something our way, and at dusk a magnum stag vaulted through the woods right at us but each time I got crosshairs on the deer, he disappeared behind an oak until I managed a quick shot and scored a shoulder hit. Martin the outfitter and Cheri picked up the blood spoor in the gloaming and tracked while I watched ahead, and in near-darkness I spotted the downed stag's condensing exhalations above a blackberry bramble, and finished it. We grunted him down the slope to the truck, and it all seemed fair chase to me. However, reputable members of the local hunting organization told me days later it was not fair chase, and their evidence made sense. Piecing it together, I believe the outfit fed deer, possibly in an enclosure, and then chased them toward hunters at the right time. Yes, the deer "could go in and they could go out," but they didn't because out there in the common areas, many other hunters shot at them, but in the private property only very few paying hunters could hunt them. What can you do? The stag's 11 x 10 pt. head gear weighed in at 14.5 kg, a king kong stag. He looks astonishing on the wall, too.

So far we haven't talked about mountain game. We'd had no luck with chamois on a Bosnian hunt many years ago, and the guide offered to arrange to get a chamois from a nearby hunting estate turned loose in the scarps. Of course, I nixed it, and so we aimed west to Croatia and bagged a fair chase goat. Pretty clear cut.

What about this one? After applying for a fair chase trophy bison permit in Custer State Park in South Dakota for nearly a decade, I finally scored! We hunted in January of 2018, right after they'd contained a wildfire that scorched much of the park. Fortunately new snow covered the scorched wild lands, and enough feed existed and enough generous souls donated hay that the bison and other beasts did fine. I think of CSP as a miniature Yellowstone Park, with bison, deer, pronghorns, elk, cougar, coyotes and all sorts of wildlife. And tourists. The bison are unafraid of people because they see them all the time.

We located a bachelor gang of three Paleolithic bulls of from 10-12 years old the first day, then hunted into other country and glassed other bulls. Next morning we ogled new geography and trophy bulls not quite as old or big as the trio we'd seen, so we searched out our three musketeers. After discussing the merits and demerits of this one and that, we decided the 10-year-old had the best cape and probably the best horns. The 12-year-old, my sentimental favorite because of its age, had one horn broken back two inches. We walked up to the bulls, and since they were used to people they had no fear. At 30 yards, I dropped it with a shot from the .375 behind the ear. Adrenaline enough for me, and a stunning trophy and country. Chad Kremer, the Park bison honcho and whom Cheri dubbed the "Bison Whisperer," thought like a bison and was fine company. The bull weighed 2200 lbs. Since the entire park is high-fenced (who wants to lose a $6K bison to a neighboring ranch?), was this a fair-chase hunt? Keep in mind this is the largest state park in SD, and I understand it's the second largest state park in the country. Fair chase? I'm told the B & C Club accepts it as such. Bagging a bull was a given, though, but I buy the hunt as fair in spite of the boundary fence.

Decades ago a Super cub swooped into the head of Old Woman Creek well above the Arctic Circle, circled three times, landed on a gravel bar, and two sports debarked and stalked and bagged a ram that only showed to me as a white spot, I was that far away. Of course they had no idea they were watched. They'd skinned it, and flew off to the camp on Red Sheep Creek. I recognized the Cub as belonging to the outfitter's camp there. Definitely not fair chase, and on top of that, illegal.

In some places, it's illegal to have been in a plane within 24 hours of shooting. Is that enough time? What about those sports that spot sheep from planes days, weeks or months before the hunt? They'll fly periodically to keep track of the ram, and come the paying client or opening day, they've got it pegged. Fair chase? Not to me. In the old days, whenever they were, you scouted afoot or ahorse and spent money on boot leather and grain instead of hydrocarbons. And you committed time and effort to score the ram. We're never going to get rid of airplane scouting. Humans are too enamored of their machines, including quads, Fords and Cessnas.

On my first snow sheep hunt in the Dzhugdzhur Mountains of Khabarovsk Territory in the Russian Far East (RFE), the outfitter urged me to shoot a tremendous ram from the ancient and gargantuan Aeroflot helicopter ferrying us into camp. I refused, to his surprise and disgust. Seems it was standard practice in the early and mid-90s when Western hunters began filtering into the country. I straightened out the guide and outfitter, and they morphed into terrific fair chase hunters on later shindigs.

Nearly the same thing happened on the Kamchatka Peninsula across the Sea of Okhotsk a few years later. The guys wanted me to bag a grand bruin from the 'copter on the flight to camp. I didn't, of course, and they couldn't understand why, since many clients did. Indeed, two of SCI's top honchos resigned after a moose helicopter hunting snafu (they got caught) organized by a top U.S. hunt broker who was also prosecuted (they got off).

Killing clean is part of the fair chase equation. That's a given, and if we've done much hunting during those bad old opening-day melees, we've seen examples enough of bad shooting and wounding. From what I've seen, sheep and goat nimrods are the best of marksmen. With the price and scarcity of sheep tags, and the distances they sometimes must shoot, they've gotta be.

More than a few nimrods out there disagree with this one, but I won't hunt non-native big game, be they Barbary sheep in Texas, mouflon in Hawaii, or African antelope in Mexico. I've been called a zoological chauvinist, and worse. For me and plenty of chums, much of the hunt's cachet involves hunting beasts where they evolved. Who could get their jollies stalking elephants in Iowa? Ridiculous, I know. Then what about African antelope in Florida or Mexico or mid-Eastern sheep in Texas? Plenty hunt them.

Obeying the laws is part of the fair chase concept. The consequence of breaking them these days is too costly not to anyway, but I like to think most fair chase hunters would stick to the rules regardless. At least in part, game laws are set to reduce the vast mental and technological distance between nimrods and the quarry—in other words make the hunt more fair. Anything, especially game laws, that reduce the overwhelming superiority humans have over the game, is worth supporting.

Technology, like robot riflescopes that plot wind drift, compute distances and bullet drop, and any of half a dozen other parameters, black-and-white increases the mental and philosophical distance between the "hunter" and the game. Hunting becomes pressing a button, a technical exercise only. What happened to reading spoor, stalking, tracking, wearing out boot leather? I published "The Tenth Commandment," an essay about technology abuse in hunting. If anything reduces the chance a hunt is fair chase, it's too much technology. Each time we increase technology, we reduce the "fair" in the chase, and hunting becomes simply reading a dial and pressing a button. After hunting no longer was a matter of survival, humans ventured afield for challenge and thrill. We could have walked into any farm pasture for a quick and sure kill, but that wasn't the idea. Alas, too many "hunters" today do just that.

Modern anthropologists are convinced *Hominins* are well into the Technological Revolution, and as we speak it's altering human culture in vast ways (the Agricultural Revolution 10,000 years ago and the Industrial Revolution 300 years ago each drastically altered human cultural evolution). Which may mean that technology such as airplanes, quads, robo-riflescopes, lasers and gadgets I can't comprehend, are evolving into part of the hunting equation. Many nimrods seem to think so, and I'm astonished at the techno-junk I see afield and in the conventions. I've still got faith, because some nimrods feel as I do about technology. Some puritans got disgusted enough they gave up the centerfire rifle and associated gadgetry and turned to hunting with a long bow or recurve.

Similar, we should not eliminate any chance the quarry can detect us. Ultra-long shooting does just that. The ram, buck or bull can't scent, see or hear you so far away. Instead, strive to close the distance. Heck, stalking is most of the fun anyway. Are we spiraling into technology so fast that the next thing will be drone hunting, without game having any inkling they're in danger? When that happens, I'll shoot drones.

Related, is trying to honor the customs and habits of the place hunted. In some places it's completely accepted to hunt leopards at night over a bait with a spotlight, and in others it's illegal. I've bagged Spots at night, I'd never pumped more adrenaline, and at least where we hunted with PH Russell Tarr in the Zimbabwe bush, the hunt was as fair chase as anyone could hope. On the other hand, the practice leaves itself open to all sorts of abuses, including menagerie cats, shooting a zoo leopard beforehand and freezing it and placing it in the tree for a client, and so on.

Baiting can be absolutely fair chase, as with baiting leopards as mentioned above, or lions or even waiting at a rotting beached whale for brown bear, but it's too often abused. Waiting at a steel drum chained to a poplar tree that's kept filled with rotting restaurant food all season isn't hunting, it's assassination. I've mentioned this before, but *Outdoor Life's* two top editors, *monsieurs*. Byers and Bourne back in the '90s, resigned their jobs over taking a stand against such bear baiting.

I like to think this should go without mentioning, but the quarry must be wild-borne and come to maturity in the wilds, not born in an enclosure and nurtured with antler-growing mixes and pumped with hormones all its life.

Yes, it's done, and shooters often select beasts by computer, eliminating chance and hunting altogether from the equation. Hard to believe? The practice is turning execution into sport, or the other way around.

Okay, so what's the "fair-chase" definition? I still can't put it into a sentence, or even two, but I'm working on it. If you won't settle for any but a short definition, *Wikipedia* does as good a job as anyone. But remember our premise? It's often best to define something by telling what it's not. Many of the Ten Commandments Moses hauled down from the Mount tell us what we shouldn't do, like "Though shalt not steal." So far, "fair chase" hunting may be best defined in the same manner, by telling us what not to do.

1. Don't use too much technology.
2. Don't hunt game restricted by high fence.
3. Don't break the laws.
4. Don't increase the mental, philosophical and physical distance between quarry and hunter.
5. Don't violate the ethics and customs of the place hunted.
6. Don't eliminate any chance the quarry can detect you.
7. Don't hunt domestic beasts. (In other words, the quarry must be wild.)
8. Don't wound game. (Kill clean.)
9. Don't hunt transplanted, non-native game.
10. No unethical baiting. (Trust your sense of right and wrong.)

If you're addicted on too much technology, withdraw slowly. Like quitting tobacco or jelly donuts. Each time you venture afield, leave something else home.

Nobody's perfect. We all fudge a bit. Sheep and other hunting tags are expensive and may take a lifetime to draw, so we've made them so important we're tempted to stretch to score that ram. Too often that means breaking a commandment or two. How many of you haven't coveted your neighbor's wife or husband, or fudged on your taxes? Like I said, nobody's perfect, but we can try.

Is It Twilight?

Honest. I planned to pen an easy and upbeat article this time. I began typing a story of a white ram hunt in the Arctic, airy and light, no editorializing. Instead, that narrative's remains lie mouldering in the catacombs of the computer, the creative dust blown away into cyberspace.

Blame the October 2017 issue of *National Geographic's* feature entitled, "Should We Kill Animals to Save Them." I'd scarcely tossed my *NG* issue aside, miffed at the lead photo of a horseback adolescent girl with bontebok tossed carelessly across the saddle with the bullet exit wound in gory display (label that sensational photo a visual argument fallacy—it biases the audience before they read a single word). The omissions that would have presented the hunters' side more accurately didn't help, either. On cue, three hunt buddies emailed me that evening asking my take on the piece, then an email from an anti-hunting colleague at the university, furious at the omissions the article owned from her perspective, glared at me. I saw her point, too, and scratched my dome and reread Michael Paterniti's *National Geographic* feature story.

Over the next week I polled three anti-hunters (common enough in the ivory towers of academia, but not to be confused with anti-hunting *activists*), three hunters, and two neutral non-hunters. Hunters were miffed, but they weren't furious. Ditto anti-hunters. Non-hunters thought it an accurate presentation of both sides. For fear of a fist-fight, I avoided anti-hunting activists; they're an irrational and noisy fraction of the debate, anyway. My conclusion? I still think the article shorted we hunters, for example it practically ignored the fact that major causes of big mammal disappearance in Africa are habitat loss and poaching, and trigger-happy Western millionaires are minor in comparison. It didn't even pay lip service to the fact that many species would not exist in Africa without hunter shekels.

But all things considered, it's a reasonable picture of how the billions of Western non-hunting humans *view* sport hunting and hunters. Today, most non-hunters see hunting as an unsavory occupation from humanity's lurid past. The article is must reading for all hunters, whether or not they hunt Africa (the article's focus), if only to give them a more un-slanted perspective. We hunters prefer cloistered environments like hunting camps and conventions where everyone thinks and speaks the same, and we embrace an in-your-face attitude towards those that disagree with us on hunting, so our thought on the topic becomes stilted. We're like Neanderthals comfortably lodged in ice-age Europe when faced with the sudden appearance of modern humans, *Homo sapiens*. They retreated into themselves and were inundated by modern human tools, adaptability, and new ways of thinking, and became extinct in an evolutionary moment. Are hunters next? Remember, we're a tiny fraction of the total planetary human population, and too many non-hunters exist to battle with any hope of winning. Yes, we're victorious in small legal battles here or there, all the while prolonging the inevitable loss of the war. Instead, we must work with non-hunters, not battle them. Darwin's base theory *Perpetual Change* states that the planet is constantly changing, and organisms must adapt or become extinct; this applies not only to organic evolution but to cultural evolution and to hunting as a sport. For nimrods, it's adjust to the evolving hunting changes or disappear altogether.

To adapt, we must guard our image and stop hunter practices that disgust and horrify others, because we need those others on our side. The vast majority of Americans are not anti-hunting activists, but what we do—hunting—is often politically incorrect to that majority. Like it or not, we must live with it. The topic makes many Americans uncomfortable in polite conversation. Heck, it sometimes makes me uncomfortable.

This isn't my life focus, but I've written and talked about hunting and its justification in 21st century Western culture for a decade now, often in universities where the usually younger audience is still open-minded about hunting and its existence. I've used all the old, stale arguments, too:

Killing your own supper is more humane than buying feed-lot, slaughter house meat.

Regulated, expensive hunting for lions, markhor, elephant, bighorn sheep—you fill in the blank—in their dotage is a sustained way to protect the species.

Money hunters pay for the privilege, goes to conservation of many species that ecotourists enjoy.

Costly trophy hunting is the best economic model we've got. Include that over-used related cliché, "if it pays, it stays."

The hunting *industry* provides millions of dollars for native peoples, locales, jobs, infrastructure, whatever. Hunting puts billions into conservation coffers, and some species wouldn't exist without hunting dollars, *ad infinitum.*

Note that most of these arguments are money-justified. The flip side, and the argument non-hunters too often present, is that you can't justify immoral acts with dollars. That's a tough one to counter. Those stale arguments are now cliche, and a sophisticated audience has heard them all before. Under critical examination, they may contain only particles of truth. Worse, these arguments largely ignore morality and ethics, often more important to our non-hunting brothers than hard statistics and logical reason. How would you answer the objection that sport hunting in the 21st century, when we no longer must do it to survive, is largely killing for fun? I hunt because I enjoy it, the solitude if I can get it, the silence if I can find it, the scenery, the challenge of stalking, tracking. I'd be lying if I said I didn't enjoy the kill at some level. Yes, if we're to be honest, we hunt and kill for fun. Is that ethical in the 21st century when many of us are too well-fed and many species are threatened? Can you justify it to our non-hunting fellow humans? Or do we retreat into ourselves and our hunting conventions like Neanderthals? I don't have a good answer.

We've seen the gory and often horrifying viral hero poses and kill scenes. Many of these demean the dignity of the animal. Too many of these disgust even me and I've hunted four continents for half a century and know what blood looks like. What on earth are shootists thinking to post such visuals? Can't they half-imagine what someone sensitive to animal rights must feel? How would the offended persons respond to hunting next time they register an opinion or vote? Safari hunting clients seem the biggest offenders, and more megafauna has disappeared from Africa in the past few decades than any place on the planet—think 70% plus in sub-Saharan Africa, in spite of claims by hunt organizations and others that safari hunters spend so much money (SCI's stats said that nearly 20,000 hunters spent more than $400M; other groups aver it's less than half that) that they largely finance conservation efforts and programs ("If this is true," I can hear the non-hunter say, "why has half of Tanzania's big game disappeared in two decades?"). Many of these gory and ill-considered kill scenes went viral even after the Cecil the Lion/ Walter Palmer debacle in Zimbabwe in 2015, so some safari clients learned absolutely nothing from the event. Wisely, many safari hunters pulled in their heads and ducked out of the way, but some still equate slaying animals using modern technology with power and virility, and must use social media to brag of it online with the idea that their money buys invulnerability. Is there a way we hunters can censure those that venture beyond good taste, morality and ethics? If so, we should use it.

Canned lion hunting in the Republic of South Africa has become a multi-million dollar industry, and it's drawn planet-wide censure and disgust. Most ethical hunters find the entire concept unethical or immoral. I'd use a stronger word. Thousands of lions are raised like so many cattle in captivity in inhumane enclosures and released for guaranteed, high-fence shooting; we'll not call it "hunting." No surprise, they're far cheaper to blast than fair-chase, wild lions. Mozambique businessman, entrepreneur and professional hunter Grant Taylor told me that hunting in high-fence hunting ranches or reserves in South Africa isn't natural—"there's only males," meaning antelope, and that the situation isn't anything like wild since no breeding females exist because you can't shoot females for a trophy, so why have them at all? "Bloody hell!" Willie Phillips, Botswana PH and veteran of 60 years in the bush and hundreds of dangerous game safaris said, "they're f@$ %&*g perverts." He referred to both the fenced lion hunting operators and the clients, and he painted the air with purple adjectives in the process.

"Yeah," you say, "but that's Africa. Sheep and other animals live in mountains in the wild and it can't happen in North America." What about *moufloniformes* and African antelope and other sheep hunts on many fenced North American ranches and elsewhere? Then we've got canned ranch-bred, tagged, inoculated and otherwise handled desert bighorn sheep hunts in Mexico; the rams have become commodities, shipped from ranch to ranch in cattle trucks to satisfy the demand of an incoming "hunter"—the bigger the trophy, the higher the price tag. Then there's canned fenced hunting in Europe for mouflon, red stag and other species where animals are inoculated with antibiotics and hormones, fed in winter and released from corrals while a shootist lurks in a nearby blind or hide. It's not hunting fenced lions, but it's not far removed. How long before anti-hunters scream about the practice? More important, how will the majority of non-hunting Western humans judge it? They've already given a verdict on fenced lion hunting, and I suspect that "sport" will disappear soon enough. What shocks me is that too many shooting clients see absolutely nothing wrong with hunting non-native animals behind high fences where they cannot escape.

Canned trophy hunting has exploded into a multi-billion dollar industry. Hunters select their trophy beforehand and eliminate chance altogether from the equation, like selecting a box of cereal from the shelf or an auto from the showroom. If it weren't for various government agencies and pressure from the public, little thought would be given to conservation of the species.

Public good can seldom stand against the profit motive without oversight. Perhaps wrongly, many shooting and hunting organizations—we'll not give examples here—are dedicated to battling those agencies, the U.S. Fish & Wildlife Service for example, and they rail against any public voice, organized or not, that cries out against hunting abuses, and there are many. Should we instead look more closely to see if there's merit to those voices? Hunters aren't perfect, and uniting in knee-jerk reflex against any of those we nimrods deem a threat may simply bring us all down in the end.

The point of this essay is we must look at the other side of the issue, that of the non-hunters in civilization, and to consider their views as more than those of an uninformed majority, or we'll disappear, period. We're simply too small of a minority to last any length of time, and if we don't consider our own abuses and end them, there's no future for the sport hunter in modern culture.

NG's "Should We Kill Animal's to Save Them?" owns an anti-hunting bias. Take not only the lead photo described earlier, but other photos in the article show hunters in an unfavorable light—for example the morbidly obese husband and wife clad in skin-tight camo attempting to grunt a black bear into a tree, or the slain and crumpled giraffe.

Some quotes, for example the rhetorical questions on page 99, "Might it now be time to stop killing the dwindling herds for sport and display?" or maybe this one—"Was it moral to kill such an imperiled creature at this moment in our history?" show a decidedly anti-hunting slant, too. I can imagine a similar protest from my anti-hunting colleague on the other side of the fence, but I still argue that the article shows a reasonable view of how most of our civilization sees sport hunting, and as such, we hunters must take note. A wise man changes his mind many times, a fool never.

The Death of "If"

Western commerce is enamored of guarantees—the "three-year power and drive-train warranty," the "one-year full replacement" deal, the "lifetime guarantee," *ad nauseum.* How many "sub-minute-of-angle" rifle ad assurances do we see in the magazines? I own a Zeiss binocular with a lifetime full replacement warranty; true to promise, it's been replaced twice. I'm about to re-roof my house with shingles guaranteed for life.

No surprise, we're carrying that commercial mind-set into our hunting, and that's changing the basic premise. Chance must play a major role in ethical hunting. Without that "if," we're simply buying the trophy.

I hunker in the tussocks as much out of the wind as I can get on a knoll on Alaska's Upper Peninsula. It's May, and patches of snow hang on from the storm two days earlier, and we're glassing for brown bear. Cheri and R&R outfitter Rob Jones and guide Scott Ruttum scan from the backside of that knoll. Maybe a mile away, I ogle a grand boar slip out of alder tangles in the river bottom, ghost across a meadow and vaporize. I strain so hard to glass him again, I get a headache. The wind drops so I duckwalk up a ridge to get a better angle when I hear it. A plane drones upriver. I'm disappointed because it's the first one we've heard since we pitched camp, but not surprised because every other guy in the Far North owns one, and every place in Alaska you can land a Piper Cub is littered with gas containers and plastic siphoning hoses from last autumn's caribou slaughter—all this in remote geography, too.

The sun glints off a wing miles downriver and I swing the Zeiss onto the unusual multi-colored bush plane. *Is it a Cub?* I ask myself. It drones nearer and then that windy maelstrom kicks in again and I no longer hear it. I see it, though, and it makes tight, low circles in the same spot for a full two minutes before floating upriver toward me. I hunker out of the wind and watch the plane, and it begins again that tight circling most of a mile away and below. *What's he doin'?* I wonder. The wind dies a moment, and I hear it—*thump,* a long pause and that tight circling, and then *thump, thump,* and then *thump,* and more of that circling and the wind howls again and I no longer hear the plane or what I conclude was shooting. He disappears upriver and I resume searching for that bear, but figure it's a lost cause. I spot something big and dark in an opening, and it wasn't there when I glassed the place earlier. I can't tell what it is, but it's not moving. I'm not going to trek an hour and then swim the swollen Nushagak River to find out, either. It lay motionless for two hours until I hoof back to camp.

I'm back two days later glassing again, note what little is left of that probable carcass and the scavenging ravens, when that polychrome plane swoops in, that's the only word for it, lands on a bare hogback, throws up a tent, and then roars off in what must be a record for pitching a tent. Then he's back, and he and another camo geek shoulder rifles and trot downhill—I'm watching all this through my 10x Zeiss. Later I hear a shot and another, but see nothing in the dense black spruce timber across the river. Hours later, they fly out and up the canyon 200 yards below my ridge-line perch. I clearly see both of them in the plane with the binocular, but they don't see me. The next day the tent is gone.

We're having no luck with our bruin, so Rob ferries us and our camp to another drainage in the Super Cub. He spots a skinned bear carcass from the Cub near where those "sports" pitched their tent.

The campfire consensus that night is that the pilot is an outfitter flying upriver shooting moose from the air for bear bait, and when a bruin responds, he hauls in his dude. Clients dislike paying 20 grand for bear-less hunts, and the guide/outfitter has his reputation to consider, after all. He couldn't just hunt and rely on bush skills and chance to kill a bear, he *had* to kill one. He's got a Super-Duty truck payment and a mortgage, no doubt.

In May in the Far North, nights are getting longer. I'd been rereading Ortega y Gasset's *Meditations on Hunting*, that says if you think you can "…do whatever you like—even the supreme good, then you are…a villain."

(Later in 2003 an ADF&G boy interviewed me telephonically about the incident, but the trooper kept mum on particulars and I never learned more. If it went to court, as I recall, the year was 2003 if you care to Google it, but I suppose any court action might be in 2004.)

Hunting has become a big money proposition. As such, it can't leave much if anything to chance. It's murdering the "if" in hunting. We sportsmen spend so much to hunt, we insist on having something to show for it. We won't rely on chance, and after all, chance is a key component of ethical, fair chase hunting. The more we reduce chance, the uncertainty in hunting, the less we hunt and the more we buy. Pay your money—shoot your game.

Big money? Last season's single Tajikistan markhor hunt went for $120K, and that's not including transportation, tips, hotels, taxidermy. Then there's those $150K Mongolian argali shindigs; multi-species dangerous game safaris that exceed $100K; auction block black rhino, bighorn sheep and other tags pushing half a million bucks. Heck, most North American serious sheep hunts soak the nimrod at least $50K! To this college prof and most hunters, that's big money. Yes, I know—much of those shekels go to conserving the species; but that doesn't make it swallow any easier for the vast majority of the planet's 8 billion hominids. I lecture university students about the topic often enough to see and hear their concern. "Yes," I'm often forced to answer their questions if I'm to be honest, "hunting has become the realm of the wealthy." I'm forced to admit to them, too, that one of the causes of the French Revolution was the fiery hatred the peasantry aimed at the gentry because hunting had become the exclusive "right" of wealthy nobility; one of the first rights the nobles relinquished was hunting if they were lucky enough to keep their heads.

The good news—students, the next governing generation, are still open-minded about hunting and its existence, though current hunt costs and many practices stick in their craw. The bad news— older humans aren't so broad-minded, and one of many examples is most of the admin and faculty in the English Department at Weber State University where I've taught for decades (yes, I also teach in the Zoology Department). I suspect Aldo Leopold was right, that "… growing up, is…a process of growing down;…[isn't] experience… actually a progressive dilution of the essentials by the trivialities of living." Did you need a guarantee and $10K when you stalked that buck in the back forty after high school classes?

Yes, if you're spending that kind of loot, making that kind of investment, you must be sure of the dividend. Not many would respond to a $100K "maybe," even if that's hunting.

I'm not perfect, either. I started hunting when I got my first Red Ryder BB gun, and haven't slowed down half a century later. Heck, we've just returned from a Mozambique safari, and it wasn't cheap. By the time the smoke clears, it might gouge me $50K.

Yes, I spent too much on expensive shooting shindigs in places like Tanzania, Mongolia and Europe, and like most of us, I wouldn't have spent those bucks unless I was reasonably sure of something to show for it. What do I remember most? Not the trophy in the salt or the head on the wall, but glorious days afield with guys like Jon Kibler, Alvaro Villegas, Erdogan Avci, John Wamback, Willie Phillips, Wade Lemon, Russ Tarr, Vladimir Plaschenko, Sam Kapolak, Jaypatee Akeeagok, Arif and his sons, Luya, Zorig and scores more, too. (Without a doubt I missed dozens of my past stellar guides. Sorry, guys! I'll catch you next time around.)

Coincidentally, Cheri and I just reminisced the other evening about our favorite hunts over the 30 years we've been together, and odd, they turn out to be the least expensive—nearby DIY elk, deer and pronghorn hunts; float affairs in the Far North for multiple species back when we lived on the Yukon River; DIY-ers after desert bighorns, and more. Sure, we acknowledge, we had grand fun with most of our guides, but the point is we didn't need a guarantee on those hunts we remember most.

Then there's the human infatuation with gadgetry. We evolved into it when hominids lusted after meat and crafted more effective projectile points on African savannas a million years ago to get it, and we never looked back. We can't do much about that genetic predisposition but consciously control it, and in the last decades we've done miserably. (See "Hunting's Tenth Commandment" in the summer 2016 issue of *Wild Sheep*.) The more gadgetry we use to insure the kill, to kill that "if," the less we hunt. Every piece of technology removes us farther from those things we went afield for when modern humans graduated to sport hunting—simplicity, challenge, and escape from the salt mine (after nine months in my salt mine—the lecture hall—I strongly anticipate sleet-numbed fingers, 70-lb. backpacks, black flies and *tsetse*). In other words, we desire dumping the AC and predictability, whether we know it or not.

"Why don't you just use a spear," a guy that probably wears camo to church challenged me in what I hoped was a discussion and not a brawl.

"I learned with a centerfire rifle, binocular and folding knife. It's tough going back to an earlier time and forgetting what we know," I said, though I knew that wasn't exactly true; a few guys dumped the modern rifle and took up a wooden long bow—heck, some even crafted the bows and arrows themselves.

On a recent Altai Mongolian ibex hunt, I struggled to judge the distance to a magnum billy across the bare hillside. Nothing grew to give me perspective. "290 meters," I heard behind me. It seems guide Zorig had scored a range-finder as a tip from a client. Of course I didn't ignore that info even though I won't use a rangefinder, and placed the crosshairs accordingly. The grand ibex dropped at the shot.

Ethical hunters and non-hunters have an especially hard time with high-fence hunting, because it absolutely eliminates the "if" in hunting. High-fences mean, of course, that the game cannot ultimately escape. Pay your money, *ka-ching* goes the cash register, grab your receipt, and select the more robust specimen. That's the general consensus.

At my taxidermist years ago, I ogled one of the largest wapiti I'd ever seen—something over 425 points typical, if memory serves. The owner was just picking up the shoulder mount.

"Where'd you bag that brute?" I asked the young man.

"Saskatchewan," he said. "Chased it from one corner of the fence to the other. Not much of a hunt, but my father-in-law paid for it." At least, there's hope in youth.

I know a double handful of nimrods that own what's called the Triple Slam—all four varieties of North American sheep, 12 varieties of world goats, and 12 varieties of world sheep. Of course I'm going to say that the "Triple" is perhaps the top accomplishment in hunting, since I own one, but all those other hunters I know have at least one high-fence animal in their collections, and some own many. I made it a point to make sure all my trophies were free-range, native and wild, without high fences in thousands of miles. Many of their collections also included farm animal hybrids and feral animals, which I will not hunt, but that's a separate concern. I've bent an elbow with a number of those "Triple" guys, and to be fair, several assured me that a chase after Mid-Eastern sheep on a Texas ranch is no slam-dunk. One brought to my attention that the fence was only "about four-feet high," but if you're a diminutive Iranian *Moufloniform*, that's high enough.

"Did you score your ram?" I asked them. Each admitted they had.

I just thumbed through a current hunt organization magazine. Of the 89 total ads I counted (guns, clothing, real-estate, optics, high-tech gear, ammo, jewelry, aircraft, fair-chase hunting destinations, taxidermy, knives, baggage, camping gear, cruises, art and so on), 20 peddled, as best I can tell, high-fence hunting destinations. Two decades ago, you'd count them on the fingers of one hand in the same magazine. You do the math.

*****

What can we do? Is there a cure for the malaise? How can we return to a purer form of hunting? I doubt many want to. When I attend the conventions, every other guy gets a paycheck from some aspect of the "hunting industry" (I cringe whenever I hear that term)—aviation reps, hawkers of electronic gear I have a hard time even associating with hunting, jewelers, auto peddlers, purveyors of camo undies, insurance traffickers, African wine mongers, smart phone vendors, publishers, travel agents, ad nauseam.

"'ate the bloody place," Russell Tarr, a Zimbabwe PH I've known for decades said. He referred to the convention itself. "Bugger the hucksters! Best feed 'em to the Zambezi crocs."

Later at one of a myriad of Vegas casino bars, we reminisced about our first safari together three decades earlier. By the second beer, we bemoaned the passing of time and the power of the hunting industry. We all knew the unasked question, the elephant in the room: "What can we do about it?"

We stared at the half-empty beer glasses on the polished, synthetic bar with gold flecs in it. A poster proclaiming "Welcome Hunters!", with a shootist astride a brand-new camo quad in a spotless camo outfit with a carefully manicured five-days' growth, hung overhead. He leered at us with perfect white teeth.

TOO OLD?

Author's note: Too many hunters these days don't apply for state hunting tags themselves, they let a company specializing in the activity do it for them. This essay is aimed at those that still apply for their own tags and know the score, like me.

"Hell, them kids are drawing hunting tags I've tried to score for a quarter century." Jack exaggerated slightly. He meant a once-in-a-lifetime Utah tag, in his case moose. "I aint got that many years left, neither." Jack had a heart attack two years earlier and survived it to make it to his 70s. "So I quit!" We're standing in his window and glass business in downtown Ogden, Utah.

His reasoning was he wouldn't draw out, or get maximum bonus points, before he died. "Even if I keep applying, I'll be too damn old to do a thing about it, if I draw the tag. Nope, I quit. Don't try to talk me out of it."

Though my health was good enough that I still climbed the sheep scarps and I'd just returned from hunting chamois in Romania, I sympathized. I teach, among other things, university human biology and knew that 90% of us will get cardiovascular disease before we check out. With cancer, it's nearer 50% (that doesn't necessarily mean we'll die of it).

I'd systematically quit applying for tags. First, I quit Wyoming bighorns and walked away from my bonus points. My reasoning: I did the math and figured I might draw out in a quarter century or more, maybe by the time I'm 90, if there's any sheep left. With the decreasing tag numbers and more young bodies getting into the tag application ritual, and they would, you could increase that date, and who cavorts the sheep scarps at 95? Then, I quit Wyoming prong-horns for the same reason, and left my bonus points right there in the dust, too. Ditto Arizona desert bighorns, and Nevada rams. I stopped applying for other species in other states for the same reason. Each summer or spring, I get warning emails from the state game boys that say I'll lose my bonus points if I don't apply or buy a bonus point this year. I won't see any return on the effort or money, so ignore them. Indeed, the only tag I'm still accumulating bonus points on is Utah bighorn sheep, and only because I have too many bonus points not to, but for getting max points and any chance on a tag, it looks like I'll be pushing my eighth decade, and maybe more.

"No sense givin' 'em money so them little cretins can hunt," Jack continued. Jack wasn't really that hard-core, because he had kids and grandkids of his own he took hunting and fishing. "The bonus point fees ain't doin' me no good. Just as soon spend it on a better brand of bourbon."

"It's age discrimination," the camo-clad and silver-haired nim-rod said. Max and I had met before. We stood in the Western Hunting and Conservation Expo in Salt Lake City's Salt Palace. "Once-in-a-lifetime!?" He referred to Utah's system where you could only draw a moose, bison, desert bighorn, bighorn or mountain goat tag once in your lifetime. Fair enough on the surface. He continued, "Hell, them youngsters have a whole life, fifty years or more to draw them tags or any tags. We oldsters have maybe a handful. Why not cut us some slack? Stack the deck a little in our favor so we get a tag before we're on the wrong side of the grass. Hell, we've been buyin' licenses and payin' into the game department coffers for decades. It's the least they can do."

Ed, another chum, joined the conversation. "They give them kids all the chances on those youth hunts. They have four times the chance of drawing a general buck tag than you and I. They've got 100% draw odds with two bonus points, but it takes eight for you and me. Gospel truth. When the archery tags are sold out, they make available more tags just for the kids—1500, isn't it? Kids that get a general buck tag can hunt all three seasons—archery, muzzleloader, and centerfire rifle. You and I can only hunt one." Ed gasped for breath and continued. "Then there's Utah's separate youth elk hunts, and 20% of general deer tags are reserved just for the kids. The kids get to jump the gun on duck hunts a week earlier than the rest of us. Those separate hunts eliminate the competition, too. Ain't that discrimination against we old-timers in aces?!" He got so worked up he choked on his *Dos Equis*.

A stranger added, "I'm with you, Pal. Name's Hal." A band of high-schoolers jostled around us. It was Saturday and the kids were out of school and at the convention applying for the myriad of big game tags available to all comers for a mere five bucks apiece, and that meant all those once-in-a-lifetime tags, including desert and Rocky Mountain bighorn sheep. The tags are good ones, so thousands temporarily immigrate from out of state to apply. No matter the chances of drawing out are as thin as getting beaned by a meteorite or winning the Mega Millions lottery.

"Look at 'em! All after that five dollar lifetime hunt. They don't see that the draw odds are worse than inheriting a grouse moor in Scotland."

"That's the joy of youth." Myron P. joined the throng in the aisle in front of Joe Jakab's Point Blank hunting booth. "Eternal optimism. We graybeards know better, and since we've been hemorrhaging greenbacks into the hunt tag lottery for decades, we know we stand little to zero chance of scoring a tag before we're dead. I ain't applying next season! I'd considered quittin' before, but you fellas gave me the inspiration to actually do it."

"I quit applyin' two seasons back," Barney J. said. "Chances of drawing nil, and I've got maybe ten years left before I'm pushin' up petunias, and the whole process got too damned complicated." Our little throng in the aisle was attracting more gray-hairs and slowing the flow of eager young eyes pushing through the SLC Salt Palace. *Good on us*, I thought.

Two more long-time nimrods from up Weber County way stopped by. They'd each applied for premium tags since well before the bonus point system even went into effect, so they had enough experience to contribute to the increasingly vociferous gray-hair gang.

"I'd applied for desert bighorn sheep since day one, before they even started up the bonus point deal," Wally said, "and continued right through the bonus point system. Had max points from the start, and it still took me 14 years in the bonus point boondoggle to score a tag in a poor area that had higher draw odds, not to mention all those years before bonus points went into effect." His chum added, "I'm not having any luck with my Rocky Mountain bighorn tag, either. I got 18 points but there's guys with 25. And lots with more than me, too. I got more chance of getting a date with Natalie Wood."

"She's dead!" someone on the north end of the crowd hooted.

"My point exactly!" Wally shouted back.

"Hell's bells!" John bellowed like a range steer, "Look at me. How many more years you think I got?" John owned the booming voice you'd expect from a trial lawyer, which he was, and he wielded a cane. I stepped back as he skewered the air for emphasis. Convention goers stared as they edged around our growing throng. We'd drawn the attention of the security boys. One stood at each end of the aisle and they glared with arms folded across trophy-sized bellies.

"Hell, them kids can buy tags over the counter," a tall graybeard with a weather-beaten tan hollered over the heads of our growing crowd. He drawled like Sam Elliot.

"Who're you?" someone else shouted from the center of the throng.

"Ira from Idaho," he hollered back. "That place with the baboon-murdering game commissioner—you heard it on the news—shows the state of our game boys, doesn't it? And they give the kids big discounts, too."

"In Montana, the kids get a separate two-day youth hunt, and a fall-break hunt, too. They got anything for we 65-and-older boys? Forget it."

"Arizona has tags set aside just for youth. They ain't got any for the gray crowd, neither," Al yelled above the melee.

The only guy in the crowd with a sports coat chimed, "It's not that we want to nix the youth hunts, it's just we older fellows want equal consideration. What's so damned sacred about being 14 or 16 with your whole life in front of you?"

"So what we gonna do about it?" someone hollered from out on the periphery of the growing mob.

"We could sue 'em!" the trial lawyer bellowed. "Age discrimination, and we'd win, too! Those fat boys in the Utah legislature would roll right over! 'Sue!' I say!"

"What about the game boys give us five bonus points when we turn 65?" a stranger hollered. "Get 'em when we apply for social security and use them how we like!"

Idaho Ira shouted, "Make it ten!"

"Yeah!!" a camo-clad gray-hair hollered. "Terrific!" a septuagenarian bellowed. "Damned straight!" echoed down the aisle. "Grand idea!" and "Right on!" and "Let's sock it to 'em!"

Gray hairs, men and women, joined the crowd like iron filings to a magnet. We surged down the aisle like we were going somewhere, slapping backs, shouting epiphanies, laughing. One graybeard shoved a fist in the air and shouted, "Gray Power!"

The security boys' eyes bulged and they stepped back and talked into their shoulders.

Hunting, Sport and Semantics
in the 21st Century

As a young professor those decades ago, I wrote on the blackboard at the beginning of each class, "A wise man changes his mind many times, a fool never." My idealism has waned, alas, but I still find reason to vocalize that saying. It's so important, you'll find versions of it in Russian, Hausa, Danish, Han, French, *ad infinitum*. It expresses the essence of learning and teaching: Without the ability to change one's mind when faced with new evidence, one is close-minded and can never learn a thing. As we age our minds stiffen, stultify, and we fogies find it more and more difficult to change our minds, or learn anything—witness our ancient and lovely batch of close-minded and dictatorial politicians. Happily, I still change my mind when faced with convincing argument or new data—perhaps a result of continued exposure to young and flexible minds at the university. Admitting I'm wrong means I learn something new.

Here's an example. I often wrote about the ethics of hunting over the years. To paraphrase, I scoffed at the idea that hunting was a sport, and said something like, "soccer is a sport, hunting is a life philosophy." I'm not sure I disagree with that opinion those years ago, either.

However, given the current and overwhelming worldwide division of hunting into either subsistence or sport hunting, without middle ground, by academics, politicians, game managers and hunting organizations, must we give in? Are they correct? Do other choices exist?

But first, let's attempt to define hunting and sport. The word sport comes from Old Spanish *desport*, meaning "leisure." In English c. 1300, sport is, "...anything humans find amusing." According to the organization SportsAccord, apparently the "...association for all the largest sports associations," sport:

1. has an "...element of competition."
2. must "be in no way harmful to any living creature." (What about boxing and football?)
3. "Not rely on any luck element."
4. "An activity involving physical prowess."
5. "...involving physical challenge and exercise."

As a noun, sport may be "a person that behaves in a good or specific way..." or "an activity involving physical exercise and skill in which an individual or team..." competes against another. As a verb, sport may mean to "...amuse oneself," or "to wear or display..."

Let's throw in a few definitions of "hunting" to keep this even: "The activity or sport of pursuing game" and "...conducting a search" hail from the *American Heritage Dictionary*. "The pursuit and killing or capture of game or wild animals" comes from the *Collins English Dictionary*.

What most members of hunting and conservation organizations pursue isn't subsistence hunting, but is it sport? We can't argue it doesn't harm animals, and doesn't it often contain strong elements of predictable luck, for example in driven game and baiting?

Let's plunge on.

I taught my logic and argumentative writing students that semantic argument (argument that relies on the meaning of words) is an admission that you lack solid evidence. Semantic argument should convince no one. Yes, that is just what we're doing here.

The insistence by those who claim that hunting is either one or the other, subsistence or sport, is a classic example of what is known as an "either-or-fallacy"—suggesting that only two choices exist. Most of us know without much mental strain that there's more than two choices on any question. The world ain't black-and-white, regardless of political babble.

So what is hunting? What about the concepts of "trophy," "patience," "bush skills" such as tracking and stalking, "persistence" as in focus on one particular animal or trophy size? None of these or any other abstract concepts hunters practice are incorporated in any "hunting" definition I can Google. Let's talk hunting.

*****

My infatuation with sheep hunting began before I was 10 years old with Jack O'Connor's stories in the old *Outdoor Life*. I read his account of the Chadwick Ram, of extended expeditions into Sonora after desert sheep, and his occasional mentioning of Marco Polo sheep though to my understanding he did not hunt them. Possibly because of its mythical quality, that last one hooked me, and I spent most of three decades researching, breathing and dreaming *Ovis ammon poli*. It took on the qualities of a quest, a silver chalice with horns. It retrospect, it seemed destined. Instead of fantasizing about the cheerleader next door in short skirts and bobby socks, my night teen visions consisted of 60-inch rams with mythic sweeps of horns on frozen Pamir peaks. Mostly.

In the year 2000, Wes Vining made it happen. He brokered a hunt with Yuri Matison, without doubt the premier Marco Polo sheep outfitter and guide (check the record books if you doubt), and in December I trod terrain that felt the tramp of Marco Polo, Teddy Roosevelt and Tamerlane. I shrugged off twenty-below-zero temps and gale force winds and dutifully lunged through hip-deep drifts and gasped in the thin oxygen of the 16,000 feet Pamirs, and I would have it no other way. One must suffer in a true quest.

Literature mirrors life, or is it the other way around? All of those day and night dreams through youth and adulthood, the physical challenge and suffering—I frosted one ear and acquired a dry hack that lasted a year—the decades of tension, were the price a hunter pays. We bagged the grand ram, for I'd settle for none less than grand, in winds shrieking like banshees and gale-driven snow curtains, then struggled the prize through the drifts to a fragment of the old Silk Road.

The celebrations of the guys in camp, the vodka toasts, the measurements and the number 229 and 63-inches to which I paid no attention because they seemed so out of place, all seemed surreal and ethereal. Not the least of it all, is the full-body mount of the ram in a part of my house we call "the clean, well-lighted place" (after the title of a Hemingway short story). It stands as a shrine amongst 50 other trophies there, and each time I walk into the room I stroke my palm along the great sweep of horns to give respect to the ram and the quest. Was there an element of competition? I think not. Was this sport? Not to me.

*****

The well-maned African lion is the perfect symbol, and it has been for millennia—of empires, of royalty, of power, of life-and-death. Well-heeled 19th century English gentlemen journeyed to British East Africa to hunt lions. Persian royalty and Egyptian pharaohs killed them with spears, often from chariots. Well into the 20th century Maasai morani warriors surrounded lions and speared them when they charged, with very frequent maulings in the "sport;" and morani status jumped upon having killed a lion and that made more wives certain and available.

I'd hunted in Africa for a decade before Charlie Goldenberg brokered a safari to Tanzania in the early 90s. My number one trophy, of course, was lion. Everything else would be window dressing without that big, hairy cat.

As in any true quest, the lion didn't come easy. We hunted in the Msima and Ugalla River country and bagged leopard, cape buffalo, an East African Greater Kudu that taped an inch more than the then world record, roan and half a dozen other trophies for two weeks, but no lions. None roaring in the night, no fresh spoor, none visiting the baits. Then we journeyed east to Maasailand.

The clients hopped a bush flight and the professional hunters drove the gear including rifles for three days over dirt tracks to south

Maasailand. We clients were stuck in the camp without PHs and, incidentally, without those rifles for those three days. The first night, lions roared in the night just down the *donga* close enough the reverberations rattled the tent canvas. I sweated and grimaced at the lack of rifles while the rest prayed the lions would keep their distance. A trophy I desired more than anything on the planet, roared out there in the black and I could do nothing about it. I learned that night that frustration exceeds fear, love and jealousy.

When the professional hunters finally turned up, of course the lions had departed. We then hunted lesser kudu, more buffalo, fringe-eared oryx, gerenuk, impala, bushbuck, and most of all, the lion. We found only old lion spoor, old lion kills scavenged by hyenas, and no lions roared in the night.

The camp sunk into silence, and we drank too much Lion Lager at the evening campfire. The safari had gone sour. The other grand trophies meant nothing without that lion. Then one evening too late in the safari for comfort and as we stared at scorpions crawl on the acacia logs in the campfire, a Maasai wandered out of the night. He huddled with Gabreli, our tracker and a Maasai elder, who then conferenced with Larry Richards the PH. A lion pride had killed a buffalo in the big thicket, a two-mile tangle of wait-a-bit thornbush down the donga. Suddenly, the camp came alive. We talked, we laughed, we drank another lager in the firelight.

We loaded the Land Cruiser in the pre-dawn dark and drove down the sand track and through the stream as the Maasai filled gourds with water, and then off into the gathering dawn. A bushbuck darted across the track and disappeared. A magnum impala posed at the edge of the thornbush but no one gave it a glance.

In the just-light, Gabreli the tracker hissed, "Simba!" and pointed at the vultures in the fever trees. Vultures in trees meant lions on the kill. We debarked and eased ahead, when Gabreli crouched and pointed as two hirsute male lions glared from across a buffalo carcass 200 meters into the thornbush, but in the shadows it was tough to tell where the manes began and the black buffalo carcass ended. I couldn't find the shot in the shadows and poor light, and then they were gone. We trailed and saw one trot through thornbush and mist into the tangle, and we circled hoping against hope to find the second male. As we neared the carcass, the lion growled a deep warning, but then vaporized, and we trailed on. At last, he turned to glare over his shoulder and uttered that low, guttural cursing growl you felt through the ground. The crosshairs settled low behind the shoulder and I squeezed and the cat leapt at the blast, stumbled in the dust and streaked for the bush. I fired again and the cat stumbled and the PH loosed off the big double .577 and kicked up dust and the lion disappeared into the tangled thornbush.

"You gutshot the sonovabitch!" the PH hissed. The trackers looked as happy as kittens in a bath, but I remembered those crosshairs solid behind the shoulder, the crisp trigger release.

We trailed into the thornbush so thick we had to crawl under it, expecting the charge at any nanosecond. A blood fleck here, strands of lion mane there on a thorn, then a francolin partridge flushed and we all tangled the guns in the bush trying to point them at a bird and the trackers flattened. On again, me without spit, Richards pale beneath the sunburn, the trackers sweating great glistening beads.

"Kufa!" Gabreli exhaled, almost in question. "Kufa!" Estoni echoed. "Kufa! Kufa! Kufa!" the Maasai that had joined the party chanted. Dead, dead, dead! I thought. The big tawny cat lay like a kitten in front of a fireplace. A tiny dark hole in the shoulder where the 300 grain .375 bullet exited, with a single drop of blood on the fur, underscored the finality. And the success.

Was this sport? Was there any competition? Without those record books which I don't care about, the drama lacks that vital element of sport as it's defined. That word, *drama*, might be a better description. Or perhaps *tragedy*, because most hunts involve strong elements of a classic tragedy. Semantics again.

Polar bear wasn't on the radar. I simply did not respond to the few polar bear videos or films I'd seen—two planes flying the ice-pack in search of the great white bear, and once located, one of them landing ahead of the bear in ambush while (perhaps) the other plane hazes the critter toward the waiting shootist. Or snowmobiles in the equation. Was there any doubt in the kill? Where was the challenge, physical exertion, the drama? In hunting, there must be that question of death, of success and possible failure. Without it, it's simply that euphemism "harvesting," of whatever word that's fashionable to say "killing."

Once again the greatest of hunt brokers, Wes Vining, changed my mind (we're talking the 1990s here, and alas, Vining has long-since retired, to my sorrow). He had a new area for polar bear that should come on line for importation within the year. Hunting was already open, but importing wasn't. "In a year," Wes said, "we'll be able to import. Just a matter of paperwork working its way through the government bureaucracy." I took his word for it and plunked down my deposit and before I knew it I was sleeping on a mound of duffel in the chill of the Yellowknife airport, and then off in a bush-adapted Boeing 737 for Banks Island, and then off again in the same plane for Resolute Bay, where I wandered the frozen early March streets in 20-something below temps waiting for the Twin Otter flight to Grise Fjord three days later. Grise Fjord was the northern-most community in North America, all 100 Inuit natives. The intense cold at minus 36 degrees frightened me in an old place, and for one of the very few times in my life, I had second thoughts. This would be no airplane or snowmobile hunt, I'd made sure of that. We were to aim out onto the polar icepack in the full winter of early March on dogsleds. We would survive in wall tents, I hoped.

I'd made up my mind not to shoot any but a truly grand bear, even if I went home without one. Ten-foot would be grand enough, but I would settle for a nine-footer, maybe just less. "You'll recognize a big bear when you see it," Wes said over the phone, and I believed.

The Inuits outfitted me with caribou clothing—parka, mitts, mukluks, pants—that slipped over my box store cold-weather gear, and one dawn our two dogsleds mushed west onto the icepack. To shorten a very long and frigid story on a dogsled expedition of hundreds of miles, we camped on the icepack for near two weeks, moving camp nearly every day. We glassed one or three bears each day, two that might square eight-feet, from the tops of icebergs frozen into the pack ice. We took six hours to break and re-pitch camp each day, too.

I'd begun to wear out. I put off loo trips until I might burst, it was that cold. No vegetation with which to make a fire for warmth.

Never truly being warm at all, unless it was in the two down sleeping bags in the tent with Coleman stoves for heat at night. I longed for warmth, but we hunted. Hard. Here was physical exertion, challenge and suffering. One ear suffered frostbite. I would perish without the guide Jaypatee Akeeagotak and his assistant.

We'd begun to hunt our way back, toward Grise Fjord, because we'd seen nothing I would shoot. *Perhaps not this time*, I despaired, and added, *you're too damned stubborn*.

As we shopped for a camp site one sundown we found those tracks—as big as a watermelon, a day old, wandering in a direction away from Grise Fjord, a direction we did not want to go. I did not want to go. With camp up and the sun down, the sled up-stander thermometer hanging at minus 38, we glass from the iceberg and spot a bear far off. I'm glassing, but really thinking of hot food and crawling into the tent and sleeping bag and don't want to mess with another under-sized bruin, but Jaypatee wanders out into the dusk and shortly he is back. "Get your gun."

The guys harness the dogs again and we mush out into the lingering twilight and soon the dogs spot the bear and in a crashing, yelping, caroming chase, we try to catch the sprinting, bus-sized bear. I grasp the lashing with one hand and the .375 with the other and then the dogs are free and they bay the bear and I am off and I shoot, then gawk at more than half a ton and 10'4" of the toughest trophy I can remember. As I stand in a stupor of awe, I touch the freon rifle barrel with bare skin and hear the skin sizzle like bacon on a skillet. It's 41 below-zero.

As we skin the bear and the hide crackles and twists in temperatures that freeze spit in midair, we toss chunks of meat and guts to the ravenous dogs. They snarl and fight in primeval fury. The Inuits hack off chunks of raw meat and chew as blood freezes on chins. We quarter the bear and load it onto the sled, even the guts which will become dog food for the return trip. No Inuit wastes meat.

There's that endless hundred miles by dogsled back to Grise Fjord that we make in two days, and the reverse flights back out to civilization and warmth. Because the bear is not importable from that area, I drop the trophy with Robertson's Taxidermy in Yellowknife and they work on what will become a spectacular life-size mount for a full year, and by that time, the bear is importable. It makes the trip to the border in Montana in a truck and in another truck to Cheyenne, Wyoming, where I gather the crate as it sits in a puddle in a shipping company yard, nothing damaged, thank the Red Gods. Through some miracle we are able to cinch the big crate onto (not into) a big pickup and make the trip home to Utah on Wyoming's back roads to avoid the high speed interstate traffic.

The vertical, full-body mount towers across the room from that Marco Polo ram we mentioned earlier, without doubt one of the top trophies I own. The trophy is part of the hunt equation, too, and it has been since at least ice-age Europe hundreds of thousands of years ago when Neanderthal man hauled bear skulls and stag antlers back to the cave. Check the fossil record, if you disbelieve.

In this essay, we really attempted to define "hunting." I'm not sure we succeeded. As it's defined, hunting is not "Sport." The element of competition often doesn't exist at all, lest we accept the quest as competition with the trophy animal, and I don't. Those enamored of record books and acquiring a game trophy a silly millimeter larger than Joe Everyman's critter might disagree.

There's also the idea of earning a trophy. I've often made expeditions motivated mainly because I wanted that particular game animal trophy or mount for a specific spot in the house. A recent Zambezi Delta crocodile from Mozambique jumps to mind, and that Animal Artistry life-size mount is spectacular. No "sport" definition I've seen deals with the trophy concept. A book publisher I know makes safaris to Africa and leaves his kills there, and to my mind he's a sportsman, not a hunter.

Hunting always involves death, or at least the attempt at it. In some definitions, that fact excludes hunting as a sport. Most hunting involves at least a minimal of luck and often a great deal, and in some forms of hunting luck is built in, another point that might exclude it from being a sport. I don't know how many hunting articles where I've written, "gimme luck any day." It was certainly lucky that we found those great polar bear tracks very late in that hunt. If we'd taken a different turn beyond that last iceberg, we'd have missed them and returned without a bear.

But if hunting is not sport, what is it? Good question, but not easily answered. I lean toward "drama" "…to portray life or a character usually involving conflicts and emotions through action…" The term "tragedy" works too, defined as, "…a serious drama describing a conflict between the protagonist and a superior force (such as destiny)…"

I tense when someone tells me hunting is a sport, or that I am a sport hunter. Tell a bullfight aficionado that has just finished running the bulls in Pamplona that his passion is sport, and he'll slug you.

THE ACCIDENTAL HUNTER

I t's my guess many of us have one of these. And we're lucky if we do. It's the accidental hunter in the family, or out of it, for that matter.

Remember those good ol' days? On my first mountain game foray with a full 17-years under my belt, I could at last grow some whiskers and knew I was bullet-roof in my L. L. Bean wool Maine guide shirt and White logger boots. I met my first honest-to-goodness outfitter in Kamloops, British Columbia. We tracked the "cook" down in a red-eye honky-tonk, and corralled the wrangler in the Lumberjack Bar. If anyone lit a match on the icy, greasy logging road drive into Crooked Lake with those 80-proof fumes oozing from the guys' pores, the Jeep would have blown in a fireball they'd still talk about in the logging camps. I slept the next two weeks in a wall tent with those guys, too, and they snored like chainsaws. In spite of the shaky start, we scored a 10-inch mountain goat.

And what about that whitetail hunt in Saskatchewan? The outfitter roomed me in the Country Inn with a guy that snored loud enough to shatter plaster, and I hollered about it, too. And then two weeks in a double wall-tent on the polar icepack chasing polar bears in full winter where one dawn the thermometer climbs to a wilting 31-below-zero. My two Inuit guides never remove a stitch of clothing the entire expedition, so imagine the odor when we heat the tent with Colemans each night. They snore, too. We score a 10' 4" stud bear from those dogsleds in spite of the eye-watering fragrance.

That accidental hunter caroms into my placid bachelor life those decades ago like a bowling ball into the strike pocket. She's an urban Michigander, and except for her enthusiasm, she's useless in the bush. Cheri screams when a grayling I'm teaching her to clean twitches. But she has advantages. I no longer share tents with the guys—we get our own. She stalks peeved lions and annoyed cape buffalo right along with us, and she refuses to stay back and watch. When we finger-and-toe a glacial scarp for King Kong tur, she clings at my heels with a 200-foot drop at hers. When bull elephants charge and the trackers vaporize, she pats my bottom to let me know where she is as the safeties click off.

Her bush role morphs. She gets so good with the binocular she often spots the trophy before the guides or me—very recent Hanghai argali, brown bear, Altai ibex, and desert bighorn sheep jump to mind. One spring hunt, she ogles a grand bezoar ibex that despite her directions, neither the three guides nor I can find. I gotta admit—with her little 10 x 30 Zeiss and diminutive stature, and after all, she is a girl, the guides don't take her serious. I know better. After we guys search for a full half-hour without finding it, we decide she's having a blonde moment (hey, I'm not gender insensitive here—nobody takes blonde jokes serious, right?). When we stand to leave, she says, "I see it, dammit!" I take a last ogle with the 15 x 56 binoc, and I do, too! Five inches of horn jabs above a cedar snag far up the scree. We score that 48-inch ibex after an hour-long stalk.

She has little desire to hunt, good news, since two sheep hunters in the family gets expensive. That said, she does hunt—for the odd leopard or croc impala bait; or maybe a trophy caribou on a two-month-long wilderness expedition, largely for the meat; or a 375 pt. muzzleloader wapiti at 25 yards.

Let's flash-back a quarter century. In those days, I'd take 5-8 week backpack and float-expeditions into the Arctic bush each year. She's on her first, and largely to please me, she's hunting trophy caribou. Weeks downriver we find a bull dozing on the river bank in the freon dusk. I coach her, and she touches off the .270. The slug slaps just where it should for a heart shot, and the bull leaps into the river and plunges toward us but loses steam half-way across. I wallow through bank ice to the struggling bull, grab an antler to horse him ashore, and he catapults me over his back into deep water. I sputter and stagger to the bank, she shoots it through the neck, and I wade back and grunt the caribou in. My teeth chatter so hard I nearly yank a jaw tendon. That 'bou is her first trophy. Over the years, she bags another one, and on a moose float-hunt with two pals, she scores the largest of the three bulls taken. I'm so proud of her, I gloat, darn me.

Over the last dozen years, she's beaten the pants off me on Wyoming public land pronghorns. We've both drawn the same number of buck tags, and her buck average is an astonishing 15-inches. My average? Don't ask.

A decade back, I draw a Utah desert bighorn tag with my maximum bonus points, finally. After 35 days of scouting and hunting, I slap the 11-year-old ram in the salt. No surprise, she found it with her little Zeiss glass. It's my ninth North American sheep and completes all four NA varieties.

The following year, Cheri draws out in a better unit with her max points. We scout for two weeks. We glass so-so rams opening morning then return to camp for breakfast. As we sip coffee beside the juniper deadfall fire, two rams saunter out of the pinions 50 yards away. We lunge for the .270 and the rams streak over the rim. We track them without luck.

It's late afternoon, two gorges east. Cheri spots—no surprise there—two desert bighorns half a mile across the gorge. I get my 15 x 56 Swarovski binoc on the pair, and one's a magazine-cover ram. *Holy Stuff!* I think.

Willyalookitdem 15-inch bases?! Grammar suffers when I get stoked. The mass carries to the broomed tips, too! But half a mile is a long shot, even for those techno-geeks with the digital scopes, sniper rifles and heat-seeking bullets.

The rams browse beneath the sheer rim across the canyon toward its head. We parallel them along the opposite rim, and as the canyon narrows, so does the distance. We're at 500 yards, still too far, then it's 450, 400. We can't let the rams mist into the tangled blackbush and willows at the canyon head, so we find a scrub juniper hanging out over a 300-foot sheer drop. Cheri stuffs her jacket into the branches for a rest, I grasp her belt with one hand and a sturdy pinon tree with the other, she gets as comfortable as possible hanging in space with that pucker-class drop beneath her, and touches off. The ram pogos twice and tumbles down the slope. It takes 25 hours to fetch that ram because we can't finger-and-toe down that sheer cliff without tech climbing gear. Need I mention? Her ram tapes 11-inches more than mine and is the second largest taken from the only Utah unit containing 100% native bighorns, too.

My accidental hunter has other uses. She wades through the paperwork for those overseas junkets. She plasters herself to the computer and shops the airlines for the best prices and schedules, and researches and reserves the hotels. We tour before and sometimes after the hunt, and she decides what to see. I'm glad she does, because I detest the busywork of hunting in other countries—gun formalities, securing visas, booking flights. She keeps me from getting too vocal at airport and airline indignities, and if I do her knuckles slug into my ribs to remind me to stay off that "do not fly" list. Guides are on their best behavior with a woman along, too; they drink less, belch less, and often try to impress her.

If we've got to change airline tickets, tweak touring reservations, or adjust anything else overseas, she does it, and she suffers no guff. My pal Don Jacklin nicknames her "Bear Cat" on an urial hunt in Turkmenistan, and not because she's subtle.

*****

I'm not the only guy with an accidental hunter in the family. Take Doug Allen in Huntsville, Utah. Doug's hardcore about his hunting, but his wife Susie is now the family pronghorn guru, and she just bagged a grand Shiras moose. And what about Joaquin Carballo's wife Pilar? She's scored jaguar, puma, and peccary in south Mexico's Chiapas rainforests, where they live. And she just wants to go along, not shoot. I won't mention my New England hunting pal's name, because he's got a new lady friend, but he hauls his women along on those hunting junkets, too, and gets the same benefits.

Cheri won't spend money on a guided hunt for herself, but encourages me. She applies for tags so we can take self-guided she-bangs, too—she owns even odds for limited-entry trophy elk this year, a long-shot on a bighorn tag, and she's applying for one of those Wyoming public land pronghorns. If she scores an almost accidental tag, she's ecstatic not because she can tack another trophy on the wall, but because she's got an excuse to hunt and camp. And that should be the real reason anyone goes afield.

ROGUES

"**N**o goot," Majara, the m'Shona tracker said. "No rain." We stood on a bluff above the dry Limpopo River and watched a dozen scarecrow Shengani cattle shuffle through the dust in a futile search for water.

The rains came late that season, and they ended weeks too soon. The Native mealie-corn plots withered before they ripened, and sand storms howled up the waterless Limpopo sand river. The elephants shoved over the vertical steel train rails planted in concrete and stepped across the three-inch braided steel boundary fence and left Gonarezhou Park. Gonarezhou means variously "place of many elephants" or "elephant's tusk," in the Xitsonga Shengaan dialect, or in the Shona.

Even in the wet years, Gonarezhou fed only half its 5000 elephants. They crossed the Park fence and raided the tribal area mealie plots, and faced the Natives hurtling fire brands in the night and beating 20-liter petrol tins year in and year out, but this season promised to get worse than even the grandfathers could remember. Already, the Natives starved. Robert Mugabe was busy coalescing political survival elsewhere, too.

The rangers tried. They peddled cull hunts to sportsmen ("You must kill the entire herd," the Park Director briefed the sporting groups), but slaughtering matriarch herds with screaming cows and wailing calves disturbed clients far more than they'd imagined. A matter of ethics, too, they said. Too, you couldn't trust the clients to kill them all. And you couldn't let elephants escape, either, because they remembered and killed people later.

After that snafu, platoons of rangers night-ambushed matriarch herds with spotlights and AK-47s, trucked the meat to the starving Natives those rare times they had gasoline enough, but word leaked and those in London and Copenhagen objected, and that ended that. Because of world opinion, too many elephants in their daily quest for a quarter ton of vegetation stripped the mopane forests of bark and browsed acacia down to the dust, and the Park turned to desert. Even more elephants raided the tribal lands. Those refined consciences in Europe and North America raised no cry when elephants trampled farmers into gore.

*****

They called the elephant safaris PAC, problem animal control. One safari hunter shot one problem elephant, but the math said PAC safaris wouldn't faze Park elephant populations. No matter, few clients hunted them for the good deed, anyway. For whatever reasons, no one objected to the PAC safaris in Edinburgh or Sausalito.

We "camped" in a rondavel at the Buffalo Bend tourist site, though no one at the Park had seen a tourist in months, and we drove into the Tribal Area each dawn with the idea of ambushing elephants retreating back into the Park after a night raiding what little remained of the Shengaan crops. Elephants knew the Natives would do their best to kill them, and they returned the favor. The farmers could not afford black market firearms, even the ancient AK-47s you bought in Harare or Bulawayo alleys for a pittance in South African Rand because Zim money was worthless, or those smuggled across the Limpopo from Crook's Corner and Beitbridge, so they snared and speared elephants. With luck. Without luck, the jumbo trampled them into sausage. If the Shengaan killed a jumbo, they dried the meat into biltong that fed a clan for a year, and it repaid in part the leveled crops, an uncle trampled into dusty gore or an infant stillborn in a thatch hut because the mother had nothing to eat.

"Bloody illegal, of course, the snaring," the professional hunter said as the Land Rover wash-boarded the dirt Park road in predawn black. "Do it anyway. Fasten cable snares to one-ton logs and when the Natives spoor up, they spear it, or blast it with a sewer pipe loaded with rebar and black powder. Can't say's I blame 'em, can you? Rangers turn a blind eye." As a result of the war between Natives and elephant, the Gonarezhou elephants became the most deadly in Africa.

"Trophy bull, that one," Mackay the professional hunter said as a bull elephant shuffled out of the ghost forest into the headlights and bluff-charged, then whirled back. "Thirty kilos in the salt."

Quick math said a tusk might weigh 65 pounds and though broken short from fighting, each was thick as a man's thigh. Plenty good enough for me, I thought, but of course you couldn't hunt them in the Park.

In the dawn, the Rover clattered past the shrapnel-pocked Park entrance gate blasted when Robert Mugabe and the over exuberant Black patriots ran Ian Smith's White apartheid government out those years earlier. No one had repaired it. Indeed, we daily heard distant explosions when a hapless Native or unsuspecting buffalo tripped a landmine.

We wheeled onto a track paralleling the steel-rail and braided-wire boundary fence. "We" consisted of Majara, Mackay and his .458, me with a solid-loaded .375, Cheri, the AK-47 toting Park ranger, a tribal area factotum, and an unarmed n'Dbele assistant professional hunter.

We motored along the boundary fence—me and Majara up top on the Land Rover's high seat in the freon dawn, Cheri and Mackay in the cab, the rest huddled in filthy blankets in the Rover's bed.

Majara hissed, "Zhou!" as the sun bled onto the withered acacia.

Three elephants grazed the mopane scrub 400 meters into the tribal area, the gray backs surfing above the mummifying gray-green canopy like whales. The great swell of muscle on necks and shoulders said they were bulls. Majara kicked the cab's back window to alert Mackay.

We off-loaded and trailed into the nine-foot mopane bush as silent as lizards on sand, cut the tracks and the green corn-flecked manure and trailed the jumbo as they edged toward the boundary fence. Wrinkled footprints the diameter of a woman's waist guaranteed bull ivory.

Majara raised a hand. A truck idled somewhere ahead. Dammit to hell, I thought. Majara climbed a mopane tree and stared toward the rumbling. It stopped, and started in another place. Couldn't be an engine. I remembered something I'd read—elephants gut-rumbled to communicate whereabouts in thick bush.

Majara duck-walked to scan beneath the three-foot mopane canopy, then grabbed my wrist and pulled me down and pointed with his chin. Fifty yards ahead we spotted the pillars of legs as the elephants stripped branches. We crouched and circled to get the wind more directly in our faces. The ranger clicked the AK safety on and off behind me in nervousness. The elephants heard it, and they stopped browsing and listened. The ranger clicked the safety again.

One bull pivoted and caromed through the mopane tangle at us and the .375 jumped to shoulder as Mackay and the ranger threw guns up, too. The bull exploded through a bush screen and braked in a dust cloud at 20 yards, shook its Volkswagon-sized head and flared ears to threaten and I aimed upward at the sixth wrinkle down its trunk and hoped I had the right angle for a brain shot. We backed away. The Native PH grabbed Cheri's belt from behind and dragged her as she photographed. False charges too often turn to real ones if you don't retreat. I read that somewhere, too. If the camera's auto flash triggered in the shadowed bush, the bull would charge.

Back at the Rover, the PH hollered, "Toothpicks! No client of mine shoots bloody toothpicks!" The tension had burst like a water balloon and we all got loud, Mackay more than anyone. "Twelve kilos to the side, hey!" I didn't know then that Jumbo Safari's professional hunter Mackay had never hunted elephant, let alone PAC elephant. Everyone must start somewhere.

Within the week, the elephants figured out we hunted them. They retreated to the Park from the tribal area earlier each day, too often in predawn black, and didn't set off raiding again until dark.

If we couldn't catch them at the boundary fence, we stalked into the tribal area at night. With these rogues, we could legally kill them anyway we could. Mackay toted a Vietnam-vintage starlight scope with the idea that he'd spot them in the dark, Majara would trigger the big spotlight, and I'd shoot. Simple. The starlight scope wouldn't work, though, so we listened for rumbling bellies or the slap of an ear against hide or the plop of dung.

The wisdom back in the States said night hunting and spotlights were unsporting and unethical—an American article of faith, if it served the person making the judgement—but Gonarezhou reality said you couldn't hunt anything more deadly and a spotlight might save your life if you had time to use it. Hunting these rogues at night pumped more adrenaline than even the charging buff I dropped so close it sprayed my chukkas with gore. When we got close in the dark, Mackay talked loud again, and that ended that.

"Seventy-five pounds if an ounce," I said as we caught a bull leaving the Park in the late sun. *Can't hope for better anywhere, chum,* I thought.

We motored down the boundary fence until we heard the singing-twang as the bull stepped across the wire cable into the tribal area. It browsed the bush 200 meters down the fence as Mackay gathered gear—spotlight, star-light scope though it didn't work, rifle, flashlight—he'd become oddly silent, and he took far too long at it. I'd loaded the .375 and fidgeted, because we could stalk and kill that bull before sunset, without any gear. Hell, I could see the bull just inside the tribal area. If it had been non-dangerous game, a nyala, say, I'd kill it from where we stood.

The bull shuffled into the mopane as the dusk gathered. When Mackay finally got himself ready and we'd cut the spoor, the bull had sauntered away into the gathering night. Majara spat and stalked off, his way of counting to ten. We all knew we should have killed the bull. Cheri *tss-k-ked* and sighed aloud. The tribal area man palms-upped in frustration, because a dead elephant meant meat and survival to the starving Shengaan—the real reason he'd come. When Majara returned, he and Mackay hissed at each other like hood-spread Mozambique cobras. Fifty-five-year-old Majara could now confront the white man in Mugabe's relatively new Black Zimbabwe, but he wasn't used to it. Mackay didn't like it, but what could he do? Too, he knew Majara was the better man in the bush, and that knowledge challenged the inviolate authority of the White Hunter.

We snaked into the savanna and sat against trees in the dark and listened. I located the Southern Cross in the black sky and heard mile-distant Natives drumming and singing, and grinned at the joy and rhythm. *Like an old Clark Gable film*, I thought.

Later, elephants slapped ears and shuffled toward us and Mackay and Majara hissed again and Mackay got loud, whether from fear, or from the back-talking and wiser Black man, I wasn't sure. The ele rumbled and plopped in the dark and moved off again at the noise. We trekked back to the Rover and left a man with a radio along the fence, then drove to the Park gate and waited for the radio to click twice to signal a crossing elephant. Too, if a jumbo stepped across the braided steel fence within half a mile of our fires, we'd hear the cable twang.

The Black men sat around one fire to ward off the night chill, and the Whites—Mackay, Cheri and me—at another, and waited for the radio signal or the singing fence. I didn't wonder at the separate fires, because a century of apartheid dies slowly. *When in Africa, do as the Africans do*, I thought, my way of rationalizing away the separate fires. *Hell, you can't speak the language anyway*, I further rationalized, *even if you sat at their fire.*

"Too bloody many of us," Mackay said. "Somebody's bound to die, and I'm responsible. Some must stay behind."

He looked at Cheri. She didn't say anything. He continued. "No place for a woman. Too bloody dangerous. You must stay behind with a Boy."

Now, Cheri tipped the scale at 103, stood five-one, took university parchment cum laude and owns a master electrician ticket and contractor's license in a male-dominated industry, and she's afraid of nothing, least of all superior males. She aimed an index finger between 250-pound Mackay's eyes for emphasis and said, "I paid to observe, and dammit, I'm observing." The fur flew so fast, and Mackay owned most of it, I couldn't get into the fray to act as peacemaker. Beyond, the gang's grins reflected the firelight. The native PH chuckled aloud and walked away from the safari and into the night and that was the last we saw of him. When we heard the two clicks on the two-way, Cheri went with us, which surprised no one.

We stalked along the fence a mile until we found our radioman. He led us another quarter mile to where fresh bull spoor crossed into the tribal area, the dung just steaming in the chill. Majara eased ahead with the spotlight. If we got up to jumbo, Majara would trigger the light, I'd step around and shoot, and Mackay and the ranger would back me up. That safety-clicking ranger worried me, though. *Bastard's liable to put a burst through the back of my skull*, I thought. Cheri'd keep behind and pat my butt to assure me of her whereabouts.

Not quite. Ears slapped hide beyond the acacia tangle. It neared, and we heard the rasping breath. Majara triggered the spotlight at the same moment I slipped the .375's safety. In that instant six tons of fury blasted through bush as broom-handle branches spiraled through air and Cheri slapped my butt when unarmed Majara faltered with the light but caught himself before he could run, and I thanked the Red Gods because we'd die without that spotlight. I got the crosshairs on a glowing tusk, but you can't shoot tusks through tangled bush if you want to live. The tusk disappeared and the endless bulk passed behind that tangle like a ship in the night. I centered the crosshairs on what I thought was the crease behind the shoulder for a heart shot, but I wasn't sure through the intertwined branches. The bull misted into the Tribal Area. He'd circle back into the Park and we'd never catch him before he did, unless he wanted us to, and in that ambush somebody would die.

"Bloody hell and praise the gods you didn't shoot!" Mackay hollered. He scanned to see who had run.

We walked back to the Rover, each with his thoughts. *We should have killed that bull*, I thought again. Majara periodically shook his head from side-to-side. The Shengani man wanted to stop at the village bottle store to spend his wages; he no longer believed in any of it.

In a day, or two, the elephants left the Park only after dark, and they'd return to the refuge before first light. Fewer of them left the Park at all along our section of fence. They'd shifted their movements elsewhere. We ate grim suppers at days' ends, and spoke little on the predawn drives to the fence. Most of the gang had abandoned the deadly and hopeless game. Even the assigned ranger found duties elsewhere.

"Damned nonsense," I said. "Let's quit. Drive on to Chiredzi." We sipped Gordon's gin and tonic sundowners at Buffalo Bend in silence watching the kudu and the nyala dig in the sand river for water in the last light. "Waste of time here."

Our chances had dwindled, and we'd only catch night-raiding elephants unafraid of man. The danger if we did catch one had expanded exponentially. Hunting is one thing, someone dying another.

We discussed it as a matter of form, but everyone wanted out, Mackay more than anyone. How much of it was the responsibility he felt for us stalking very dangerous elephants in the night, and how much of it was something else, I wasn't sure. Up north, we'd stalk hippo, bushpig, and kudu with no danger, and finish up the safari without the bile. Without the elephants looming in our dreams, we grinned again in the Rover cab, and the guys in the bed laughed aloud on the day-long drive.

As the Red Gods would have it, we hadn't quite finished with elephants. While hunting bushpig along the Chiredzi River one dawn, we startled a cow and calf elephant herd in acacia forest. Two cows instantly charged the Rover. Mackay ground gears into reverse and revved backward down the track with pistons screaming. I clutched the .375 between knees as two cows closed and expected Mackay to smash into a tree at any moment. When he did, I planned to vault free and shoot as fast as I could jack the bolt. Just as the first cow closed the final yards, she lifted her head and broke off the charge as the Rover revved backward at 50 per through the forest. Point taken.

Gonarezhou Epilogue:

Two years later, another Zimbabwe pro-hunter showed me a photo snapped where we'd had the near thing in the night at the Gonarezhou fence. In the photo, you saw the dark greasy channel through pale sand from the screen of acacia bush to the boundary fence. A rogue elephant had caught a hunter at the acacia and crushed and trampled him along the ground as his gore darkened the sand.

"Put the carcass in a mealie basket," the PH with the photo said, "save for the boots."

EASTERN CAPE, 2004

"Eh! Still interested in a bloody nice PAC jumbo?" I heard through the crackling phone connection in that distinct southern African accent. I'd left word with outfitters I wanted a rogue bull, and the hairier the ordeal, the better.

Five days later, we motored into the dawn on another continent and in another hemisphere, me suffering from acute jetlag. The private game reserve manager said, "Let's do the dirty and get back for the breakfast. Mustn't offend the clients out for the family photo safari. Apt to get nauseous at the sight of blood."

Apparently, two young bulls had chased an open touring Land Cruiser lorry, and tourists got sensitive about that sort of thing. That teenaged elephant exuberance sealed their fate, too.

We ambushed the problem bulls next to a road within thirty minutes and climbed out of the Range Rover. "Shoot 'em both if you'd like," the reserve manager said. At ten grand per trophy fee, I didn't like. I put a .375 solid through one bull's brain at 105 measured yards, and that was that. Before we got back for breakfast with the tourists without a drop of blood on our pressed britches, two lorries complete with hydraulic hoists had hauled the young bull to a warehouse butchery. As much adrenaline as swatting a fly, I thought.

CAPRIVI STRIP, 2008

We'd just cleared Namibian customs in Windhoek aimed at a leopard and crocodile safari.

"Care to shoot outlaw ele?" professional hunter John Wamback asked as he wheeled the Toyota Land Cruiser through downtown traffic. He sounded cheerful, but I recalled those two PAC failures. *Is this the third strike, or the charm?* I wondered.

My late hunt fantasies all dealt with leopards, though I'd bagged several, so elephant hunting wasn't on the radar. I'd forgotten how much I wanted rogue ivory. Hunting rogue elephants can jade anyone, to the extent it's tough to take much interest in stalking other game. I can't sit through a Super Bowl or welter-weight title bout, either.

"Problem beasts up on the Caprivi Strip," Wamback said. "Migrating 'cross from Botswana to Zambia. Wreck the Native mealie fields in the process. You put an end to their bloody mischief, or the rangers will before they bugger someone else. All they found of one chap was the head." Elephants had stomped two Natives into molecules a week earlier. "You put a rogue bull in the salt, and the Natives score the meat and your trophy fee—in the form of HIV medication and schoolbooks, of course. If rangers kill the bull, Natives get only the meat."

Wamback knew all about my rogue jumbo infatuation. He'd hooked me like a tiger fish on a Rapala within two stoplights, except I didn't fight like a tiger fish. Yeah, the medication and textbooks were worth the thought, but I wanted rogue ivory so bad my stomach knotted when I thought of it.

Next day, we motored north on Namibia One and over-nighted with assistant professional hunter Isaac (EEEt-sok) Grobelaar, and next dawn we offed east into the Caprivi Strip and collected two Kung! trackers complete with the ultimate bush status symbols—cell phones—from dirt-floor, thatch-roof huts, and made East Caprivi's hub of Katima Mulilo in afternoon. Wamback and Grobelaar sorted out the permits and arrangements with the local ranger and phone calls and faxes to the ministry in Windhoek.

When they'd finished, Wamback said, "Shoot as many as you can afford. Bloody beasts tearing up the whole Caprivi." As a college prof and scribe, I'd settle for one trophy fee.

"Must get the local chief's permission," Wamback said as the Cruiser granny-geared up a yard-wide footpath through dreadlock thornbush. "More important than the bloody endless paperwork. Wait here." We parked at a pole-fenced kraal. "Might take a bit."

An hour later, Wamback said, "Bloody ordeal, that. You crawl in on knees staring at the dirt floor clapping hands. Our gov game scout explains in their lingo, and he and the chief back-and-forth while I crouch and sweat and the chief's wives giggle at me, the fat White man. Bloody formality it is, but we must do it. Toss me a Fanta, even if it is warm."

Later, we drove two miles through trackless bush to visit a Native complaining of problem ele. "Chap says crop-raiding bulls watered at a pan out in the bush last night," Wamback told us. "Saw the tracks and mealie in the dung and everything. Don't quite trust it, but best to look."

We drove to the pan and found ele spoor. "Right-oh. Bloody three-days old. Natives see ele a week ago and send us on snipe hunts. Nothing lost, to them. Time means nothing. They reason we might find jumbo, and if we do, they get first meat. If we don't, they've had a grand outing, and we've wasted half a bloody day."

Next dawn we trekked an hour into the bush listening to the doves *coo-coo-COOah*. Otherwise, the mopane tangle was oddly silent for anywhere in Africa. I saw why. Natives had set the entire pan or waterhole shoreline with tiny snares made from bent twigs and twine. For any bird to drink, it shoved its head through a loop in a snare and when it did, one dead dove or partridge. Elephants had trampled the snares where they'd watered. We saw old antelope snares along the trails to the water, but the Natives had abandoned them because larger game no longer existed.

"See why no bloody game lives in the tribal lands, save goat-eating leopards and migrating elephant?" Wamback said. "Can't say as I blame them, though. Natives're starving thanks to the ele. Good thing is, a rogue bull watered here four hours ago. See the maize kernels in the dung? He'll shade-up in an hour and we'll spoor 'im up 'fore day's end."

The Kung trackers led, then Wamback and his .458 Lott, me with the .470 Champuis double rifle, Cheri, and Isaac and his .458 Win brought up the rear. We trailed past abandoned huts and a five-acre ruined mealie field and trampled squash plants. The Natives had retreated from the nightly elephant terror to Katima town. A five-inch scorpion lay flattened in one ele track, and a chameleon in another. The dawn chill had turned to sweltering heat in the tangle. The spoor led toward the Zambezi River and safety in Zambia if the ele crossed.

Three hours later, Wamback turned and put an index finger to lips. Everyone unlimbered the big rifles. I squeegee-ed sweat from my eyes. Cheri grinned at the thought of pending action.

The trackers eased along the trail of 21-inch footprints and torn branches. Instead of staring at the ground, the Kung trackers stopped dead and squinted into bush dreadlock to one side of the spoor. The bull had circled onto its back trail and waited five yards from it, absolutely invisible in the tangle. Lucky, he'd had second thoughts before we'd caught up or he'd have charged onto us before we could shoot.

We slowed more. Wamback thumbed the safety. So did I. Isaac carried the .458 half way to shoulder. Cheri's eyes danced and she looked as though she were on the way to a Jimmy Buffet concert. We spoored through the jungle that way, then pushed into an open, meaning safe, maize field, and huddled.

"Bastard's hunting us," Wambach said. Isaac nodded. "Knows we're on the spoor. Bloody apt to do something about it."

We trailed on, huddled again, and discussed it, and spoored farther into the bush and found where the bull had circled again on the backtrail and waited in ambush. He'd moved off when he heard us huddle half a mile away.

The trackers didn't like it. *Who would if they were unarmed?* I wondered. Wamback read my thoughts and said, "Better men that I to do it."

A muscle twitched in Grobelaar's jaw. I wanted the bull to charge and give us a shot. Wisdom of a fool, perhaps.

"Bloody bull tried to ambush us twice now," Wamback whispered.

The trackers wanted out, but they spoored on, across a flattened mealie field and a hut with its roof torn away, into the bush jungle again. One tracker held up a hand and we stopped and stared where he stared. Something rustled 40 meters into the jungle we couldn't see two meters into. Thumbs on safeties again.

The bull trumpeted and charged and the trackers evaporated and rifles jumped to shoulders. Wamback could see nothing behind impenetrable bush but I had the bead of the big double very high on the charging rogue's shoulder, the only part I could see, but shooting guaranteed a completed charge where at best we'd kill the bull so close he'd fall on someone, or he'd kill us all. We'd get no other shot until the bull broke out two yards from us, and if he did, someone would die.

Lucky—the bull trumpeted and broke off the charge and crashed away like a Peterbilt through Utah oak brush. Part of me wanted the bull to have shown enough to get bullets into him.

We huddled again, but no one could think of anything to say. Wamback gestured with his chin and the trackers started off along the spoor without enthusiasm. We carried the rifles with thumbs on safeties. Grobelaar looked pale beneath the suntan and I had no spit. The spoor led into thick bush and circled and we found where he'd made another ambush, then moved off. We huddled again.

"Best to end this foolishness," Wamback said, "before the bastard murders someone. Only a matter of time. Better than bodies on the ground."

So, it's just like Gonarezhou, I thought. The rational part of me knew Wambach had it right, but Grobelaar saw my face drop. "Plenty ele about," he consoled. "No problems. We'll find another without the blood in his eye, and live to drink to his ivory in the salt."

We trailed back to the Toyota. The trackers chattered and Wamback grinned again. Once the trackers pogo-ed at a mamba, but after trailing the rogue, what's a snake? The trackers joked at the mamba's manhood.

Next dawn, we motored from the circa 1960s tourist-less tourist lodge on a channel of the Zambezi with the tiny frogs crawling up the walls and the bush snake in the shower, and as sun hemorrhaged onto the mopane tangles, a tall Native waved us down.

"Says he heard elephants last night," Wamback said. "Watered back at a pan he knows. Probably another bloody snipe chase, but let's look-see."

We motored two kilometers down the track. The Native and trackers hiked into bush toward the pan and we waited at the Land Cruiser. They returned in an hour.

"Best grab at the .470," Wamback said. "Three bulls just left the water."

We trailed at half trot, found the big pan and the elephant spoor and corn-flecked dung, and spoored along the trail. The ele had browsed the mopane at their leisure as we closed. In an hour, we heard them. Wamback raised a hand to hold everyone back.

While the gang waited, Wamback and I snaked ahead on the silent sand, careful to move aside the mopane branches so they wouldn't scrape. In 200 meters, we saw the bulls shuffling in that ground-eating gait and Wambach vaulted ahead and set the acacia branch shooting tripod, I aimed the bead between the ear and eye of the largest bull as they shuffled away and slapped the trigger. The bull threw the trunk in the air and collapsed like we'd rehearsed it. Just like the videos.

"Shoot it again!" Wamback said. "Shoot it again!

I put the second barrel's 500-grain solid into its skull. When my ears quit ringing, I heard the gang running up through the bush.

"Load up!" Wamback said. "Put another into it."

The bull's trunk lifted feebly. His previous client wounded a bull in Botswana and a sudden rain had wiped out the spoor and they lost it, so he wasn't chancing this one.

"Shoot again!" Wamback said. "The dead ones kill you."

I got the bead on the shoulder and pressed the trigger. I heard the muzzle blast as though in a dream and saw dancing lights and black spots and heard wind chimes and chirping birds and back-ped-aled to keep my feet under me. When I could think I examined the double and expected to see the barrels peeled like bananas. They weren't. I shook my head to clear it, and again, until I realized that I'd loosed off both barrels of the .470 Nitro Express at once and sent 1000 grains of solid metal God know where into the bull.

"Always thought those stories of clients offing both barrels at once were bloody safari myths," Isaac said. "Know better now, by hell."

Everyone thought it a fine joke. I felt much too grand about the rogue ivory on the ground to notice the ringing ears and throbbing shoulder, or to care that I'd become immortalized in safari jokes throughout the Caprivi.

The trackers talked and texted on the technology that branded them sophisticated 21st century men, while the rest of us photographed, hacked off the bull's tail as a trophy and elephant hair bracelets later, and stroked the rogue ivory. No better feeling exists than that release of tension, most especially with dangerous game, the sudden ecstasy like a long slug of chilled Gordon's gin, and all of it mixed with just enough sorrow.

Wamback and company hiked back to retrieve the Toyota. Natives began drifting out of the bush toting baskets and machete-like *pangas* within ten minutes. Give credit to the trackers' cell phones, not the mythological bush telegraph. By the time the crew had worked the Cruiser through the downed and tangled acacia, 60 natives circled the ele carcass. We held them off to finish the photography. Then, the mob hacked at the carcass and two dozen fires smoked in the bush as they broiled ele tidbits while they gathered gory mountains of meat to haul back to the huts. Each bloody pile meant a year's supply of dried meat protein—biltong—to one family. One man offered me crinkly tripe, and a woman handed me a char-blackened bit of trunk, and I ate that, too. I photographed the bush butchery, and grinned at the laughing and hollering and gory glee. Twenty men hefted the severed skull and tusks into the Toyota bed. In four hours, they'd finished butchering and had hauled off six tons of bull. They left only gut contents, the largest bones, and toes.

Caprivi Epilogue:

Next day, Wamback and the trackers hacked the tusks free with a chainsaw while Grobelaar, Cheri and I battled tiger fish on the Zambezi with ten-inch gaudy Rapala lures. In another day, we'd buried the tusks in Grobelaar's yard and a week after that the soil microbes had cleaned off the clinging flesh. The largest tusk weighed just over 50 pounds. The other was broken off a foot from fighting.

*****

A college pal became infatuated with climbing Denali—Mt. McKinley on the old maps—from its base. Weather turned him back his first two attempts, and he lost half a ring finger to frostbite. On the third try he fell and broke out two teeth and frosted an ear, but he made it.

"What's next?" I asked him.

"I'll look out the window for a while," he said. "I'm content."

Man-eaters and Naked Ladies

Crocodiles…are so dangerous in some places that the villagers make a stockade in the water, so that they can draw water and bathe in safety. Denis Lyell, *Memories of an African Hunter*, c. 1923.

…there was taken from the stomach of a gigantic crocodile over six yards long, an assortment of twenty-four copper bracelets and a large ball of frizzy hair, which the horrid beast had been unable to digest… Edouard Foa, *After Big Game in Central Africa*, c. 1899.

"M*an-eater?*" Pro-hunter John Wamback hollers into the cell phone from the front seat of the Toyota *baakie.* "You don't say. Bloody hell." We're motoring down Namibia's Caprivi Strip after putting a rogue bull elephant in the salt, aimed at a Kaokoveldt safari in the wildest bush in Africa. Wamback is talking to our Himba guide in the frontier village of Opuwo two days west, and the last place to buy petrol before disappearing into the great desert wilderness of Kaokoland.

Wamback grins at Cheri and me in the backseat and shouts over the engine noise. "Story is, the croc heaves out at night and grabs Himba natives hauling water from the river. Good at it, too. Bagged nine of 'em."

Crocodiles horrify me in a deep place, ever since I'd gaped at the gut contents of a croc natives had speared on the Ugalla River—the undigested human arm with fingers intact, three metal bracelets, the mostly digested human foot from an earlier meal, what must have been an entire human head with ears and eyes dissolved from gastric juices, and two yards of heavy fishing net. A native poked at the head with a stick and the scalp peeled away revealing the greasy white skull. When the breeze shifted I gagged.

As horrifying is how they kill—dragging the struggling victim into deep water and drowning it, then spinning to rip off chunks they can swallow. If more saurians are about, each grabs an appendage and death-spins and in moments a wildebeest-sized carcass disappears down maws of Jurassic nightmares. As often, a lone croc drowns its victim and stuffs it under a submerged root until it rots enough to tear chunks off and swallow them. A 400-pound, 10-foot croc can catch, drag and drown you with minor effort. To a one-ton 15-footer, you're a *canapé*.

Though they can't chew and cut, their jaws are so strong that once they grasp prey, it's done for. Our tracker on an Okavango safari was an exception. Three years earlier, a croc hauled him under in less time than it takes to tell of it. He somehow had the presence of mind and positioning to jam his thumbs into the croc's eyes. The croc released him and he made shore choking water. Around the campfire that night, he hiked his jersey to show us the neat, parallel scars on his back and stomach. I thought of this, and remembered wading chest-deep as we spoored buffalo in Botswana. We crossed one at a time, with .375s at the ready on either side. And I remembered paddling the croc-filled upper Msima at its confluence with the Ugalla in Tanzania in dugouts with the sterns cut out to let out the fishing nets; I sat in the bow. Crocs followed the dugout, too, because they'd learned to snatch natives letting fishing nets out the open stern. They'd scored 16 of them in seven months. And other times on the Zambezi and Lunde Rivers. Perhaps most frightening, is crocs have absolutely no respect for our humanity. We are food, no more, no less, and they'd as soon eat us as wildebeest. We're easier to tear apart. I think of this while we drive the two days of dirt track so rocky we seldom shift out of first gear through a people-less desert the size of some nations. We sand river bivouac, then descend into a valley green with recent rain—the last gasp of the wet season—and motor through 800 migrating springbok. One of them 50 yards off must be some sort of record. Ostrich and the odd zebra graze with them. Though Wamback has them on license, I don't shoot because I want to make the Kunene River croc country by dark. We pass staring oryx, then top a last pass and gaze into the *Inferno*, the sere plain ghosting into heat and sand haze toward the invisible Kunene Valley. *We* are Cheri, pro-hunter John Wamback, Kwe San trackers Moses and Koos, our Himba guide, and me in the first Toyota *baakie*. John's wife Anneli, three-year-old son JC, and cook Gabriel follow in the second Toyota. Journeying into the remote Kaokoveldt requires two vehicles, because if one alone quits, someone might die in the desert wastes. We see no trace of fence, utility line or pavement in the xeric wilds, and my soul soars like Icarus.

We motor another half-day into the treeless dunes and rock Hades of the Marienfluss then descend through scattered camel thorns to the lush bush paradox of the Kunene River. Himba women naked save a tiny loin skirt haul water between great *anabaum* trees to conical stick-and-dung huts. Men and boys herd goats and fat-tailed sheep just as they have since the Magna Carta.

We recce downriver late that afternoon and spot crocs in nearly every pool. In half a mile, we glass seven saurians of at least eight feet, as many as I've seen in so short a time. A good one slips off a mid-current rock polished smooth by croc bellies. Wamback and our local guide question the locals. Suspicious Himba say no man-eating croc exists. Others won't speak to us at all. Some are friendly, but what we can glean from them is vague. We find spoor in the sand where a king-kong crocodile hauls out thirty yards from the river, unusual behavior. Could this be the man-eater?

We piece together the clues at the fire that evening: A man-eater probably exists, but the locals mistrust our motives, because we're the first safari hunters they've seen and they reason no sane man would travel so far to kill a crocodile. The Himba believe that the sooner we leave, the better. And if a man-eater does exist, it's the Cretaceous relic dozing on the Angola side of the Kunene where we can't shoot it. Hope drifts up and away like the campfire smoke.

A second sundowner does nothing to improve our moods, but Cheri tries. "Still, we've seen plenty of crocodiles."

Wamback owns the Kaokoland concession, and he's allowed one croc every three years. We're the first to hunt them. He hasn't visited the Kunene before, but he says, "From what we've seen we could shoot thirty a season and it wouldn't faze croc numbers. The Himba'd be glad to be rid of 'em. Aside from the odd auntie, the crocs dine on their livestock."

I'm disappointed, of course, but I hadn't flown half a planet to Namibia expecting to shoot a man-eater, because that would be too wonderful, the stuff of fantasy.

We trek downriver at sunup hoping crocs will climb out of the water and into the sun. One skids off a beach and disappears in a swirl just below. We spot a 13-footer on a boulder on the Angola side. Just above, a man throws rocks into the river to frighten off crocs before he allows his goats to drink. He shouts at us and waves his arms.

"Wants to know what we're about," Wamback says. Our Himba guide shouts back across the river that we're hunting crocs. The Angola Himba launches into what I take is some sort of polemic, at us or the crocs, I'm unsure. "Says we should shoot every buggering croc we can. Offers a goat for bait. E'd probably give you a wife, too."

We don't see crocs in the numbers we saw them the evening before. Apparently, the water is warmer than the sun at this time of day. Later, when the air warms, more crocs climb out into the heat. We trek back to the camp on barren sand and rock a hundred yards above the riverine bush.

From camp I watch the Himba water their goats. They throw rocks into the shallows for some minutes to frighten off crocs before they allow them to drink. Naked men bathe in shallows. They won't go into the murky water over a few inches deep and won't get within 20 yards of water deep enough to conceal a croc. They and I watch a croc weighing its chances at dinner from deeper water. Women wash clothes with similar precautions.

Later, a Himba man shuffles into camp and wants us to blast a croc with a sweet tooth for goats; I'm not interested because the croc isn't big enough, though I'd like to help. Another wants to show us a donkey-eater downstream. Women water individual corn shoots planted in craters dug into sand. They haul the water from the river but toss rocks into it before they do. Himba cross the river in dugouts back and forth between Angola and Namibia without a customs officer within a hundred miles.

At lunch, John says, "Didn't want to tell you earlier, no need to get you nervous, but pull the trigger and it costs you $3000." The usual rule is wound an animal and you pay the trophy fee, but I'd never heard this one—paying even if you miss. It makes a guy sweat, because he's got to smash the croc's tennis ball brain or spine just behind the skull to anchor it. Hit elsewhere and it will slip into the water, and with this current and the croc numbers, it's gone.

"What if I miss clean?" I counter.

"That won't happen." His reasoning is that the croc may not bleed and leave evidence it's hit before it's in the river.

A white South African couple motor to the river on a pilgrimage. A croc killed a missionary relative at a beach a mile downstream two years earlier; he and a companion arrived late that fatal night biltong dry, blistering hot, and trusting in faith and bathed in the river. A croc grabbed the relative, and that was the last of him.

A six-inch black scorpion stings the South African man while walking across that same beach in flip-flops that night to pee. He spirals into early anaphylactic shock but he's turned the corner when we hear of it, and I so wanted to try my intramuscular adrenaline shot to see if it worked. He nearly dies, but he's up in two days, though part of his face and the muscles along his spine are numb, and his joints pain him to walk. His face muscles twitch in the firelight.

We trek downriver in the late afternoon and spot good springbok, but I'm not interested. Wamback and I edge along bluffs above a smaller channel of the river and peer over every hundred yards. The gang—Cheri, the trackers, and the local guide—follow. Crocs sun on the beaches and boulders, and others float in the pools. A magnum croc dreams of Himba entrees on a beach across the channel, but we can't figure how to get closer without spooking it, and if I brained it someone would have to swim rapids and tie a line to it. Our crew seems sane, so I doubt anyone would volunteer. A seven-foot croc spots us and torpedoes into the pool. Eight-footers litter the shallows. I wouldn't stick a toe into that water for a tryst with Nicole Kidman.

The sun plummets behind the ragged volcanic peaks when we spot a big croc lying across that same polished crocodile rock midstream of the river channel. It's not as big as the earlier croc, but it's big enough. We back out of sight behind the bluff and snake downriver. The jury's still out on how well, or even if, crocodiles scent, but we're taking no chances. I'm certain they do, because I've seen a half-dozen homing in on an impala bait on the Chiredzi River in Zimbabwe, and the only way they could know about its existence was scenting it. We keep the breeze in our faces.

The terrain and wind are perfect, and when we belly over the crest, the croc sleeps on that crocodile rock 60 yards below. It faces away and a soft-point in the back of the skull will split that lemon-sized brain. If I'm a bit low, the slug will shatter the spine. If the croc twitches, though, it'll slip off the boulder and into the river. I'm prone and aim, but I'd shoot through grass, and at three grand a trigger pull, I won't chance it. We lizard to a bush twenty feet below, neither croc sees us, and the wind drifts into our faces. I ease to sitting and anchor the rifle to a branch with my left hand, but that $3000 trigger pull spooks me. My breath comes ragged and the branch wobbles. John shoves his shooting sticks in front of me. My pulse pounds in my ears. *Steady it, boy*, I tell myself.

John whispers, "Hit that bulged scale just right of center. See it?" I do.

Wamback's shooting sticks skid on rocks, so I discard them. I'll rest elbows on knees. I concentrate on relaxing my diaphragm, and after an eon, I steady, then touch the .300 Winchester magnum trigger. Except for the companion croc's swirl and the muzzle blast, nothing happens. The croc makes no twitch, not the slightest movement. *Did I miss?* I work the bolt and get the sight picture, then notice blood trickling down the crocodile's rock.

"Can't do it better!" John slaps my back. Cheri and gang rise from the crest a few yards above and grin. I put another core-lokt through the croc's chest just in case.

Now what? I wonder. The croc lies on the boulder mid-channel, and the trick is to get it to our side and downstream where we can haul it to the Toyota. *I ain't swimming to the boulder*, I assure myself. Wamback treks back for the baakie. Moses and the local guide boulder-hop the current downstream and get to the opposite small island. I watch with my hands sweaty on the Remington and thumb on the safety in case a croc makes a try at them. They make it and shove through the tangle on the island opposite my croc, then edge along the bank prodding with poles to spook crocs away. The guys strip and Moses wades out to the boulder prodding ahead with a stick. My hands sweat even more on the Remington. Koos throws a rock tied to a stout line from our side and Moses loops it around the crocodile. I skid down the bank to get closer to the action, but I won't stand close enough to water for a croc to grab me, rifle or not. An hour later the guys float the beast downstream as the Toyota grinds over the rise.

The South Africans and Himba pilgrimage to the camp that evening to view the crocodile. A native spits on it, and a child kicks it. In the morning Himba women in their naked finery tote infants to see the reptile. They're smeared in ochre and goat butter and glisten red in the Himba equivalent of formal wear. We photograph them, and they charge $100; apparently, they're not totally innocent of civilized habits. After the guys skin the croc while keeping an eye on another eyeing them back from the shallows, we slit its belly.

I desperately want to find a human hand or leg, or at least a Himba necklace, but the gut contains two crabs and a gallon of ballast pebbles. It's a fine trophy, but I'd fantasized slaying man-eaters and getting carried on natives' shoulders since I was eight. I'm reminded of a lesson learned long ago—life is mostly a process of losing illusions.

THE PECCARY PARTY

"So, my berry good Yanqui amigo," Homero Canedo Carballo, the corpulent city outfitter said, and looked at me out of the corner of his eye, "Wha'choo want to choot now?" I was paying by the day, so he didn't want me escaping just yet.

That first morning we'd collected a big, Sierra Madre cow-killing puma out of a blackjack oak after a dozen, tree-climbing, mostly Walker-mongrel hounds had run him there. No one kills an honest, dry-ground lion the first day, let alone the first morning. Thirty years astride horses and mules chasing hounds hot on molten lion scent taught me that much, anyhow.

It was embarrassing, too. When the guides Armando or Jesus walked by, with a "con permisso," they'd run a calloused hand down my sleeve, so the luck would rub off. Later, other vaqueros sidled up, straw sombreros in hand, and did the same.

Homero looked hopeful. "You like colas blancas?"

"Maybe." Why not? Stalking Coues whitetails is always great fun, and they eat better than most anything in the hemisphere. After bartering the trophy fee, I killed a dandy 10-point macho the first dawn and was back where we started.

Homero looked worried as Rosa, our ample cook who'd slung frijoles since Pancho Villa days, fry-baked her *tortilla especial* over mesquite coals in the ranch yard as a chill December sun rose in typical wild rose Sonoran splendor.

"My berry best Gringo friend," Homero wheedled, "why not huillotillas?" I'd shot acrobatic December doves just down from running the gauntlet of gunners from Canada to the Arizona border before, and didn't want to attempt the mach-two feathered demons with a borrowed smoothbore with the fore-end duct-taped to the barrel. They were tough enough with my pet scattergun.

"Forget it," I told Homero. His fleshy jowls dropped to his collar. I let the likable rogue suffer as he imagined gringo dollars disappearing into the clouds. I didn't tell him, but I didn't want to quit yet, either.

"But my berry good Yanqui friend, eet ees mas early to leef." Homero looked at me out of the corner of his eye again. "Javelina! Thass eet! We haff javelina on zee rancho!"

I'd been angling for him to suggest it, but I looked reluctant. I didn't want him to bilk me too much for the trophy fee. I'd hunted with Homero before, and he'd charge four times the ranch owner's harvest fee if he could get away with it. Besides, I liked watching him sweat. Beads of it clung to his upper lip in the chill desert dawn.

I hemmed. I kicked the dust. More satisfying, I was scamming the scam artist. "Well," I said, "I dunno. I've shot plenty and ain't that interested in another." I had to give Homero credit, though. He kept pitching. When he'd dropped the price to a tolerable level, I gave in. "I guess so," I said.

Jesus Campa Miranda, Homero, the kid go-fer named Humberto, and I rode cow *caballos* to a canyon thick with *palo fiero*, agave and more cactus than a Palm Springs country club. The arroyo was so thick you'd never see a knee-tall pig, so Jesus and Humberto pushed up the miniature gorge to where Homero and I perched on a rimrock overlooking an arroyo that topped onto an open mesa. We heard pigs squealing and splintering through the tangle, but couldn't glimpse them. Homero sighed with relief. He wanted to drag the hunt out as long as possible for the extra dollars.

"Nada," I called down to Humberto when he staggered from the spiny tangle with T-shirt in tatters and arms and face checker-boarded with scratches. Jesus, a six-foot-two Mayo Indio and the rancho foreman, had taken a path of less resistance and emerged as he went in, ahorse and looking like a Hollywood vaquero complete with pencil mustache.

We tried again. This time all of us, except Homero who was too fat to make it down and out, afoot or ahorse, plunged into the thorny dreadlock. You'd never talk Jesus off his horse, a real vaquero would rather die than walk, but Humberto and I battled through the tangled spines on foot. I stalked along the rimrock base while Jesus and Humberto tried to push the pigs into me. They did, too—half the javelina population in Sonora. Trouble was, the pigs bolted in and out of the tangle without warming and so fast I couldn't shoot. When a handful exploded out behind me, I'd whirl with the Winchester Model 94, then half-a-dozen more rocketed out and back where I'd faced a moment earlier. I never fired a shot. I couldn't.

We visited a *mescalero* camp on the ride back to the ranch. Illegal mescalero boot-leg stills dot the ranchos, with a wink from the rancheros in exchange for a jug now and then. In this part of the Sierra, the wild agave produced a fine mescal called Bacanora, named after the nearby town, or the other way around. Gato del Mundo, the head mescalero, offered a fruit jar of the clear liquid lava. When the kid Humberto reached for one, Gato swatted him with a sombrero. By then, I'd nicknamed Humberto *El Javelinero*. Humberto is now a grown-up desert sheep guide, but the moniker has stuck, and he resents it, too.

Gato told of a cantankerous *viejo*, an old man, that would sooner shoot than talk if you neared his still, that drank his share of Bacanora one night and staggered away to sleep it off under a mesquite tree. During the night, a puma ate part of him, to the relief of his Indio neighbors. After a second fruit jar of the mescal, we thigh-slapped and wiped mirthy tears from our cheeks at Gato's story. I didn't get much of it with my high school Spanish, except the part about a drunken puma, but everyone else though it was so hysterical, I did too. As we sat saddles back to the ranch house, I felt like Lee Marvin in *Cat Ballou*, though my *caballo* was sober. A plate of puma-head tacos that night probably kept the next dawn's red-haze hangover from being worse.

Each time my caballo missed a step that next dawn, my skull throbbed like a Mexican cantina on fiesta night. Humberto, of course, hadn't sampled the Sonoran white lightning and he irked Jesus with his whistling. He bugged me, too, especially when he got too lively with "La Cucaracha." Armando Vacame Andrade hadn't touched the stuff, either, and he was altogether too cheerful for my liking. Finally Jesus had enough. "Silencio, Javelinero!" he roared. I applauded the silence. We rode up a long barranca and ground-tied the caballos.

The plan was to drive the pigs again, hopefully into me this time. I was to still-hunt through the tangled ocotillo, palo verde and cacti of a dozen species, then scale a three-story rhyolite spire and wait for the drive. I shoved into the tangle while the guys siesta-ed under a spreading mesquite. The tangle was so thick, I crawled on hands and knees. At that level, the place was tunneled with pig highways. I jumped two from their beds, but couldn't shoot on hands and knees. Others snuffled or bolted ahead. Six or eight nearly ran over me in their confusion. Hands-and-knees isn't for fast shooting. You'd have to stand, in which case your head tangled in thornbush, sit, which took too long, or flop prone. I flopped on my belly the next time I heard pigs ahead, but wasn't fast enough. I tried it again and almost got a forty-pound boar in the '94's sights. While I lay prone trying to get a shot ahead, a pig jumped across my back. After two hours hands-and-kneeing it, I made the pinnacle, *sans* pant knees, various irregular patches of skin, and a pint of blood.

The view from the rhyolite spire was right off a *National Geographic* cover. Rifle-barrel palms hop-scotched up the creek below. Organ pipe cacti shoved twelve-foot pipes from volcanic outcrops. Acacia of various species tangled below, and the slopes of Cerro Chihuahuilla shimmered dark emerald in a blanket of blackjack and white oak. For a moment I forgot my pounding skull.

"Ayii-Yi-Yi-Yi!" echoed off the volcanic bluffs. That meant, I assumed, the guys were starting their drive. I thumbed cobweb off the front sight.

Nothing happened for an hour, except I slugged back a gallon of water, vowed never to touch Bacanora again, and waited for the hombres. Then brush splintered, I heard steps on dead oak leaves and caught a nanosecond glimpse of two pigs below. Three burst into the open ripping faster than I thought possible for pigs, then vaporized into creek willows. Two zipped across the only opening in the acacia tangle and disappeared. I glimpsed I don't know how many javelina crossing the skyline half a mile up the ridge, and that was it.

Jesus and Armando, always vaqueros, let the horses and chaps take the beating, and emerged from the thorny tangle as they went it, sombreros in place. The Javalinero, on the other hand, looked like he'd lasted two rounds with a she *tigre* in heat.

We hunted another spiny dreadlock thicket on the way back to the ranch house, without luck. The pigs were there, alright, but you couldn't get sights on them.

After the gaudy sunset, half a dozen vaqueros strummed guitars and sung songs of lost love, yearning souls and *revolucion* battles in the courtyard, while Rosa baked whitetail enchiladas over the open mesquite-fired adobe oven and coyotes wailed right along with the vaqueros. The evening was right out of Hollywood. And no Bacanora, Dios be praised. A fine Mexican cerveza Bohemia killed off the last of the hangover. Homero, the rogue, had driven into Bacanora, the village, or Hermosillo, the city, for supplies and whatever. Probably whatever. No one missed him.

Homero hadn't made it back the next dawn, and though no one else on the rancho spoke English, I didn't care. All hunters speak the same language, anyway, and you don't need a phrasebook to interpret it.

Armando, Jesus and I swung onto the caballos, and the Javelinero jogged along behind on a burro the next dawn. Armando and Jesus made lively conversation, and from what I could pull from it, we'd hunt a tangled *canon* so thick with pigs, the only problem was selecting the more robust specimen. Their body language shouted something was up. An hour later we topped out onto a mesa as the desert sun bled across the *chollals*. We sat saddles and stared into the most fearsome, tangled, on-end geology I'd seen in the Sierra. Jesus and Armando grinned with too much satisfaction, I thought. I grinned back, but it was bluff. Javelinero moaned.

Jesus and Armando aimed their mounts down and skidded off the bluff and into the tangled acacia. Javelinero and I would ride to the head of the canyon and push back on foot. We'd meet up at a prehistoric *Indio* bean field, or campo, and the pigs, Jesus assured, would trample us into the dust. So many javelina would charge out, we'd have to shoot in self defense.

Javelinero cinched the burro to a palo verde, I tied the buckskin to a mesquite and we slalomed down scree into the acacia and greasewood dreadlocks. You couldn't see farther than the end of the short .30/30 barrel. They were right. The only way you'd get a shot was if they charged you. We heard them ahead and to the sides, but didn't glimpse pig hair. An hour later, Javelinero and I had worked to the creek without seeing a pig. But we heard and smelled them and we stepped in their scats.

Jesus and Armando hadn't yet made the campo when we broke out of the intertwined thorn scrub. Even so, the campo was a dust storm of fleeing pigs. Thirty or more disappeared into the scrub at the other end of the field 300 yards away. Pigs darted upslope and vaporized. They ghosted below and behind us. I couldn't shoot.

Armando crooned a love song and splintered brush from the opposite slope. His white sombrero flashed into view and disappeared. I checked the '94's action, made sure the barrel was clear, and got comfortable below a mesquite snag. Javelinero faced upslope so we wouldn't miss anything.

"Ay-yiyiyiyi," echoed up the canyon from below.

A moment later pigs raced across the bottom end of the campo so fast I didn't get the .30/30 to shoulder. A band sprinted into the open to our left, spotted us and swapped ends and vaporized back into the tangle. "Senor Yanqui!" the Javelinero hissed. He couldn't pronounce my name, so he called me whatever came to mind. Half a dozen peccaries streaked across the upper campo. I'd begun to believe I'd be lucky to get any shot, let alone one at a trophy boar. I heard Jesus's caballo splintering brush and Armando's negro gelding splashing through the creek. "Ayyiyiyiyiy!"

The Javelinero hopped from rock to rock in his excitement. Pigs whirled and pivoted in the dust. Peccaries sprinted everywhere you looked. I got what looked like a *macho* only to lose it in the dust and other racing pigs. Another boar sprinted straight at us, but veered into a band of smaller pigs as I pressed on the trigger.

"Senor, Senor!" The Javelinero was beside himself.

"Ayyiyiyi-YI! echoed from across the clearing.

"Son of an illicit woman!" I cursed as a pig disappeared as I was about to pull off. An outsized pig raced down the campo broadside and I shot over it. Another broke from cover to the left and streaked above but I couldn't shoot because the Javelinero hopped into my line of sight.

"Senor, Senor! But shoot!" The kid again.

More pigs broke from cover ahead of Jesus, then right-angled and sprinted up the campo. I got the buckhorn sight on a boar's shoulder and touched off. I saw hair in the air before losing the band in the dust. Javelinero hurtled the bisnaga cacti and volcanic boulders.

"Que bueno!" he hollered, thumbs-upped and pogo-ed at the dead boar.

The pig melee hadn't slowed. I motioned and the Javelinero loped back.

I handed him the .30/30 and gestured at the swirl of pigs. His eyes bugged at the Model 94 in his hands. I gestured again at the pigs, at least a hundred of them. The kid could shoot. He hammered a single below just as Armando splintered his lathered mount into the open. A moment later Jesus "ay-yi-yi-yi-ed" into the campo.

"So, my goot Estados amigo, what we can choot now?" Homero was still angling for those Gringo dollars. "We have berry many coatimundi on zee rancho." Coatis are odd raccoon relatives. "Another cola blanca? We can buy zee deer tag next year and mail zee trophy to you." Illegal, of course, but that's Homero for you.

"Forget it," I said. This is a javelina story, after all.

A WISE MAN…

S ame drill every semester. First day, I walk into my university classrooms and write on the board, "A wise man changes his mind many times, a fool never." No matter if it's an animal ecology, human bio or Chinese lit class. Unless we're willing to change our minds, to grasp new ideas, we can't learn a thing.

Trouble is, I should take my own advice. I just knew European hunting was too cushy, too predictable, and what kind of hunting is that? You should bleed on any hunt worth the name. For decades, I kept Europe in my "old age" bucket while we stalked man-eating crocs on the Kunene River, chased polar bears on Arctic icepack in 41-below temps that snapped leather dogsled bindings like taffy, and hounded Tajik Marco Polo argali in banshee gales in the freon December Pamirs. All great fun, too.

In very recent years, though, we've stalked half a dozen European countries, but Spain remains our favorite because it owns native quarry hunters drool for. That means the four "ibex" varieties to me, though biological wisdom suggests they are probably more closely allied to the tur of the Caucasus. (See my four-part series, "The Great Arc of the Wild Goat," in *Wild Sheep* magazine.)

Espacaza co-outfitter Jose Mallo collects us at the baggage carousel, and in minutes we're streaking through Madrid's traffic bedlam, then Jose's Land Rover scorches westward toward the Gredos Mountains, smoking Porsches in its wake. We "camp" at a tiny former pepper farm *cum* designer hotel and restaurant run by a Brit couple, and after supper and a double Scotch, I stagger for bed to shake the jet-lag before the dawn's hunt. I'm so fried, I don't remember what we ate.

In a black-dawn deluge we motor to the Gredos Reserve, collect two rangers and then switchback the mud-greasy roads up and up even more. We make trail's end, don rain gear and packs, and trek into the rain so thick you can't see the sodden Gredos. It seems the rain in Spain doesn't fall mainly on the plain, after all. To underscore that epiphany, the creek has morphed into torrent enough to drown you. "Don't shoot ibex on the other side," Jose tells me.

We trek into the downpour, and rain blasts us in sheets and in spite of name-brand raingear, we're drenched. The sodden togs might otherwise concern me in the Gobi or Arctic, but in European hunting you end the day at hotel or lodge to dry out, then dine on camp "grub" to turn Julia Child green with envy.

One reserve guide raises his Swarovski binocular. I squeegee rain from my eyebrows and squint into the Zeiss glass, and Cheri does the same. Sure enough—three grand Gredos ibex browse the heather near the stream—on the other side. I don't much care about record books, but I know enough about trophy sizes that I'm certain one would top-off any record book. Many Spanish hunt prices include the cost of the trophy up to a certain, generally mediocre, size; after that, you pay big shekels for larger horns, and King Kong might own an eight-grand surcharge for that headgear. Earlier, Jose and I discuss how much I'd spend for a magnum ibex, and a $2500 trophy surcharge would max me out.

"Don't look," Jose says, because he knows I'm staring at that freak's outlandish horns. I've never lusted after anything more, but I heed Jose's advice and shift the binocular to Number Two. Normally, Number Two's horns would give me the quivering fantods, but not when King Kong stands right next to him. Jose repeats, "Don't look."

I rest the 7mm Remington magnum over my pack, get the crosshairs behind Number Two's shoulder as he dreams of past loves, because the rut is winding down, and touch off. The ibex doesn't bat an eye.

"What!?" I say no one. The ibex profiles a mere 175 yards across the creek with the crosshairs as solid as Gibraltar. I jack another up the throat and settle the crosshairs behind the shoulder again, when the billy sways. "Momento," someone says, "Wait." The ibex topples over backward.

After the back-slapping and hand-shaking and hollering, we climb upslope to glass that torrent for a place to cross. Like I said, those rapids would drown you. You couldn't cross without swimming, and unless you're Mark Spitz, even that's iffy. We hike back out, get dry, warm and fed at the lodge, and trek up the opposite side of the stream next day to retrieve my 13-year-old ibex. Without King Kong to compare him to, I'm giddy enough that those magnum horns are worth that $2500 trophy surcharge.

We streak back to Madrid at the speed of sound, overnight in a 5-star hotel, and Jose's man Carlos Arbex collects us the following dawn and we race east toward the Beceite ibex scarps. Carlos is a NASCAR wannabe, too. I'm so happy to make "camp" alive, I kiss my palm and slap the ground with it. "Camp" is Jose Manuel Monteys' converted century-old stone farmhouse that owns much more cachet than that 5-star Madrid hotel.

Before we unload, Carlos herds us into a Land Rover with local guide and mayor of the village of Bel, Joaquin Sabater, and we're racing through orchards and farm fields and believe it or not, spotting rutting ibex just off the pavement. One is a grand 11-year-old trophy, too, and Carlos wants to slap it in the salt. "Sorry," I tell him. "No road-hunting for me." Hunting is too much fun to hurry it.

Next dawn we motor toward the scarps, Joaquin gives us the VIP tour of block-long Bel village including his home and the 11th century stone church, and we park as high in the peaks as the Rover can go. We'll foot-hunt down the cordillera and rendezvous with a vehicle at the bottom at day's end.

We spot ibex, too, including what to my eye are trophies. Many own horn configurations similar to those of Gredos ibex, though geography says they're Beceites. For one reason or another, mostly having to do with age and future trophy potential, Joaquin nixes them. The geography isn't a federal reserve; rather, local villages manage the hunting. Trophy surcharges don't apply, to my relief. You shouldn't have to use a calculator to judge trophy beasts.

Joaquin winks and nods and says, "Muy bueno," later that afternoon. A grand billy and five nannies bed on a mile-distant slope. The ibex owns classic Beceite horns; they flare out at nearly right angles from the face rather than spiral up and back like the Gredos. The horns are heavier than anything we've glassed. "Viejo grande," Joaquin affirms—a big, old ibex.

We skid into the tangled thorn scrub behind the ridge, hand-and-knee up a bluff and pray the ibex don't spot us, slalom into a canyon and claw another ridge. We can't snake closer, though the band beds 350 yards cross canyon.

The ibex are oblivious, I get prone, we discuss distance and bullet drop in low voices, and when the billy stands, I touch off. The ibex staggers. We expect the ibex to drop any moment, but it doesn't. He steps, and I break the 12-year-old billy's shoulder.

We don't rendezvous with our ride down canyon until dark, and we celebrate at the lodge with local Mediterranean shrimp paella to make the Galloping Gourmet cry. Our cook stacks champagne glasses in each other three high, and then she pours into the top one and it overflows into the next one down and so on, then she serves them out. Who says hunting should be tough?

We've scored two ancient high-end trophies in two hunting days. I haven't changed my mind about Spanish hunting.

The next December, we collect our baggage from that same carousel and locate our outfitter, Eurohunt owner Alvaro Villegas, texting under the stairs. Same drill—we speed through that Madrid traffic bedlam and out onto what Americans call a freeway, southbound this time. We're chasing Ronda and Southeastern ibex that will, with any luck, give us all four varieties of Spanish ibex—Spain's Big Four. I'm even more jet-lagged this time around. I submerge into a deep sleep and when I claw up into consciousness somewhere in central Spain, Alvaro's texting at 130 klicks per hour. Jet lag or no, it takes time to get back to sleep.

We're after the Ronda ibex first and we bivvy at a quaint hotel outside the village of Aloainza. An hour before dawn, Alvaro steers us to a tiny smoky bar where olive-pickers quaff brandy and cafe before trudging into the orchards. We munch tapas and slurp coffee that take the enamel off your molars. The place is out of a Humphrey Bogart movie set.

We meet the local village guide and motor to trail's end in a cloudless cobalt sky, then trek into the ibex scarps. Seems the guide eyeballed a heroic ibex weeks earlier. We ignore other trophy ibex as we claw up, too. Two-thousand vertical feet later, we glass for that magnum goat but don't find him, so we aim down another route. We jump a grand ibex, discuss whether or not to collect him, but while we discuss he vaporizes. So what if we don't collect ibex the first day every time?

Same drill next day. We can't find King Kong, again. We blow a stalk on another ibex, and see no others. At second day's end, it's Ronda ibex two, hunters zero. Spanish ibex stalking isn't slam-dunk after all.

"What you want to do?" Alvaro asks in Aloainza later. The question takes me aback, because I'd assumed we'd hunt the Ronda again the following day.

"We have only two days to hunt the Southeastern ibex at the Tejeda Reserve. After that we cannot hunt them." Outfitters buy two or three-day slots on the federal reserves. Normally, that's plenty of time. If you miss your slot, though, you're out of luck. "We should hunt there tomorrow."

Where's the choice? We motor easterly in the night, me fuming and Cheri positively steaming because our hearts are set on completing that Spanish ibex slam. We dodge wild pigs and hares on the two-lane, bypass Malaga and aim at the Sierra de Tejeda Reserve. We bivouac at B & B *El Refugio*, another designer hotel-and-restaurant owned by Belgians Ingrid and Peter.

Alvaro tries to reassure us, Cheri more specifically because when she gets mad, she scares guys that don't give charging pachyderms a second thought.

"Paco Navero, the ranger, thinks we can shoot ibex very quick. After that, we go back for the Ronda," Alvaro says. *Sure*, I think. I'd heard that before in Tanzania, Russia and Zimbabwe, and we never went back, either.

Paco's Land Rover parks at road's end as Sol clears the peaks. In two-minutes, a magnum ibex skylines in my Zeiss two miles up ridgeline. Cheri, Paco and Alvaro ogle another a mile west.

We're all plotting stalks, but their ibex is the easier approach. Forty-five minutes later, one shot puts a magnum 14-year-old Southeastern ibex in the salt. We're celebrating at a tiny cafe in Canillas de Aceituno village an hour after that.

"You want to go back for the Ronda now?" Alvaro asks me over Cokes. I'm taken aback again, but so tickled with the ibex success I'm in no hurry. I was all wrong about Alvaro, too.

"Tomorrow," I answer. "We'll leave early."

Ingrid and Peter, owners of *El Refugio*, once operated a famous Antwerp restaurant, and they can cook! They out-do themselves with a grand paella, Mediterranean lamb, seafood hors d'oeuvres, and Spanish bubbly. I love Spanish hunting.

This time we collect two town guides at Aloainza and motor into the Ronda geography. We park at a defunct marble quarry and glass far up the peaks. We've done this before, without luck. I'm losing the faith after half an hour, when something skylines two miles up. I've got the Swarovski 15 x 56 this time, and even at that distance I see horns against that azure south Spain sky.

"Got one." I'm trying to sound relaxed, cool, like those astronauts on Apollo 11, but I'm not pulling it off. I direct Cheri and the guys to the ibex.

"Bueno," one local guide says. "Muy bueno."

"Muy, muy bueno!" the other guide tells Alvaro.

We stalk out of sight a mile upslope and deposit the local guides and Cheri to watch. Alvaro and I claw up a ravine through the thorn and scree, belly across a bluff and hope the now bedded ibex doesn't eye us, and hand-and-knee through thorny brush. I spot horns above the scrub, but can't see fur. We belly farther in mortal fear the ibex will spot us. The Force is with us, and I shove the pack onto an outcrop and rest the 7mm WSM across it. Alvaro scratches "200" into the soft limestone, and we wait for the ibex to stand.

When the goat at last stands, I squeeze off. It's hit, but the trigger on Alvaro's Model 70 throws me off. "Wait," Alvaro says, but the ibex won't drop, though I now see blood low on the shoulder. To make certain, I sock it again.

The guys shout from below and we all trek up the ridge to the ibex. Ronda are the most distinctive of Spain's ibex varieties. Instead of some version of the black and white pelage patterns you find in the other varieties, they're reddish with little black. Instead of spiraling horns, theirs spiral very little. To my eye, they're the most stunning Spanish ibex.

"You have all four Spanish ibex now, yes?" Alvaro asks, though he knows I do. (He doesn't know that the Ronda ibex also completes my Capra World Slam—12 varieties of wild world goats [in all my collections, that means absolutely native, endemic, unfenced, and no feral or hybrid varieties]; and the Triple Slam—in addition to that Capra Slam, the Triple includes the Ovis World Slam of 12 varieties of world sheep and the Grand Slam of the four varieties of North American sheep, for those collection hunters.)

*****

While Alvaro capes the head, I pinch thorns out of my ear lobes and dab blood from my talus-scraped hands. After three days chasing Ronda ibex, major angst, minor blood loss, and tattered togs, who says Spanish hunting is too cushy, too predictable? Like that wise man, I change my mind on that score.

Rite of Passage

The twin-prop Piper shuddered itself free of the crumbled tarmac and groaned up into the equatorial sun and out of the Arusha slums, banked toward Mount Meru with its summit hidden in clouds, then it droned southwest above twenty-mile dust plumes blown north out of the Athi Plain into Kenya, over arid thornbush wastes then mopane scrub forests and hippo-filled pools along the rivers now evaporating into the climaxing dry season. Hundreds of ebony buffalo flattened with altitude lay in the scant shade, and then a thousand wildebeest fled the plane's tiny shadow in that rocking-horse gallop and the dust.

"Bloody rite of passage, that." The professional hunter gestured with his chin at the spear. I ran my thumb down the spear's long double-edged blade. "They kill the lion with spears. A simba scar or two makes 'em the devil's bloody own with the maidens." I'd just traded the spear from a wandering Maasai warrior for an elk antler belt knife and a dime-store ring I wore as a kid when I killed my first buck. We both walked away grinning.

*****

Years earlier, the Tanzanian central government outlawed lion hunting with spears, but they'd only just got around to enforcing it this far out into the bush. Lions were too valuable to the economy, because Western safari hunters paid many tens of thousands of dollars to kill them. The southern Maasai did not know this, nor care if they did. They only knew you had to prove manhood to get the equivalent of a western financial portfolio-cattle. Cattle bought wives and gave status. Hunting lions with spears had always proved manhood, and it was a critical last shred of the warrior life, now that they could no longer raid neighboring tribes for cattle and women.

"Out here in the remote bush, no Maasai belle wastes favors on a moran who hasn't blooded a lion," the PH said. "These chaps aren't the tourist Maasai you see in the Parks. Never tasted liquor save fermented blood and milk. Never journeyed to Arusha. Haven't changed since the Kaiser decided he wanted Tanganyika."

When they learned of the law, the southern Maasai speared 11 elephants in a month. The government outlawed that, too, but they couldn't absolutely enforce it because they were too poor to pay and arm game wardens, the south Maasailand too remote, and they wouldn't risk a spear-driven rebellion. Plenty would give them AKs, too.

"Still do it," the PH continued. "That abandoned boma we hunted through yesterday—they're grazing their cattle off west where there's grass left—spear lions. Keep it a bloody secret, though. Won't admit it to other Maasai, let alone the white man. They won't talk to us because we've a government game scout along. They bugger off into the bush when they see our dust." The PH let the Cruiser coast to a stop and we glassed a trophy impala in the thorn scrub.

"They isolate the cat in thick bush, encircle it and close in pounding buffalo-hide shields with the spears and coughing like lions. Like the old Roosevelt film you saw as a laddybuck in the cinema. Hell of a racket. The simba charges, a dozen spears fly. Some slice through the cat and glance into another moran. They pick 'em up if able, bend the soft-steel spears back into shape over a knee, and get back to it. The lion takes long enough at dying to maul a brace of warriors. Too many warriors died for the Arusha governors to tolerate, or so they claimed. Real reason, though, was the Maasai didn't pay thousands of dollars to kill them like American Safari bwanas." He spat in the dust and glanced at me from the corner of an eye.

*****

We'd already used 18 days of the 28-day safari, first to the west along the Ugalla River upstream of Lake Tanganyika; then to the fringes of the Serengeti near the active volcano Ol Doinyo Lengai, god's mountain; and finally in south Maasailand. Early, we baited the dry flood plains where we'd seen old lion tracks with carcasses of the antelope or buffalo we killed. We'd hunt the mopane thickets for the antelope—a roan here, a bohor reedbuck over there, and we ambushed buff coming to water in the evening. We scored a 7' 3" tom leopard over a topi bait, but no lions. No angst and the pleasantest of all hunting, looking for whatever came along with the faith that sooner or later we'd get a crack at lion. For the first time in years, I wasn't pushed. We had plenty of time.

No one comes to Tanzania on an extended safari without hunting lions. I'd come solely to hunt them. Sure, the leopard was as good as you'd get in the Msima scrub, and we bagged a top-ten-class Lichtenstein hartebeest, for whatever that was worth. But we had time then.

Later, as I became too aware of its passage, we found the kind of East African greater kudu no one ignores. By then, I didn't want to take time away from the lion hunt. I declined the shot. We single-filed through the mopane scrub to check the buffalo carcass lion bait two miles up the thicket.

The grand bull sauntered a second time out of the scrub and across the open flood plain. The PH motioned me to shoot. I still wasn't tempted, much, because I wanted to get to that lion bait. The trackers looked at me with raised eyebrows, gestured with their chins in that way they had, but I shook my head and said, "hapana." They shrugged, spat, and stalked on toward the lion bait. Within ten minutes, that kudu strolled out of the scrub ahead of us a third time.

The PH Larry Richards whispered, "*That,* is a very big kudu." Sweat beaded on Estoni's lip and Gabreli wrung his hands, and their disgust at me smelled mongrel dog acrid. "You'll never kill another like it. Bloody world record, that. Or damned near."

This is the same beast that became Hemingway's obsession in *Green Hills of Africa,* and later Ruark's in his Hemingway wannabe book *Horn of the Hunter*. But they'd already killed their lions when they took after the kudu.

In the end, I succumbed to the treatment and killed the kudu. After all, what good is it to get the client up to a trophy of a lifetime he won't shoot? Grand trophies are the trackers' and pro-hunter's proof; the grander the beast, the better they are at their job, the more clients and status they get. Like the Maasai's cattle.

For a moment I forgot the lion obsession as I came out of the .375's recoil and the bull sagged into the dust and the trackers hollered in the Maa and Swahili and the PH grabbed my hand and shook and slapped my back and grinned.

"Lengai told you to shoot that bull, Bwana," Gabreli said. "Three times he tempts you."

But in the next moment I regretted pulling the trigger because now we couldn't get to the lion bait before dark. The trackers started that bounding Maasai dance, but quit when they glanced at me. I forced a grin, and they shouted again and pulled my thumb in the best of all hunter sensations, now only slightly soured by the lack of lions. Cheri took Polaroids and handed them to the trackers, and grinned. Later in camp the PH measured the bull at one-inch larger than the then world record. Still, it was no lion, and we hadn't made it to the lion bait.

We'd had no luck with the lions. We'd seen none on the Ugalla. Later, we'd seen only immature males in the Serengeti. I awoke sweat-drenched to nightmares of a thick-maned lion-god misting into bush and a jammed rifle and failure at a thing that meant more to me than anything had in decades. Obsession was too weak a word. I felt the morans' lust, the pucker in the groin. When I thought of it too long, my bowel knotted and I spat. I snapped at Cheri across the fire over sundowners and regretted it again, and drummed my fingers over Gordon's gin-and-tonic and the chilled buffalo tongue as the PH small talked at the dusk fire. Into the fourth week with the time running out and no hint of them, Cheri had retreated into herself in that practiced way and the PH Richards barked too often at the staff.

"When you get the chance, don't hurry it," the PH said out of nowhere one evening. "You'll get that chance, ol' Sport. I've no doubt," he reassured. Himself, or me? He shouted too loud, "Cocktelli!" at the Warusha man waiting table.

The Land Cruiser ground south in the dawn, beyond the dirt tire tracks, and bushwhacked through the thornbush with the trackers and me up top on the high-seat, me bleeding from the thorn. It felt right, the blood and rip of the wait-a-bit through an ear lobe when the Toyota forced through the acacia.

From the high-seat, we spotted fringe-eared oryx—we didn't have one yet—and a tracker slapped the cab roof to signal the PH. The Cruiser coasted to a stop and the PH and Cheri climbed up top to glass.

"Good bull, that," the PH said. The Maasai tracker Estoni motioned at the .375 across my knees with his chin. The PH said, "Best take it." I paused, but we duck-walked through the acacia. After that kudu treatment, I knew better than to refuse, but it would take time away from the lions, wherever they were.

The shot took the lungs and the bull leaped and sprinted that final dash across the dead-grass plain. You didn't need your Baedecker Swahili phrase book to know what the trackers shouted. "Piga m'uzuri! Kufa. Kubwa sana! Kubwa!"—Good shot! Dead. Very big! Big!

"Kubwa!-Kufa!-Kubwa!-Kufa!" the trackers began chanting and dancing. I forgot the lion.

It took time to skin the head and hoist the oryx into the Toyota bed. Then the trackers wanted to grill the tripes, though the remote Maasai only varied their milk-and-blood diet on special occasions, so we drove to a hill in a strong wind that kept off the *tsetse*, and that took more time. We'd gotten into pepper ticks, and it took kerosene and time to get them off our legs. Then a family of Maasai wandered out of the bush and I tried to photograph them but they refused. Cheri took Polaroids, handed them out to the Maasai, and then in fair-exchange goodwill, they allowed photography with the SLR and the video camera. She smiled again. They gave her a bead bracelet, and she grinned. We at last drove off, cross-country through the acacia scrub and wait-a-bit tangles along the dry dongas, trailing a half-mile red dust rooster tail over the dead-grass plains, me thinking only of the lack of lions and time running out. I ignored a rare and very desirable gerenuk browsing in the thorn.

"Bloody hell. They'll never believe this in the camp. No client passes up gerenuk," the PH said when I declined the shot. Gabreli, the head tracker shook his head, pleaded "Bwana!" and smacked his lips. The 'Cruiser clattered north again in thick and absolute vocal silence—the treatment—and downwind in a cloud of red dust and when we removed sunglasses we stared with pale raccoon eyes in a face of ochre. We killed an impala for the pot in the last light.

"Lesser kudu off east," the PH said at the fire that night. "As good a chance at lion in that country, too."

We drove east in the dawn, giraffe lumbering between *sansevierra* in the distance, Grant's gazelle out on the dusky plain. The sun hemorrhaged above Kilimanjaro so far north that when we looked again we weren't sure we'd seen it. We quizzed Maasai boys herding cows for any lion spoor. Later, Gabrelli slapped the cab roof. He'd spotted kudu tracks in the dust.

We trailed two lesser kudu an hour, one of them a bull from the spoor, into a donga and spotted them hiding in the thorn tangle at eighty yards. Gabreli gestured and the PH whispered, "On the right." I couldn't see the horns invisible in the tangled brush, and I doubted the PH could, either. At the .375's blast the two kudu bounded out of the donga and through the dead grass, the bull squealing with each bound. I swung through it and when the crosshairs passed touched off again and the bull disappeared. It had horns, all right.

The trackers circled twenty minutes through the long grass and I'd begun to worry when Estoni stumbled over the very dead bull. The long horn measured 33-inches, but the other was broken off six. No matter, I didn't care about record books and we'd scored a heavy-horned Methuselah of a bull.

The trackers shook hands in the way they had of pulling the thumb. The first slug shattered the heart, but I didn't know that when I hit it again.

"Could hunt a month and never better it, Bwana. Bloody grand bull, that." They'd hear of it at the Club and the Convention and the kraal, and for more proof Cheri grinned and took Polaroids and handed them out to the trackers, the best of gifts. Still, this was no lion, to any of us.

We drove on in silence. In a mile I no longer thought of the kudu luck, only the time running out and the lack of lions and the sour taste and dust grit in my teeth.

At first, it seemed a dream. I sat up in the camp cot and listened in the dark. A very distant rumble way off toward Lake Manyara, increasing in intensity, the rumble morphing into an express train roar as it neared until the tent canvas rattled and that keepsake spear clattered to the floor and cartridges rolled off the night stand and someone hollered from the skinner's hut. And then it passed and faded in the distance. The Great Rift owns fumaroles, volcanoes, and yes, tremors.

After another lion-less day, a second quake rumbled and roared and shook out of the north to disappear again into the south as we stared into the sundowner campfire. From the direction of the trackers' huts the Maa word *lengai*—god—floated out of the darkness. "Bloody omen, that," the PH mumbled to no one.

We counted the days now on the fingers of one hand. After another day without lions, we subtracted one more finger. We spoke little at dinner.

I came out of sleep to a rumbling roar and sat up in the cot. I'd done this before, it seemed. It quieted, then, and someone spoke in the Maa very low, then that African night silence so thick you felt it. I lay down and listened and drifted off somewhere when it rumbled again out of the night. That's no quake, I thought. Cheri rustled the bedding and sat up.

A roar blasted out of the night, then gut-deep grunts I felt in my bowels. Another roar from the distance, and the grunts echoed along the stream. *Lions! Hunting lions!* I thought, but I said, "Hear that?" She had, of course, and she came out of herself for a moment in the night and touched me. Muted Maa and Swahili words fluttered out of the dark like bats, and you felt the excitement floating out there in the night brush against your face. Everyone hoped the same thing— the pride would kill a buffalo in that thornbush tangle we called the

Two-Mile Thicket, because a buff-sized kill might anchor them until we could find them in the dawn.

The tent man hung the lantern and set the tray with the morning tea on the nightstand and squeezed my foot under the blanket until I came out of the sleep. It was black dark through the tent flap and the dawn frog chorus hadn't started. In the past, we awoke to the trilling frogs in the dusky half-light. Maa voices drifted out of the pre-dawn black. The cooks argued at the cook fire.

"Bwana," the PH's morning-hoarse voice said through the tent canvas.

"Awake? Chacula. Breakfast." In a moment Cheri slipped through the flap and I followed double-checking the .375 cartridges in shirt loops and shivered with the chill and angst. In minutes, we'd drunk the coffee and poked at the mealie and eggs and climbed into the Land Cruiser and splashed it through the stream and up the sand bank as the Maasai ghosted through the headlights with gourds to fill at the water. We turned south in the coming dawn toward the Two-Mile Thicket and flushed francolin partridge from dusting chores, and a bushbuck bounded out of the stream bottom in the just-light.

In a mile, Gabreli knuckle-wrapped lightly the cab roof and pointed at the vultures hunched in the fever trees. "Simba," he whispered. The Cruiser braked and the PH and Cheri climbed out of the cab. "Vultures in the trees means lions on the kill," he whispered. "My shillings say under that big fever tree." A jackal floated across the track toward the tree. "Our luck has turned," he said as he slipped two panatella-sized .577 cartridges into the double rifle. "Ready?"

I jacked the Remington's bolt and a .375 cartridge into the chamber, checked the safety, and we—Gabreli, the PH, me, Cheri and Estoni in that order—snaked along the track in the silent sand, the light coming but still too dim to see into the shadows. In two-hundred yards, Gabreli crouched and pointed. A lioness slinked into cover, and another.

"See 'em? the PH whispered. Two grand hirsute male lions crouched over a buffalo carcass facing us at near 200 yards.

"Got 'em." My voice sounded odd. The light was still bad in the shadows.

"Just below the chin of the darker lion to the left," the PH said. I looked through the scope. The dark below its chin seemed part of the buffalo they'd killed in the night. The second lion glared and its tail whipped in the air twice.

"Six-inches below the chin, mind you, and a three-seven-five bullet into Black Mane's heart." The black below the chin still looked like buffalo carcass through the 4-power riflescope, but the shadowed half-light was bad and the PH had the 10x Polish binocular.

The crosshairs wobbled too long in my lust, and I fought with myself not to hurry the shot, and it seemed an unconscionable time before they settled solid below the chin and I squeezed the trigger. I lost the lion in the muzzle flash in the half-light and recoil and then found it again in the riflescope as the lion tumbled, regained its feet and sprinted into the thornbush tangle before I could shoot again.

"How'd it feel, Bwana?" the PH said.

"Solid. Right below the chin." But something felt wrong.

We approached with rifles ready, the trackers armed now with spears, and Cheri following. We all saw the white ragged rip running the length of the buffalo rib where I'd aimed when we'd thought it was the lion's chest. The slug had glanced up and hit the lion in the mouth and a gory canine tooth broken off at gum-line lay in the dust. We stood silent as the first vulture planed from a fever tree into the dead grass and waddled toward the buffalo carcass.

Gabreli edged to the donga and tried to see into the tangled thorn. "Hatari, Bwana," the PH warned him. The Warusha assistant drove the Land Cruiser up to the buffalo kill to keep off the vultures.

We took up the spoor—the seven-inch pugs clear in the dust, the odd blood drop from the lion's mouth, a mane hair caught on wait-a-bit thorn—and followed into the thornbush so tangled we couldn't force through it unless we got to hands-and-knees along a bushbuck trail. The lion kept to the bushbuck trail, too. The trackers hands-and-kneed with the idea they'd flatten like postage stamps at the first hint of lion and we'd shoot over them, but no one believed in it.

Then the spoor led out of the thornbush tangle and into an opening and the trackers followed at a trot, spears glinting in the rising sun, and we found where the lion spat saliva and a bit of blood. The trackers said something in Swahili to the PH that ended with "hapana." I'd picked up enough Swahili in three weeks to know it was a negative.

"They don't think he's much hurt," the PH said. "Let's spoor a bit." Thirty minutes later we glimpsed a very healthy lion gallop through the thorn, and the lion vaporized into that bush of my nightmare.

"Hapana," Estoni said.

We single-filed back toward the Toyota in silence. As we neared the Cruiser, Gabreli pointed with the spear at a pug cratered in the sand and the PH nodded. The PH and Gabreli discussed something in Swahili, low, and it didn't take much to know they thought it was the other male lion. Then the trackers followed on each side of the spoor with the PH and me watching ahead into the thickets and our thumbs on the safety. The track circled into the open through the sand, easy to follow, back toward the buffalo kill. We heard a low growl from the thick bush and the trackers crouched so we could shoot over them, but I stepped to one side because I didn't want one to jack-in-the-box into my line of fire should the lion charge. I wanted it to charge, too, more than anything I could remember.

Estoni pointed the spear at a lioness trotting away, and then a hairy male lion misted into the bush. We jogged to catch up and another lion growled, deep and rumbling, and we swung to face it, then ignored it and kept to the spoor, trailing the dream now at a trot.

Then we all saw Him standing between thickets and looking back over his shoulder, the tail thrashing now, reluctant to retreat more. I put the crosshairs behind the shoulder as He stood quartering away and roared so you felt it through the ground, the trackers had the spears up, and as it turned to charge I touched off the .375.

At the blast the quarter-ton of cat pogo-ed, stumbled in the dust and got its feet under it and bolted for the thick bush in the donga. I fired again and the lion stumbled and caught itself and the PH shot and dust geysered behind it and the lion disappeared into the bush.

The trackers began pulling thumbs and grinning, when the PH said, "You gut-shot the son of a bitch."

My mouth became ashy. I remembered the crosshairs steady behind the shoulder. I'd never felt more certain of anything. But that was the way with it with anything important. Then I thought of the rifle banging around in the Land Cruiser. The rifle and scope had shot perfectly for three weeks, but the scope could have jarred askew.

The trackers had caught the PH's mood and looked like kittens in a bath. Cheri had retreated into herself in that way she had and the driver escorted her back the open Land Cruiser, which would have been no protection. We took up the spoor into the thick bush. The blood spots were scarce but the uneven tracks showed the lion stumbled and mane hair hung from the thorns where he'd crashed through. The thornbush became so thick we could not move five feet in a minute, and most of that crawling. Two trackers first, then the PH wormed ahead and I had no chance at a shot even if the cat charged. A francolin partridge flushed and the trackers dropped to belly and the PH tangled the double rifle in bush and I shoved the safety off so hard it jammed the thumb. A charging lion would have killed us all. We crawled on, me no longer wanting anything but to get out of Tanzania, to go anywhere else. I felt disgusted at the mess I'd made. The PH looked sick-pale beneath the sunburn.

"Kufa," Gabreli quavered almost in question, then he repeated "Kufa!" in half-surprise.

"Kufa!" Estoni exhaled in a gust. *Dead*, I marveled as I hands-and-knees bulldozed the PH aside and shoved past Estoni and looked to where Gabreli pointed and there He was stretched on the dry-season dead leaves as if asleep.

"Hatari!" Gabreli shouted at the danger as I pushed past him, too, and on to touch the lion. "Hapana," he said and then a stone whistled past my ear and dead-meat whunked the cat's flank and I reached to touch and caressed the face, caressed its flank, fingered the black-red bullet hole behind the shoulder, and worked my fingers through the tangled mane, before anyone else could touch Him.

And then, the deluge. The PH slammed both palms against my shoulders from behind knocking me onto the lion and hollered and then the trackers slapped and they all reached to touch Him and the trackers began chanting and we heard the Maa voices from the distance and then the Maasai morani forcing through the thorn naked with the red shukas wadded so as not to catch on thornbush and more Maa voices in the distance and Cheri there and touching the lion and touching me.

Somehow we crawled out of the thornbush thicket with the warriors still struggling six-hundred pounds of symbol out of the tangle. Coquettish n'ditos streamed into the opening from the local village, giggling, touching the lion slayer, one placing a beaded bracelet on my wrist, touching and taking long enough to fasten the strap and staring into my eyes, and another doing the same on the other wrist and taking even longer. When they struggled the lion out of the bush I kneeled to stroke it again and Cheri squeezed my shoulder and the n'ditos reached to touch my shirt, my arm.

"Sit, Bwana," the PH said. Someone pushed me into a canvas chair and then it was to shoulder height, the trackers and warriors carrying and if not supporting reaching to touch and chanting, "Simba! Simba! Ungh-ungh-ungh!" while Cheri videotaped. Twenty warriors lifted the lion and danced around the Land Cruiser chanting until it collapsed in on them. More children, warriors, n'ditos, and matrons drifted out of the scrub and they touched my sleeve or arm and everyone touched the lion and crooned as they loaded Him into the Toyota and we drove slowly past the manyatta and more boys fell in behind singing and shouting "Simba!" until we crossed the stream and drove into the camp.

"Look, Bwana." The PH prized open the cat's mouth and pointed at a gory stump that should have been a canine tooth. "Greedy bugger wouldn't let a toothache keep it from its bloody share of buff."

The Maasai at first trickled into the camp beside the brook under the big yellow acacia trees, then streamed in and they lifted the lion and carried and chanted out to the skinning huts and the n'ditos said something with their eyes to me and Cheri touched and held. "You're the Devil's Own with the ladies now," the PH said. "Could have any one you want. They'd put you on the cover of that news magazine, *Time*, is it?"

We sat at the fire ring away from the skinning shed bedlam with cold Lion Lagers trying to absorb it. The PH walked up. "Ten-foot-three between the pegs," he said. "The Old Hunters, chaps like Selous and ol' Alfred Pease, drove pegs into the ground at the nose and end of the tail, and measured between the pegs. Hell with the Safari Club measurements. Keep it simple. You bloody won't see a better simba, Bwana."

We drank more lagers, and the Maasai misted back to their boma beyond the stream and then in the dusk and distance we heard the chanting.

As we listened, the chanting shifted and we followed it in the dark now, across the stream and up the track and down into our camp. "The n'goma is building," the PH said. "It's party time, Bwana Simba."

They drifted into the camp with the black m'pingo-handled best-dress spears glinting in the firelight and the hissing gas lanterns, chanting in Maa with the odd Swahili *simba* echoing through the fever trees. The numbers swelled until twenty warriors and more n'ditos heavy with bead-and-wire jewelry, chanted and danced into the camp and the elders and matrons and kids followed. The matrons and oldest of elders sat beneath the trees with toothless grins and sipped the blood beer from gourds and the rest danced and chanted and played the musical instrument made from bits of bent metal and a carved wooden box and strummed with the thumb. I bought three cases of the Lion Lager from safari stores to help the party along and gave the head elder, the one dressed in western clothes, a C-note to promote general goodwill.

We sat beside the fire and listened to the guttural chanting and watched the leaping dance where the moran leaped from a standstill so high it was impossible to understand how they did it and the n'ditos urged them along by bouncing the great circular beaded neck-laces on their breasts. The warrior that jumped highest and longest became the n'goma hero and owned the most desirable of women, at least for the night. Two warriors with ochred faces wanted wives and they competed in the leaping with gusto. The n'ditos often danced past bouncing the elaborate necklaces and touched me and looked into Cheri's eyes as she held my arm.

A moran left the leaping, chanting bedlam and approached, his crimson shuka against the ebony polished skin looking more elegant than any urbanite in a tux. Gabreli translated the Maa into Swahili, and the PH translated that into English. "He says your *simba* chewed him up while herding cows." The warrior about-faced, bent over, and hoisted the shuka exposing the purple scars on naked buttocks. He handed me the black-handled, best-dress spear as a gift, and disappeared back into the leaping and chanting mass. I ran my thumb down the long double-edged blade and grinned.

Saga of the One-Eyed Bull

I recognized the old bull by the odd dark patch of fur against the blond of his shoulder, and for two years now, the empty eye socket. There'd been no heavy roundness to the barrel of his body when I'd seen him early that September before the rut, only the shoulders and hips sharp in silhouette against the dusk sky, the sway-back, and the careful old-man steps back into the timber. There were still six points on each antler, but the beams were shorter and thinner.

He won't make it through the winter, I thought, almost aloud. I was convinced I'd have to get him that season, or the winter would. There'd be no next time for me and the bull.

I'd seen him first years earlier (was it four now?). He'd stood on the meadow in the gorge at dusk, Clydesdale-big and rounded, and bugle-roared at a lesser bull at the edge of the trees, the banshee scream and then the heavy, gut-deep grunts echoing between thousand-foot limestone cliffs.

Two weeks later and two days before the season opened, I returned to find the bull gone and the big tracks leading up the gorge onto a mile-long bench, then high into a heavy mixed stands of aspens and Douglas fir on the shoulder of the big mountain. There were no tracks leading away from that blown-down, hair-thick tangle, either.

That seemed to be his routine: summering in the tangle on the mountain and then dropping down to the meadows along the creek in the gorge in September to fight and bugle and rut, and then climbing back up the mountain again in October to rest and regain weight before the winter pushed him out.

I came back to hunt him first that October. I rode a mountain-wise mare up the first canyon and onto a high windy plateau and through the canyon heads and then down into one last valley, the bay quick-stepping silently on fir needles through a heavy, sunless timber to the foot of his mountain. I let the mare switchback her way up the steep flank of the mountain, stopping to blow when she needed it, until we were at the meadow below his cover. From the tracks, he came out of the timber to feed at dusk, and I waited there and remembered his antlers, the beams as big around as a man's forearm. He came slowly to the edge of the timber almost at dark, stood a moment, then disappeared back into the gloom. Perhaps he'd scented me, or maybe he had had some other way of knowing. Though I had three days to hunt, I didn't see him again.

I looked for the bull again the second season ten days before the hunt, and he was there, lean from rutting and fighting, and there was a black, oozing hole where his left eye should have been. He'd taken an antler tine there in a fight and the wound had the sunken look you see in toothless old people. I left as soon as I'd found he was still there, careful not to disturb him.

When the hunt began, I waited two days at the meadow without results. His fresh tracks were there in the grasses and mud of the seep, but he only came out of the thick trees to feed at night; he remembered too well the season before. After waiting those days, I still-hunted very slowly into the tangle of trees, stalking along a deeply tracked trail, examining antler rubs on aspen and fir saplings where the bark had been scraped higher than I could reach. The blunt hoofprints were as big as saucers and sunk deep where the soil was soft. The timber reeked of his musk. It took me an hour to ease 200 yards into the tangle, looking long and hard into the shadows ahead and to the sides, aware the wind quartered into my face, listening for anything that might hint "elk." But there was nothing, only the Indian Summer sun filtering through the broken canopy of autumn-dead leaves and the twitterings of chickadees searching the tree bark.

So I continued, reveling in that action-to-come feel. Then the crash as if a 10-ton boulder fell from the bluff above and through the timber, and the brief glimpse of teak-and-ivory antlers with the sun glinting off them and the disappearing creamy, heart-shaped rump. That was the last of him that season, and I knew it as I sat on a deadfall and watched my hands shake.

I had similar luck the last day of the following season, the third season, by that time I kept track, as I still-hunted back into the timber again and jumped him at 20 yards. As he crashed off through the timber, bowling over saplings and hurtling blowdowns, I couldn't quite get the crosshairs anywhere but on his rump. If I touched off the .270 like that, he'd escape and die miserably.

He survived the long, hard winter and the late-coming spring, and the next September he looked poor and his antlers were smaller as I scouted before the hunt. "He's passed prime," I told the mare as we rode to camp.

Two raghorn bulls kept him company that fourth season, and as they fed out of the timber on opening evening in the dusky half-light, I could just make out the old bull hanging back in the trees behind a screen of fir saplings. Then it was dark, and I stumbled down the ridge to where the mare waited in the night and chuckled softly at my approach. I waited and watched the meadow for three days, then still-hunted back into the tangle. I heard the bulls go far ahead, the wind had shifted, and that was it for the season.

That final season I scouted a week before the hunt and he was there. I knew then as I looked at the bony hips and watched him take those old-man steps back into the timber that this would be his last year on the mountain. There was no doubt, and as soon as the first heavy snows came he'd begin that irreversible downward spiral.

The old one-eyed bull stood in the wind in the dawn on opening day. I hesitated after settling the crosshairs on the dark shoulder spot and looked up from the rifle. You get old and you die, I thought, but I knew it was better this way than in the winter. "It's better," I told myself aloud, rationalizing a bit, the sound of my voice as soothing as if someone else had confirmed it, too. I pressed the trigger and the bull sagged forward.

I walked up to him. Though he was still a six-by-six, the antlers were no longer the heavy, massive, heavy-beamed rack they were two years earlier. Maybe I shouldn't have shot him. Maybe I should have let him have the rest of the fall until the snows got too heavy. But in my mind I saw him lying in the belly-deep, blue-cold snow, like that bull I'd watched die in Yellowstone. He took six days to do it, weakening all the time until he became too feeble to keep the coyotes from his haunches and the magpies from his eyes.

"It was right to shoot him," I told myself. A heavy, deep bugle floated up from that sunless timber at the base of the mountain, and in my mind I saw the bull in the gloom of the trees with beams as big around as a man's forearm.

Republished in the centennial anthology, *The Best of Field & Stream, 100 years of Great Writing*, Lyons & Burford, 1995.

THE GOOD, THE BAD AND THE UGLY

G ood thing we don't copyright titles, because this one's toured the planet, from a Clint Eastwood shoot-em-up up to hunting newsletters. But it's apt for an article about hunting guides, or if you prefer, professional hunters. Now, I've hunted from the ripe age of eight over half a century ago when I harried neighborhood cats and squirrels with a Red Ryder BB gun, until stalking chamois and red stag just before the Pandemic, with more hunts in the offing. I mean, I've had my share of guides.

All hunters are optimists. Why else would we crawl from a toasty bedroll into a freon black dawn, slurp coffee that peels enamel off molars, plunge through frozen tent flaps into a whiteout, then repeat next day with the same hope of bagging a 10-inch billy or full-curl bighorn? As optimists, we tend to forget the debacles and recall the spectacular. So I'm going to concentrate on the good guides and PHs, and skim the bad and ugly.

First, let's give credit where it's due. I'd just drifted into foggy dreams when Cheri elbowed me back into consciousness. "What about spectacular hunts and guides, with guys like Yuri Matison, Alvaro Villegas, and Vladimir, Rob, John, Ken, Craig, Willie…?" She was still rattling them off trying to give me an idea for another story, when I floated back into the dreamy ether. In the morning, I thought, *Why not?*

Starting with those that jump into mind first, but otherwise in no particular order, let's begin with legendary Tajikistan outfitter and guide Yuri Matison. No matter that I slapped one of my best of 20 sheep trophies, a near -63" x 17" Marco Polo argali, and a magnum ibex in the salt with Yuri's outfit nearly a quarter century ago.

He ran a tight outfit that started in Moscow when Yuri's guy met our Aeroflot flight out of NY, bribed us through customs and gun formalities, escorted Cheri and me to the Tajik embassy for visas, guided us to Red Square, then Yuri's wife bought dinner and pushed us aboard a converted Soviet Badger bomber to Kyrgyzstan. In Biskek, his people grabbed us as we debarked and escorted us to the VIP lounge; it had no other residents, so no heat, and that meant you saw your breath in the sub-zero December temps. In the dawn, they stuffed us aboard a Yak 40 Kyrgyzstan Air jet to Osh. In Osh, Yuri's *major domo* Boris Popov and driver Soli handled our baggage right off the Yak before anyone else could get out, shoved it into the Russian Uaz van backed up to the plane, and motored through the city and onto the euphemistically named Pamir Highway. Ten hours, an overturned truck with frozen bodies—it's 20-odd below—and nine Russian army roadblocks (to intercept opium out of Afghanistan; the guys bribed our way through with vodka and vegetables brought for such purposes) later, we made Matison's Lake Karakul camp.

After we'd bagged the grand ram two days on, I mentioned to Cheri in the privacy of our room that it might be nice to take a day and trek around the lake by way of denouement. The next day, we got that wish. Cheri said, also in the room, that she'd kill for a Coke, and sure enough, one materialized, complete with bottle opener. Likewise, she mentioned in passing that a porta-potty for the room might be a godsend to save her hiking to the loo through the 20-below-zero temps. Sure enough, she got one of those, too. Do you suppose the walls had ears? Yuri left nothing to chance.

Yuri and his guys—guides Dolat and Toktomat, organizer Boris and driver Soli, skinner and man Friday Vladimir—couldn't have been more efficient. I recall that stellar shikar whenever I glance at my full-body *Ovis ammon poli* mount or that ibex head high on the wall. One of the best hunt brokers ever, Wes Vining out of Wyoming, organized and booked the hunt, by the way; alas, Wes is no longer in the business. It's tough keeping the good ones around.

We all start somewhere, and the Red Gods smiled big when we latched onto professional hunter Willie Phillips for our first Africa safari in Botswana's Okavango 40 years ago.

He became a stellar guide and mentor for two Utah hicks. Not only did he produce grand trophies, including a 15-inch warthog, top-ten-class tsessebe, 42-inch buff, 52-inch kudu, and half a dozen others, he elaborated hippo habits, ID-ed polychrome bee-eaters, and we glassed hammer-head storks, chased a venomous boomslang until it decided enough was enough, and photographed swamp lilies.

Vira Safaris, the outfitter, refused to let us shoot a kudu, the main reason I'd made the safari in the first place, even though it was on our contract. "Sold out the bloody quota, they did," Willie said, "and they're using your safari to make it up." After the nightly shouting match over the two-way to the headquarters where Willie invariably won, he said, "Bugger 'em! We'll get your bloody kudu, alright." Seems he had citizen permits where citizens that did not have rifles asked him to kill animals for the tags they'd secured—all entirely legal in Botswana back then. We bagged our kudu, too. Alas, we couldn't help but compare the dozen or so African PHs we later hunted with over the years to the standard Willie had set.

The next season he ditched Vira Safaris and hooked up with Safari South. He'd be in his late 80s now, and telling stories at Riley's bar if he's still kicking. Vira Safaris no longer exists, as I understand it. Jack Atcheson Jr. booked this safari, by the way.

Invariably, visitors to my house ask which is my favorite big game trophy. It's usually a sheep or goat, depending on my mood, such as that Marco Polo argali mentioned above, or a maybe a 40" Dagestan tur. Sometimes the 10'3" Tanzanian lion makes its appearance. As often as any, it's the 10'4" Nunavut polar bear. I dislike using arithmetic to describe big game trophies, but these days it's tough keeping it out, so I too often give in.

Inuit guide Jaypatee Akeeagok and his aid Pauloosie Attagootak and I made the dogsled hunt in early March more than a quarter century ago, too, full winter on the polar ice-pack. Temps never climbed above 31-below zero, and once plunged to 41-below. We slept in wall tents on the pack ice heated, sort of, with Coleman stoves, then broke camp each day and dogsledded from iceberg to iceberg frozen into the sea ice and glassed, then dogsledded until purple sundown and spent three hours pitching camp again. We'd repeat next sunup.

Jaypatee and Pauloosie waded into a snarling, snapping canine chaos to feed the sled dogs each evening with frozen, raw caribou chunks. Jaypatee tossed the chunks and Pauloosie stood by with a 16' green seal hide whip in case Jay lost footing or a dog attacked. If dogs threatened, the whip snapped and dog fur floated in the breeze. If a dog went down in the melee, other dogs would kill it if Jay didn't break it up.

"They're not lap dogs," Jay said to me, "Don't get near 'em." Mother didn't raise any fool children, so I didn't.

We'd dogsled 50 miles a day, glass from each iceberg, and stop for tea and soup made from iceberg chunks melted over a Coleman. We ogled bears in the 12 days on the pack ice, too, 13 of them, but none magnum enough for my fantasy. On the 12th evening, while Pauloosie and I wrestled the wall tent and blue italics floated in the breeze, Jaypatee scaled the iceberg and glassed. He slalomed down minutes later.

"Good bear out there," he said. "Get your gun." Pauloosie pounded in the last stake, swore at the tent for good measure, and he and Jay harnessed the shivering dogs again and we aimed out into the gloaming. We caught the bear within two miles, Jay turned the dogs loose to bay it, and we bagged that bear and I forgot all about the bitter cold. Next daybreak, we dogsledded two more days the hundred miles back to Grise Fjord village on Ellesmere Island, the farthest north settlement in North America.

No guides ever worked harder, and few of my experience owned Jaypatee's expertise. Without it, we'd have frozen. Of course I'm still high on that hunt, and the Red Gods grinned a big one my way, but I'm happy enough not to repeat because of that brutal cold. You can no longer import them into this country, anyhow. Wes Vining booked this one, too, so you understand my woe at his departure from the field.

Nomad Mongol guide Luya (normally, nomads own only one name) is another of the true greats. He's soft-spoken, fame hasn't spoiled him, he seldom leaves the Hanghai home turf of the Gobi Desert, and he's got his ducks in a row, whether trading goats and camels or stalking argali sheep or ibex. He's genuinely surprised when you tip him at the end of the hunt, too.

I've hunted with Luya two seasons, once for Hanghai argali where we bagged one of my most stunning rams ever. The December before we hunted with Luya and stayed at his uncle's *ger* (a Mongol *yurt*) encampment at the base of a freon mountain range in the central Gobi and bagged a magnum Gobi ibex after six days scaling the scarps in twenty-odd-below zero temps and howling sand and ice blizzards. That last day Luya scaled the scarps with a bad chest cold, too. That afternoon, my birthday, we galloped Bactrian camels, quaffed Chinese wine, and supped on camel roast and yak stew by way of celebration.

Luya's pal and famed Mongolian guide Zorig is another of the greats. On a 3000 km. cross-country argosy across much of Mongolia, we bagged a 57" Altai ibex, a grand black-tailed goitered gazelle, and a roebuck with a 14" beam. There goes that math again. Erka, his wife and our woman Friday, skinned, cooked, boiled skulls and anything required of her. If I had to choose, I'd pick Mongolia as my favorite hunting geography, largely through Luya's and Zorig's comradeship, efficiency and expertise. Kudos to Erka, too, even if she wasn't the guide.

Let's throw in two more African PHs before I forget. We first met Russell Tarr in Zimbabwe more than three decades ago, where we bagged a 7'2" leopard, a 43-inch sable, a 52" kudu and the best part of a dozen other antelope. Russ never raised his voice for any reason, he'd always throw desert-dry quips our way, he'd cheer you in a laid-back way, and we've visited several times at the conventions and he's spent nights at our manse in Utah, too. We went tobogganing once, and Russ turned pink from the cold and vowed never to repeat. I wouldn't hesitate to hunt with Russell again, either.

Then there's John Wamback. I've hunted Namibia with Wamback several times and bagged an elephant, a croc and three antelope. Wamback is Tarr's antithesis. Both are efficient, though, and I'll hunt again with Wamback if the Fates are kind enough.

John's visited the manse in Utah several times, too, and we've snow-shoed, hiked and jogged together while he did. We always visit at the conventions, too.

I've hunted with other Africa PHs, some okay, and others not. I nearly came to blows with one because he insisted I shoot from the Land Cruiser. Another was petrified of the elephants we hunted, and we missed a chance at a 70-pounder because of it. One wanted to sneak us into Kruger just across the Limpopo from Zimbabwe, but I nixed that; thing was, I wouldn't have realized it was Kruger if he hadn't chosen to tell me. You got to watch 'em in Africa. Outfitters could be worse, too, including the Zimbabwean who saddled us with a tourist photo guide that never hunted elephants before; the out-fitter now manages a safari company for two wealthy Americans in Mozambique, and I understand from a pal that hunted with him, the Zimbabwean hasn't changed much.

But let's get back to the good of those good, bad and ugly guides.

Vladimir Plaschenko and I've clung to rotten limestone scarps and rafted through bergs in the Okhotsk Sea breakup over the course of maybe ten years starting back in the early 90s. No doubt, those Red Gods we keep mentioning winked and grinned again when I became his first western client. For all I know, I'm still his only west-ern client.

Olga Parfenova then working with the Tor Company out of Khabarovsk city organized that first snow sheep hunt with outfitter Yuri Cherneyshchevich for Cheri, me, and college pal Peter Spear. In those days, a ram was a ram to Russian guides just after Glasnost. Meat was meat, so Vladimir couldn't understand why I kept passing up rams, especially those near camp. It took a while, but he finally grasped the idea that all rams weren't created equal.

Probably he thought me loco, stumbling from camp and warm bedroll each dawn and finger-and-toeing the scree day after day and passing up ram after ram, and staggering back to camp in the black. But he kept at it, and he learned not to hike along ridge lines because he'd be obvious even to a one-eyed octogenarian ram. He learned to judge trophies, and figured out with some precision just what sized ram I lusted after. He actually got into the thrill of the chase and

punched both fists toward the cumulus when I finally bagged my 40"
x 15" ram (those numbers again).

I hunted more rams and bears with Vladimir in later years, and
I like to think we became friends, too. Heck, when I disagreed with
his boss, the outfitter, he took my side in the shebang.

Vladimir lived in Okhotsk village on the Sea of Okhotsk in the
north of Khabarovsk Krai, in the Russian Far East. Olga now works
with Spartak (get contact info from their website) in Khabarovsk city
and could probably run Vladimir down if you wanted to hunt with
him. You can't go wrong.

At the moment, I'm trying to figure how to work another hunt
with Eurohunts outfitter and stellar guide Alvaro Villegas. I'm getting close, too, and with any luck, might swing a shindig in May or
June or as soon as I can get that Coronavirus vaccine, for both of
Spain's chamois.

I hunted last with Alvaro for Ronda and Southeastern ibex, and
scored grand billies of both. That Ronda ibex, by the way, completed
all 12 varieties or subspecies of the world's wild, native, non-hybrid,
non-feral, and non-fenced goats. It also completed my Spanish Big
Four—that is, all four of Spain's native ibex varieties.

So what if I scored two more of those "collections" with Alvaro?
Those collections weren't as important as the grand time we had, and
the unhurried hunting we experienced. Unlike much of Spain, or
Europe for that matter, we didn't hunker on a ridge with a calculator
to compute whether or not I could afford this ibex or that one, like
I've done before. In Europe, you very often pay according to size,
whether in millimeters, CIC points or kilograms, still a foreign concept to most Americans including me, even after a dozen European
hunts, too. We stalked the biggest we could find at a fixed price and
outdid ourselves, just like North America.

We breakfasted on tortas, liqueurs and cafes in tiny cantinas
peopled by olive pickers in the black dawn, and dined in obscure
restaurants on some of the best grub on the continent. Alvaro went
out of his way to meet any need, and he never rushed us, a fact
important to both Cheri and me. Unlike some guides and profes-

sional hunters, he made you feel that hunting was more than just a job.

As I write this, I'm realizing all the guides and PHs I've left out, and that I need a book to do justice to all of them. I'm also understanding that I'll inevitably hurt feelings here, dammit. So apologies to all the guides and PHs I've not included in this limited space: Spaniard Jose Mallo of Espacaza; Ken Olynyk, Ralph Kitchen, Cliff Eagle, Charlie, Herbie and Burt of British Columbia; Craig Cross and Wade Lemon of Utah; Rob Jones and Scott Ruttum of Alaska; Sam Kapolak of Nunavut; Jonathan Kibler of Arizona; Erdogan Avci in Turkey and Azerbaijan; Arif and his four sons in Azerbaijan; Evenk native 'Cola in the Russian Far East; Anatoli and the others on Kamchatka, are just a few of the good ones.

LESS IS MORE

*...I had seen a lesser kudu bull come out of the
brush to the edge of the opening where the salt was
and stand there, heavy-necked, gray, and handsome,
the horns spiraled against the sun while I sighted on
his chest and then refused the shot, wanting not to
frighten the greater kudu that should surely come at
dusk.*

—Ernest Hemingway, *Green
Hills of Africa*, 1935

Hemingway's *Green Hills of Africa* is largely the story of his
quest for East African greater kudu. In one instance, he
passes a sure lesser kudu trophy at the chance for a shot at
a greater kudu. With proper plot and drama, he bagged two greater
kudu bulls at the last of the safari.

I couldn't have cared less about greater kudu this safari, because
I'd shot a handful in southern African countries, and to me a kudu
was a kudu. Besides, a Tanzanian greater kudu trophy fee was expensive. With classic irony, though, I killed an East African greater kudu
on the Msima River measuring an inch longer than professional
hunter Richard Trappe's then Safari Club International world record,
only because the trackers and professional hunter wouldn't speak to
me again if I didn't.

On this East African safari, my lion obsession kept me staring
into campfires late into many nights and drinking too much Lion
Lager for three weeks, until we at last put a hirsute, Maasai cow-eat-

ing 10'3" cat in the salt. In the process, we'd scored a 7'3" leopard, a brace of fine buffalo, and all the antelope I'd wanted.

Except one: lesser kudu. No one safaris to shoot lesser kudu. Clients bag them while hunting more glamorous game, greater kudu, for example. The name has something to do with it. Could you earn fame and riches as a lesser accountant, say, or a lesser CEO, or lesser mechanic? I lusted after a 30-inch lesser kudu nearly as much as that lion, though. I was more inch-conscious in those days, too, but a wise man changes his mind many times, a fool never.

Two days earlier we'd hunted 20 miles south of the last free water in this part of the Maasai Steppe and spotted a 35-inch fringe-eared oryx we couldn't shoot because I'd already bagged one, but no lesser kudu. I shot-gunned a brace of vulturine guinea fowl in frustration, though they made a fine supper. Yesterday we'd driven east toward Tarangire savannas through zebra herds, bands of eland mixed with kongoni and hundreds of Grants gazelle, and a lioness stalking them. I bagged a King Kong Coke's hartebeest, but what's a hartebeest when you're hunting lesser kudu? Driving back in the dusk the lioness is worrying a zebra carcass she'd scored. After twenty-odd days inhaling Tanzanian dust, we'd seen no lesser kudu. If you'd asked me then, that proverbial water glass was more than half empty.

"This is the place of the little kudu," the local Maasai elder tells our tracker in *Maa*. The tracker translates into Swahili for the professional hunter, and the PH tells us in English. In the dawn the Maasai elder traces a furrow in the sand to show our tracker the route. In exchange for this intelligence, Cheri snaps Polaroid photos of the elder posing with his newest wife. Cheri's Polaroid snapshots make her a great favorite with the staff, and the local Maasai bedeck her with more beaded polychrome jewelry by far than they give me for slaying the cow-killing lion.

We all suffer to one degree or another from the effects of the Maasai ngoma the night before to celebrate the death of my lion (with a C-note to oil the process), but I'm still higher than Kilimanjaro from the natives and trackers carrying me about on their shoulders chanting, "Simba! Simba! Bwana Simba!"

After two earlier days finding no lesser kudu where they were sure to live, none of us believe much in the new information. The trackers suffer more from their meat gorge at the ngoma than I do, so I'm alert enough to spot the first lesser kudu. They are cows, and the first I've seen, so I don't recognize them right off, but the trackers do. We see no bulls, but our spirits lift and the trackers forget the effects and soon spot a bull lesser kudu trotting across a plain. We jog beyond the thornbush thicket to intercept the bull, but can't find him again. The trackers then circle up the sand wash and beat back down through the bush to where we hope the kudu will flush. Nothing jumps except a francolin partridge. The bull has vaporized, but we're in lesser kudu country—their tracks crisscross the sand wash.

We eat cold buffalo tongue, guinea fowl, and drink a soda at the Toyota Land Cruiser and glass the plains. Giraffe float between the spreading acacia and Grant's gazelle graze in the spaced trees, but we spot no lesser kudu. Later, we find where poachers killed an elephant years ago and hacked the tusks out of the now bleaching skull.

We push the brushy flats along a dry sand wash, or donga. The professional hunter, the three trackers, Cheri and I work through the bush as if we're hunting pheasants in the Dakotas. We flush three francolin partridge, a brace of guinea fowl and a springhare. I'm toting my Remington .375 not because I need it for deer-sized lesser kudu, but because my 7mm/08, otherwise the perfect caliber, isn't holding its zero.

We repeat the maneuver at promising flats along the donga. On one, a lesser kudu bull erupts from a thornbush thicket and sprints straight away. I've got the crosshairs solid at the base of its tail as it bounds arrow-straight through high grass, no question the .375, 300 grain Sierra A-frame slug will punch into the vitals, and I know I have him. The trackers shout, "Shoot! Shoot, Bwana!" (After three weeks, I still look around for Stuart Granger or Clark Gable whenever they call me "bwana.")

The PH hollers, "Shoot!" then half in jest, adds, "bwana."

I'm as certain of the shot as I am of anything, but I lower the rifle. The trophy bull's horns didn't turn outward and into that last curl that normally makes a 30-incher. Since when could I afford to act so picky? *It may well be your last chance at them, Bub*, I tell myself. The bull is only the second we've seen in twenty days and the first I've had crosshairs on.

"You ain't got a prayer without lead in the air," the PH says. It's mid-afternoon of the last day hunting lesser kudu if we want to go up north after Tommies. I don't feel so good. The guys are silent as we drive along the donga. As the Toyota bounces along the track and giraffe float through mimosa, tracker Estoni spots a magnum Grant's gazelle profiling on a termite mound. We stop and glass.

Gabreli says, "Kubwa sana!"—very big.

"You won't find a better," Richards says. From their body language, the trackers want me to shoot. After three weeks with them, what I can't get from the Swahili and Maa, I can decipher from posture. I consider it, and you're allowed two, but I've already bagged a good gazelle, though the buck posing a hundred yards off is a full two-inches longer, probably top-ten class. At least we'd have something to show for the day's hunt, but dropping the gazelle would take away from our remaining kudu-hunting time—a few hours. I motion the driver on. Later, we ignore with effort the largest warthog we've seen posing in short grass along the donga bluff. In an hour, I'd passed up two of the safari's best, certain, in-the-salt trophies, and everyone wonders at my sanity, including me. A mile on, three impala wander out of the long grass, all of them inches longer than the one I'd bagged. It's legal to shoot more than one. I look away when the trackers stare with questions in their eyes. *Focus*, I tell myself. A tracker whistles low in exasperation.

The Toyota jolts along the track, when head tracker Gabreli whistles and points. We've all got the glasses up and I spot two gray, white-striped bodies in the tangled bush in the donga. The PH exhales and I sense the trackers' adrenaline, but I can't see any horns from my angle.

"Shoot!" the PH hisses. I step around a tracker and steady the crosshairs offhand behind the shoulder of the larger animal, yet still can't see a horn. My thumb's on the safety, too, but I'm reluctant. I side step again for a better angle, and still can't spot the horns. The striped bodies are poised to sprint, Richards hisses "Shoot!" again, I thumb off the safety, decide to gamble, and touch the trigger.

At the .375 blast both kudu vault onto the flat above the donga and sprint through the scattered bush. I swing through the racing and squealing bull and hit the trigger again and the bull cartwheels and disappears.

"Piga?" the PH asks the trackers. Is it hit? From his angle, he didn't see the kudu bull drop.

"N'dio!" Gabreli asserts. Yes! "Kufa!" Dead! I'm still not sure what I shot. It had horns, but how big? I hadn't time to judge them, concentrating so on the running shot at the bull, and I didn't see them at all before the first shot. The trackers cross the donga and circle and search for the bull. Cheri, the PH and I watch from the opposite side of the donga, me with the .375 at the ready in case the bull jumps. It's some time before Estoni locates the kudu.

"Kufa," he shouts across the donga. Dead. "Kubwa!" he hollers. It's big, too. We scramble into the ravine and finger-and-toe up the crumbly clay bluff and out onto the flat and to the kudu. The horns are as thick as my wrist and spiral into that third curl and I'm certain they'll tape that magic, mythic 30-inches, like that 40-inches for a North American ram, but one of them is broken off six or so inches. The scarred bull was a battler.

I'm not disappointed, though you'd like to have entire horns. Earlier, I'd bagged a gargantuan bushbuck west on the Ugalla River with a broken horn, too. The first shot socked the kudu bull low in the chest behind the shoulder and took the heart, and the second spined the bull in its death rush.

"Kubwa, Bwana!" the trackers shout and grasp and tug my thumb in congratulations. I love that "bwana" part; maybe I should put it on my office door back home. "Kubwa sana!" Very big! "M'uzuri sana," very good, Gabeli says and we tug thumbs.

"Nice bull, Bwana." Larry grasps my hand. He knows it, too. Cheri beams, and we all—the team—chatter, grin, slap shoulders and wallow in the best feeling there is.

Later, on the dusk drive back to camp, a very good lesser kudu bull walks across the track and stares. Later still, in the near dark, a wondrous lesser kudu bull profiles across another donga. Its two entire, heavy, incredibly long horns spiral against the light gold grasses on the slope as if in a fantasy. Everyone stares at me, but I'm okay with it; I'll stand with my bull, not that I have any choice.

"This is your day for lesser kudu," Richards says.

LITTLE THINGS

"...the little things are infinitely the most important." So says Arthur Conan Doyle, author of the Sherlock Holmes stories. Ditto Charles Dickens' character David Copperfield: "Trifles make the sum of life." As in literature and life, so it is in hunting, which for a many of us, is life.

Cheri has always involved herself with life's minutiae. Too often to the point it gets irritating. After all, who cares if the XKE in the next lane is the same model as her boyfriend's car 30 years ago? Or a hummingbird on a porch feeder has a missing tail feather?

She's a little thing herself, and at five-feet-one and a hundred pounds after supper, hunting guides tend not to take her seriously. They watch out for her, humor her, and grin at her little 10x30 Zeiss she slips in a pocket. How cute.

"I see horns!" she hisses. She kicks me to make sure I get it. I do take her seriously. I've seen her blast knots off a stump with a .44 magnum revolver offhand, run a marathon then party half the night, and grin at 20-below zero gales in the Gobi. She located my last argali, desert bighorn, ibex, and brown bear with her quaint little binocular.

Turk guide Hasan again swings his Leica Trinovid binocular in the direction she's looking, shrugs, then swings it elsewhere. I see zip with my Swarovski 15x56.

"See the ridgeline!?" She phrases it as a command, not a question. "Follow it down to the big cedar."

I obey. "I see two cedars."

"'The big one,' I said." She's getting irked at these dense and condescending men. "Then straight down a dozen feet. You can't miss it." She says this like she's talking to someone without all his bricks. I resent it. I'm a university professor and author, after all.

I see dead branches, rocks and snow. I scan back-and-forth, up-and-down—no horns. Hasan joins in again, but loses interest. The Aladaglar Park ranger takes another scan and shrugs. I take one last look and stand to leave. The guides are impatient to hunt bezoar ibex up-canyon.

"Dammit! I see horns!" She's so sure I look again. At first nothing, then maybe five inches of something behind dead branches of the same color and texture slips into place, like that epiphany piece of a marathon jigsaw puzzle. Horns! Hasan senses my soaring adrenaline and finds them and grunts satisfaction. Cheri smirks. After a longish stalk, we collect that grand ibex because Cheri spots five-inches of horn, a little thing.

Let's step back to our very first safari in the 1980s in the Okavango Delta—before the tourist lodges, jet boats, and shuttle planes—to a pristine part of Africa I thought no longer existed. On the bush flight from Maun, Botswana, we ogle hundreds of red lechwe—a golden-red, swamp-loving antelope bounding through gin-clear water; dozens of tsessebe; giraffes galumphing off in clouds of dust at the plane's shadow; a family herd of elephants; and lions mating on an island. The Cessna 206 swings onto the dirt strip hacked out of the bush and clatters to a stop. I'm so psyched I bang my head getting out of the plane—twice.

"Holy Mother of God!" professional hunter Willie Phillips booms in his best Queen's English as the bush-beaten Land Rover clatters over the track to camp. "Will you look at the bloody lions?!" A lioness and hirsute male lion profile on a termite mound. "No one sees lions like that his first day in the bush. With your luck, you'll have no trouble this safari."

And we don't. The next day, the first of the semi-aquatic hunt where we pole mokorros—native dugouts—from island to island, we score a magnum tsessebe, the largest of Vira Safari's season. I'm ecstatic, and Cheri slaps my back and the trackers give a "Goot, Baas," and grasp my thumb and tug, but Willie fills out the paperwork.

Ditto the next day, this time with two impala trophies. I'm flying, but Willie is reserved. The following day, we bag zebra in the mopane scrub of a big island. Willie's still cool, but I'm having fun enough for both of us. Then it's a magnum lechwe, a kudu. But we haven't scored buffalo, my target species.

Next dawn we spot a buff herd with good bulls in just the right spot for a text-book stalk, and start after them—Joseph the tracker, Willie, me, and Cheri with her protective Bayei shadow, Shorty. The wind is just right, the buff are making racket enough grazing toward us that they wouldn't hear us if we made our own racket. We're closing. They should be just beyond the line of termite mounds ahead.

Willie stops dead, brings the binocular up, exhales and crouches and motions us down. We obey.

"Shoot the warthog. Base of those palms to the right." He points with his chin. His voice is velvety, cool. Joseph hands Willie the shooting sticks.

"We'll spook the buffalo," I counter. I'm not overly concerned about warthogs, but I lust after buffalo.

"It's a good pig. Shoot it."

"Let's get the buff first," I whisper.

"Shoot the @#%&#g bloody damned warthog!" His tone brooks no disagreement.

I shoot the warthog. The buff herd thunders toward Zambia, dust billows into the Okavango blue and I trudge after the guys toward the dead pig, cursing my luck and the lost buff. The pig is a good one for all I know, but everyone else knows a good one from King Kong and from their body language and grins, this is King Kong. Willie is more animated than I've seen him, and he tapes the pig at 15-inches in camp.

We slap a magnum buffalo in the salt next evening and score another antelope in the next days and then it's over. As we board the

Cessna at the dirt strip to fly back to Maun, Willie grasps my hand, and doesn't let go.

"Bloody good job, *Baas*," he says. His eyes lock onto mine and I know he means it, and his grin is the essence of the entire safari.

Half English and half Bushman, lean as a shitepoke, and at half a century old at the time of the safari with high blood pressure to boot, I suppose Willie is dead now, but whenever I ogle those Botswana trophies, I remember first that hand shake, the eyes, the grin—little things—of the best first African PH a guy could have.

A crumb of damp soil tumbles into the hoof print—a trifle. The autumn Utah sun is touching the slopes, drying the soil, moisture is evaporating, causing dirt to shift. It's nothing.

I'd been tracking the buck most of four days, returning to camp at dark each night, and picking up next dawn where I left off the evening before. Some days I trail all day and make less than a mile. This day, the fourth, I'm still less than three miles from camp. I'd seen him first on the eve of the opening, fleeing the country across the big canyon, away from the motorized red shirts. He'd bounded down the stadium-sized slope and into the Sheepherd Canyon bottoms and then up the ravine 100 yards below—a body the size of a billboard, and antler beams as big as my wrist. But the season won't open until dawn and I won't shoot.

Tracking is my favorite mode of hunting—knowing your quarry is at the other end of the trail without doubt and that the quarry and hunter are intimately connected. Of course snow is best. Trailing cross-country through rocks, brush, forests and creeks, too many things can go wrong. Losing the track altogether is most likely, often in a maze of other tracks, then there's other hunters fouling up your work, weather obliterating the trail.

This day, the tracks look more fresh than I've seen them. Dust hasn't drifted into them, and sagebrush leaves haven't settled into them, either. No rain-drops crater the prints. Then they trail across limestone shale rock and I lose them. I circle the limestone scree and in midday pick up the trail again. Still aiming south, into Cottonwood Canyon. He's moving at night and holing up in daylight when the redshirts are out, and he occasionally buttonhooks on his back trail to check it out. No surprise. Any buck that size has survived at least half a dozen seasons, and he's nobody's fool.

The trail beelines across the big plateau at 8000 feet, right-angles down a northeast facing slope thick with chokecherry and quakie saplings. The loam soil is black, moist, and takes a nice hoof print, but the dead leaves slow the trailing. The trail meanders, first this way and then that—the buck is searching for a bed. The hoof prints seem fresh, but then all prints look fresh on moist soil. I trail on. I doubt the buck will bed here, but I've been wrong before. It's too exposed to the opposite slope in case redshirts show. It's just that the wet soil make the prints look so fresh.

Then that crumb of soil tumbles into that track. I notice it, but think little of it. It's just gravity, changing soil moisture. I step down the slope, and again, then stop dead. The buck just made that track! I sense him. I ease to sitting because if the buck flushes, he'll aim into the bottom and up the opposite open slope and I'll have a good shot from my butt. I smell him. I toss a pebble a few yards down the slope, and another. He knows I'm here. I know he's here. I wait, toss another pebble. The breeze shifts, drifting first this way, then that. I'm certain he's heard and scented me, maybe seen me, too. He's no fool. Patience, I tell myself. Wait him out. Two minutes that seem like an hour creep by. Then maybe 15, 20. My pulse slows to near normal. After all, I toss another pebble, clear my throat. I want him to hear, to make him antsy, drive the buck to jump and run for it.

It's anyhow half an hour of clearing my throat, scratching stiff fabric, shifting my boots on gravel. He sits tight. Then he busts 20 yards away, caroms downslope and as he hurtles the creek, the best part of four days' trailing and tension burst like a balloon and I miss clean. Then he's bounding up the opposite slope and I shoot and he immediately right-angles across slope. He's hit! I swing through him and touch off and the buck is down. All because a crumb of soil rolls into a hoof print. A little thing.

Two of the best Arctic bush pilots, and good friends—Roger Dowding and Joe Firmin—are dead in separate crashes, likely, because they didn't trust the instruments in zero visibility and went with their senses. Arguably, a little thing. The instruments were right in both crashes.

I'm 17-years-old and aiming the Old Man's Oldsmobile north on the highway to my first out-of-country and guided hunt. It's a combo November-December shindig on Christmas break, and I'm blowing my entire job savings and whatever I could borrow. At Crooked Lake, British Columbia, Shuswap guides Charlie and Herbie and I pack into Hendrix Valley for an unsuccessful moose hunt in two-feet of snow, then we run black bears with outfitter Cliff Eagle's black-and-tans with equal luck. I bag a mule deer.

Then it's pack to the far end of Crooked Lake and Cliff's log basecamp for mountain goats.

"No good," guide Herbie says. "Gotta git that pink squaw-catcher shirt for Xmas." The implication is that if we climb into the goat scarps in the heavy snow with a looming Chinook, we won't survive until Xmas. I'm in my adolescent prime and bullet-proof, and not the least fazed. Even by the big warm wind from the Pacific threatening to melt the heavy snow load and cause avalanches.

At dawn, Herbie and I sit horses toward the east end of the lake. No Chinook yet. Herbie frowns, but I grin at the goat trails in the heavy snow thousands of feet above. We tie up the nags with feed bags and aim up. Before long we're lunging through hip-deep snow—a thousand feet, two, then three thousand. By midday we're atop the plateau and the air has warmed and it's clouded over. I'm young and tough and I've been breaking trail, but I feel it.

I'm ahead when five billies climb out of the ravine, oblivious—a gimme shot. I'm slammed with teenage buck fever, though, and hit the goat too far back. I fire again and the goat staggers over the rim.

"Horse kick you?" Herbie asks when he catches up. He stares at the horseshoe scope gash between my eyes as I stanch the blood flow with snow. I'm leaving more gore in the snow than the goat.

We trail the billy through the drifted snow across the plateau and in an hour, maybe, I spot the goat standing in an old burn and drop him. But it's not my goat, though a good one nonetheless. In those days, you could shoot two goats, so no problem, though I didn't budget for a second trophy fee. I then notice the trail angle out of the chute beyond and onto a ledge, and there stands my first billy. When I shoot, he drops and wedges between two snags, so I scale the shear scarp—no mean feat in hip-deep snow, wrench him free and he cartwheels down the chute in a rumbling cloud of avalanche spindrift for anyhow 1000 feet. We shove the other goat into the chute, too. Getting down the avalanche chute ourselves isn't so easy. We sit facing down, raise our heels and toboggan on our butts, braking and steering by digging our heels into the packed snow. Once I blast over a ledge and bury myself waist-deep, then struggle to get out of Herbie's path. He fires across the ledge and just clears my shoulder and half buries himself. We giggle at the idiocy.

We survive the butt ride, then dig the goats out of the hard-packed avalanche snow. Lucky, we find one goat's leg sticking out of the snow, and the second billy's snout, so we don't have to search. We skin the goats and lash the trophies onto the pack board. I'm younger and a bit larger, so I haul them. It's dusk. Then it's dark.

Herbie leads down the steep gorge that will end at the lake maybe a mile from the horses, the stream rushing and roaring below the ice. At one place, Herbie steps gingerly across the ice, but with the heavy pack I crash through to waist. I'm soaked now, and my pants start to freeze. Herbie looks concerned, but we trudge on. When we rest, I fall asleep and Herbie shakes me awake and gets me going again. No doubt in my mind, without Herbie waking me, I'd have taken that final sleep and died of hypothermia. At one place, I climb over a big spruce deadfall waist high and pause to rest. The rushing creek echoes through the gorge, even beneath the ice.

I doze a moment sitting there, then rouse myself. *Enough*, I think. *Gotta go*. I swing a leg over the log to slide off the other side, and dislodge a chunk of ice. It slides off the log and I'm about to follow it when I realize I didn't hear the ice hit. I'm not thinking clear, I know. I'm hypothermic and exhausted. But I didn't hear that ice hit! I break free another piece and toss it, and it's some seconds before it smashes far below. I nearly soared that same trajectory, hundreds of feet of free-fall onto rocks below.

I ease that leg back over the log the way it came and back away. Though I'm shivering, sweat breaks on my forehead. One tiny chunk of ice on a mountain with millions of tons of the stuff, a trifle, is the essence of life in that canyon on that night.

It's not such an unusual May Sunday. I'd been sawing the scrub oak deadfall broken down from the winter's heavy snows, in anticipation of fire season, and dragging it to the wood yard. Enough is enough, I think as I haul the Stihl chainsaw to the shed. Something touches my shoulder, and I turn to the dandelion blossom Cheri holds for me, a little thing.

Joe Everyman

We stared into 130 years of smoke patina on the beveled mirror of the oak back-bar. The mirror's silver backing had peeled in irregular patches, but we could see the century-old buck head's reflection. The woman washed dishes at the end of the gouged wooden bar, and Tex Ritter moaned "Blood on the Saddle" out of the honky-tonk jukebox. That much hadn't changed, anyway, I thought. A digital cash register flashed red numbers next to the 1920s scrolled brass cash register with the bell that rang each time you cranked it. They kept it as a curiosity. Back then, we used it.

"They need to clean up this place." I stared at the cobwebs. "Smells of burger grease."

"How long's it been?" the younger man asked and scratched his graying beard. They sat alone at the counter.

"Been what?"

"Since you owned this dump?"

"Would that I still owned it. Could quit wasting what's left of my vocal cords in the lecture hall. Twenty-five years, more or less."

The younger man signaled the woman and pointed at the empty cup, then walked to the centurion buck mount and patted it. He could just reach the shoulder. "For luck," he said to the buck head. The two men met for coffee at the now Shooting Star Saloon and played Dottie West and Boxcar Willie on the jukebox once a week. Before the Beamers and Range Rovers clogged the parking spaces, we called it the Shooting Star Tavern, or just the Star. The place changed with the new owners and substitution of the more update Saloon. After that, Ray Johnson and the old timers quit playing pinochle at the back table. Whiskey Joe Stoker no longer sat in the last booth and poured whiskey into his coffee and talked to himself. No sheepherder tried to ride a horse into the tavern on the Fourth of July, either.

"How long since you wrote that last deer book?" the younger man asked. Arguing about politics, philosophy, religion or deer hunting had become the weekly ritual, somehow. This time, he'd chosen deer hunting. His eyes narrowed and the unruly beard jutted.

"Who cares? Not ten years. Where's this going?" I slid a dollar bill toward him. Tex Ritter had run out on the jukebox. "Play Patsy Cline. And 'Blue Eyes.'" When he got that mood, Willie Nelson's "Blue Eyes Crying in the Rain" made him melancholy. It might get him off it, because I'd hoped for some peace this time around. He punched the juke buttons.

Patsy came first, and in my mind I saw her sitting in a booth back in the dim. This was the place for Patsy Cline. I hung on her every line. The younger man pivoted the stool and stared at the patchy old buck head down the wall.

"How long since you bagged one like that? Thirty inches plus?" Out here in mule deer country, Boone & Crockett and SCI record book points meant little, except to the kids on quads with the designer camos, that is, anyone under 40. To we Wrangler-clad buckskin vets, spread counted, and a typical buck with a main-frame spread of 30-inches meant more than any 190-point B & C trophy.

"I kill a good buck most seasons," I said. "On public land, too. I'm democratic. Compete with Joe Everyman. Don't have to buy it, either, like you."

"Answer the question. Like that one on the wall." He'd just scored a 32-inch buck on the private ground up the canyon. Each season, they sold a handful of tags for whatever they could get.

"You're going to brag up that buck you bought. Six grand, yet. No competition from the masses. You got the place to yourself and the wranglers got every buck pegged and walk you right to it. Besides, the main frame only spread 28-inches without those trash points." So much for that peace, I thought.

"You're dodging. How long since you scored a buck like that one on the wall? You wrote those books. How long's it been?"

He had me. I was dodging. Yeah, I scored bucks most seasons—with four points or better per side, decent bucks—but no 30-inchers. Heck, I hadn't even seen one in years.

"How long since you shot one like those you got at home on the wall?"

I tried to remember. Twenty years? More. He had me—how can a deer hunting "expert," at least that's what they called me, not kill 30-inchers?

"This is the year," I said. "Already packed my camp up top, too. I'd grunted up four gallons of water from that spring down the ridge." I sounded sure enough, but didn't feel it.

"It ain't long before you get Medicare, is it?" It wasn't, either. "Ain't got it anymore, do ya?" he said. Willie Nelson twanged "Blue Eyes" on the juke and he got off it. By the end of the song, he looked distant and misty. I put another dollar in the jukebox and punched "Blue Eyes" three more times.

I'd toted three pack-loads up top on my back in the last weeks and scouted weekends from the camp, all solo. Heck, you wouldn't do that as a kid, I told myself, and then hunt this steep tangle and then grunt the buck out on your back piecemeal. Okay, so you're nuts, but where's the 30-inch proof?

I sipped from the blue porcelain cup I carried on all hunts beside the fir deadfall campfire on the eve of the opener and squinted against the wood smoke. This was the last place. The redshirts had overrun any public land they could motor to. The only places left were those few too rough to get the machines to. To find good hunting anymore, you had to buy a tag on private ground.

I poured another cup and stared into the flames and talked to myself. "When they get here, it's over," I said. "Might be anyway." I'd seen only four or five bucks, yearlings and two-year-olds, in three weekends of scouting. "No one should shoot a yearling—no meat on 'em and no trophy, either," I said to myself, but I remembered that kid that thought a yearling was a trophy. So far, though, I had the place to myself. The redshirts kept to their motorcycles and the forest service trail a mile away and walked each other up on yearling bucks across the basins with cell phones. "Cheating, you ask me." No one had fought their way through the bluffs and tangled buck-brush to get here, to "my" camp. Yet.

In the dawn, I stalked the sagebrush hogback and dropped through the chaparral tangles to the aspens in the canyon north, then circled into the brushy dreadlocks mess below the camp before the sun rose far across that big valley. I'd killed good bucks in all that country, but spotted only a doe, fawn and yearling buck. I climbed to that pale limestone spire and glassed the cross-canyon tangle, but nothing. "You killed three good bucks you spotted from right here," I told myself by way of encouragement.

In an hour I shrugged, shouldered the rifle and grunted the mile nearly straight up to the camp and grinned at two sets of fresh deer tracks. In camp, I stirred up the maple embers and heated water for the tea and dehydrated scrambled eggs and massaged an achy ankle and swallowed an aspirin. I shed the wool long johns because of the climbing sun, shouldered the feather-weight Remington 7mm/08 I used on backpack hunts, and trekked the ridge south for a look into the big, dog-hair canyon I seldom hunted because you'd have to shoot 500 yards across it if you glassed a buck. A cat couldn't stalk through that desiccated tangle. I had no faith in it, but I couldn't quit this early in the day. I'd come to hunt, not stare into the campfire and talk to myself.

When I got there, I sat on a ridge and glassed across the canyon into the shaded north-facing slope. Glassing couldn't take long, because most of the slope was too timbered-up or brushy to see into. You glassed the few openings, and you either still-hunted into the canyon, a fool's errand, or hiked back to camp. That summer had been so dry no one could hunt into that tangle, and the shed leaves so noisy even a bobcat couldn't pussyfoot through without spooking every hare within a mile.

"Stuff and vinegar!" I said aloud. I'd glassed ten minutes with the 15 x 56 binocular when I spotted King Kong bedded in an opening in the heavy shade. My hands shook so bad I had a tough time focusing the binocular. I didn't need to punch a calculator and do the math to "score" the buck—I'd hunted with that kind before and didn't care what the G4 might measure—because I knew with that first glance this was one magnum buck no one would pass up. When you spotted a grand buck, you knew it without arithmetic.

I slid into a ravine and climbed out of it toward the buck, fought the dreadlocks oak scrub and quakie sapling jungle to the next ridge and glassed again. The buck still bedded, but if you moved a foot either way you'd lose sight of him. My heart thumped like a kid. "Buck fever!" I muttered aloud. I had it so bad, I forgot my wool shirt bunched in a scrub oak, too.

If I stalked downslope, I'd shed some distance, but I doubted I'd find a place to shoot out of the big-tooth maple canopy. I refused rangefinders and other techno junk, for the weight I convinced myself, so I guesstimated the range cross-canyon to the buck at 600 yards and change. The shot was possible for the techno geeks with the digital riflescopes and sniper rifles, but not for the rest of us. When and where I learned deer hunting, and it was mostly self-taught, you didn't even shoot 300 yards if you could get closer. Sure, there were plenty of times when I couldn't, but if I saw any way to close that gap, I did it. Besides, stalking was most of the fun.

I slid down the slope anyway, first through the oak scrub tangles, then into the big-tooth maple forest where the autumn-dried dead leaves piled ankle deep. I slid my feet through them, rather than lift them and set them down again, because it made less noise, but it wouldn't work. The stalk was so noisy a deaf old birddog would hear you, and I'd never find a place to shoot out of the forest canopy and across the canyon, so I clawed back up the slope hoping for an opening I could see out of. Near the top of the ridge, I found one. It was no great shakes of an opening, but from one spot I saw the still-bedded buck. I studied the canyon with the binocular and guessed it at 400 yards, maybe more, so I'd closed some. I hadn't shot a deer that far in decades of hunting them, because I could always find a way to get closer. This time, though, I didn't see the choice.

Shooting prone wasn't an option on the steep slope. A wobbly oak sapling rest made the shot if not likely, at least possible. I'd never shot the 7mm/08 at anything that far and had no idea how the little 120-grain soft point would fly, but I settled the wobbling crosshairs three feet above the buck's back for the distance and when the wobble eased, touched off. The buck bounded from the bed and stared upslope. The little slug had slammed into the dirt just above. I lowered the wobbling crosshairs and touched off again. The buck leapt up the slope and hunched, and moments later the faint soggy thump of the slug socking into buckskin floated back. He lunged into the timber before I could shoot again, then collapsed into a rockrose thicket. Something in the way he collapsed told me he wasn't dead when he hit the dirt.

You still got it, I thought, but I felt the doubt. I'd just scored maybe the longest shot at a deer in my life. I slid down the slope through the maples, realized I'd left my scope covers in the leaves and that I'd be lucky to find them if I bothered to look, shrugged my shoulders, then jumped the dry creek bed and fought up the opposite slope through the aspen saplings and rockrose thickets all bent downslope and against me by the winter snows. I'd hit the buck at the top of the highest scattered aspens, and I'd use that to orient when I got up the slope. It took an hour to batter through the tangled brush, but when I got to where I thought the top aspen was, I noted other quakies just as high along the slope west, and some beyond the Doug firs to the east. Nothing looked familiar. I found tracks everywhere, but none stumbling and no blood. Without my reading glasses, I'd never see any blackened blood drops against the dark soil in that heavy shadow. I looked anyway, but found no evidence of where the buck had bedded, and none where he'd staggered cross-slope when the little slug socked him and none where he'd vaporized into that rockrose thicket. I couldn't even find the rockrose thicket. I circled and gridded through the tangles but found zero.

After three hours, I skewered my hunter orange wool stocking cap on a chokecherry sapling to orient myself from the other side of the canyon, then slalomed into the bottoms and clawed back up that opposite slope. I couldn't relocate where I'd squeezed the trigger in the oak tangle, and maybe find those scope covers, but I glassed my orange cap across the canyon.

"So," I told myself. "You searched a hundred yards off. He bedded upslope and east from where you looked." I didn't have the steam to climb back and search again, and even if I did, it meant fighting my way to camp in the dark in those tangles. "Tomorrow," I told myself.

In camp, I grilled chicken over the maple coals that night and drunk from the lucky blue cup and planned it out: He's hit. *You saw him go down, you heard the bullet, you saw him hunch, so don't rationalize it away. Go back and look, at least. Tomorrow. The whole day if you have to. No shooting at something else. Orient on the cap and grid across the slope from there, then make the next pass ten yards down-slope, and then repeat all the way to the bottom. He's hurt, so he won't climb and if he's bad enough he'll only go downhill. You probably jumped him with all that thrashing around looking. He's got to be there. Dead maybe. Make the cross-slope passes long enough so he'll be within them. Half a mile long, maybe. In that tangle, you'll have to step on him to find him, but you gotta try. Bring the damned bifocals, too. Might be too soon, but watch for magpies flying from the carcass.*

I sat up in the sleeping bag awakened from a dream of me bloodied and battering through the thorny tangles in desperation. In the dawn half-light, I stirred up the embers and heated the water and drank the tea and poked at the rehydrating eggs and slurped a fruit cup and two aspirins, worked a kink out of my knee, shouldered the rifle and trudged the hogback toward the tangled canyon. I'd gone 70 yards when I remembered the reading glasses and went back to the tent for them.

I found the orange cap skewered on the chokecherry sapling in the binocular from cross-canyon—the buck had bedded 90 yards up and across the slope from the cap. After the slug had socked him, he'd stumbled another 60 yards cross-slope to the east. I marked the thicket where I thought he'd collapsed. I glassed every tiny opening, especially beneath the big firs, with some hope of finding him. Then I slid down the slope, tight-roped the blade-edge ridge around the canyon head instead of battling the brush, and scaled crumbly limestone bluffs that sliced jeans and gloves.

They'd never find me here, I thought as I looked off a sheer hundred-foot drop, *if something happens*. Straight down, the highway between the city and the Upper Valley snaked along the Ogden River. One misstep, and I'd bounce maybe three times and splatter on the highway 3000 feet below. Once, a cliff section pulled loose and if I hadn't pivoted out of the way, it would have crushed me. I circled the canyon head and ridge-lined and bumped a four-point buck. *Remember, no shooting*, I told myself, but I un-shouldered the rifle just in case it was my buck. I edged along the canyon's opposite blade ridge and then slalomed down through the shiny-leaved chaparral tangles to the orange cap on the sapling. From there, I angled cross-slope to where I thought I hit the buck, hands-and-kneed 600 square feet squinting through bifocals for blood, any blood, a tiny spot maybe, or maybe bullet-cut hairs. Nothing.

If he's bad-hurt, he's wouldn't climb. He'd stagger down and maybe cross-slope, I figured. Just in case, though, I climbed another 50 yards up the slope and then gridded back-and-forth across the grade. Half a mile east, then ten yards down-slope max, and half a mile west. Repeat.

From the spoor, the place was thick with deer. I studied droppings on hands and knees with my glasses for blood sign in the stool. No luck. I found four-inch tracks I measured against a 7mm/08 cartridge, but they proved only that a big buck lived there.

At each deer bed, and I found two or three with each pass across the slope, I got to hands and knees and searched with the bifocals for a spot of blackened blood or clipped hairs where the bullet might have entered. Any blood would look black and difficult to find against the dark soil in the shadows, even with the glasses. I relearned deer always shed some hair when they bed. A handful of hair lined one bed, but no blood or bullet-cut hairs. A single large track cratered the bed but it had frost in it which meant it was 12 hours old and maybe older, because the buck made it before the first frosts and that was early last night. It might have been the buck, but if so, it meant he'd been there last evening. Possible. The track led down the slope. Tracks disturbed the fallen leaves, and you could follow them that way, but when the trail got into the snowberry and rockrose thickets, you lost it.

Stick to the cross-slope passes. Don't try to follow a track unless you see blood. Keep to the plan.

185

"Noon," I said aloud as I stared at the shadows across the canyon, "and nothing." I'd made eight or ten passes half way down the slope and had seen no blood, no cut hairs, no stumbling tracks.

I drank what was left of the water and ate the dried fruit. *Better to carry in in your belly instead of on your back,* I thought, and then, *maybe you'd nicked him and he left the country. Maybe you're wasting a hunting day. You haven't got that many,* but in my mind I saw the buck hunch again, 120 grains of copper and lead slapped, and the buck collapsed again in that rockrose thicket. "That's 27-28 hours ago," I told myself aloud.

The brush tangled thicker toward the canyon bottom. "You'll have to step on him," I told myself. By then, I'd made a dozen cross-slope passes, that's six miles fighting through the entwined rockrose tangles and picking the thorns out of ears, hands-and-kneeing the deer beds and droppings, duck-walking under the fir tree boughs, and believing in it less and less. I remembered that dream, too.

"Three, four more passes and you'll hit bottom. You can quit," I said aloud. I crossed the slope west again, turned around in half a mile, dropped down-slope ten yards, then aimed back east. The plan sounded so rational at the campfire sipping from the blue cup with a full belly, but in the reality of the tangle, I started losing faith from the start. Now, I wanted it over. This fighting through dog-hair brush for ten miles of cross-slope passes was a fool's task. I looked at my bleeding hands and felt my tattered ears.

I nearly allowed myself to step across and ignore the next deer bed to just get done with it, but I forced myself to get to hands and knees again and put on the bifocals. No blood. No bullet-cut hairs, no bloody droppings. I stood up and bent the crick out of my neck, then glanced back the way I'd come for no reason I could think of. Just down the slope under a tangle of winter snow-flattened quakie saplings, something looked odd. I'd walked two yards above it and missed it. I put the binocular on it, and it did look odd, but not like deer fur. Aspen deadfall, maybe. It seemed too big for a buck, and the texture looked strange in the shadows. I took two steps toward it and stared again. *Weird,* I thought, *and that's no stump.* I jacked a round into the chamber, thought about putting one into it in case it was the buck and it jumped, but thought better of it. No telling what it is. Two more steps.

Another step, and a shadow became an ear, a branch a tawny face, and I didn't really believe it until I grabbed the antlers, stroked the fur and grimaced at the stench. From the odor, I guessed the buck had been dead since shortly after I'd shot it, and that was a relief. The buck had run down-slope, collapsed at full speed, cartwheeled once and died stretched out on his back. I'd had no faith in finding the buck all day, and then stumbled across it when I'd already given up.

I rough-caped the head and hauled it across my shoulders to the camp, with the big lice dropping down my collar. In camp I photographed with the single lens reflex camera and the slide film. I grinned into the campfire and sipped the bourbon in that blue cup that night, too, and once or twice hooted aloud to compete with the horned owls and that coyote down-ridge. In the morning sun, I stuffed the pack with whatever I could haul and cinched the buck head on top and aimed down toward home. I'd retrieve the meat and the rest of the camp in a day or two, as soon as I could get back. I'd left the quarters in the permanent shadows in the bottoms, and it frosted each night, so they'd stay cool enough.

The next day it began snowing—three days and 35 inches worth, and when I snowshoed back, I barely found the camp. The heavy snow had flattened it, and the winds had tattered the tent fabric to ribbons and snapped the poles. With the snowshoe, I dug out the soggy sleeping bag and pad and whatever I could get. I webbed to the buck's canyon but couldn't find the carcass buried under four-foot drifts somewhere. Lost again.

*****

We sat at the wooden counter and sipped yesterday's coffee and stared into the old back-bar beveled mirror at that ancient buck head on the far wall. The same woman scrubbed dishes at the end of the counter and ignored us.

The younger man said, "This coffee must be old as that buck head. Takes the enamel off your molars. Those the bifocals?" I'd just taken them out of the aluminum case to read the jukebox. "The one you tracked that buck with?"

"Yup."

He pivoted the stool and stared at the centurion buck head down the wall. "As good as that one?"

"Close." I'd measured the spread with my arm in the camp at the second points, and it went from the tip of my left middle finger, up the length of the arm, and the opposite point passed my nose. From experience, the slick typical rack would tape 30 inches and change, maybe 33, if someone cared to measure it, but once any trophy made it to my house, no one put a tape on it—my rule.

"Why don't you carry one of these?" He took an iPod from his Carhartt pocket and punched up a pic of his CWMU buck. "So I can see the damned thing and won't have to wait for you to develop that film."

"Forget it. I like real cameras with real film. So I'm a Pleistocene relic. At least I didn't buy my buck."

He walked to the jukebox and punched in "Blue Eyes," then shuffled to the old buck head down the wall and patted it. I wondered how many more times we'd have these talks.

Turkish Delight

Turkish Delight is a confection flavored with starch and sugar, often containing pistachio, hazelnut, lemon, mint and orange. In homemade rural Delights, one nibble might be sweet, the next bitter.

Sometimes you got it, sometimes you don't. And you know it when you do. You know that card planing across green felt makes your full house. You know that overdue paycheck rests in your PO box when you walk through the door. And no question— the snow blower starts with one pull.

But I couldn't buy the feeling. First, I wandered in an out-of-sync fog because I hadn't booked our usual Xmas break expedition to an exotic locale like Mongolia or Tajikistan. Then a microbe ingested on a tur hunt in Russia kicked up, so we cancelled our New Year's Day shindig. I brawled blizzards and battled snow blowers, threatened a troglodyte copy editor with an express trip to the hereafter, and a sophomore complained to the dean about a failing grade.

So as I glared at snow drifted to eaves, Orhan Konakci's email was that card slipping across felt, the on-time paycheck and a one-pull snow blower rolled into one. I just knew it. I'd scored a 40 inch Dagestan tur and a 10-inch Eurasian boar on past Konakci hunts, too. He had an ibex tag for March. March is spring semester break. Did I want it? Does a camel spit?

The luck held—my rifle and baggage arrived with us at Ataturk International in Istanbul, our contact maneuvered us through the myriad airport bureaucrats that must sign off firearms, with less than the usual comments about ancestry, and onto a flight to Kayseri in central Anatolia. In spite of acute jet-lag, the feeling stayed so strong I didn't even buy a blue glass eye charm against the evil eye from a gift shop. I'd always bought them.

In Kayseri, famed guide Hasan and translator Aygaun met us, whisked us through the police check and into a Nissan and we roared through eight-feet of snow on a Taurus Mountain pass and in the wee morning hours clattered to Yahyali village on the edge of the Aladaglar Range. We'd stay in a pension room instead of a tent. Wow!

Two hours later the minaret's blaring dawn call-to-prayer yanks us into other world consciousness. Our 4th floor room sits eye level with minaret speakers owning remarkable fidelity a long spit across the street. So much for sleeping in. Later we fetch the Aladaglar National Park ranger and motor out to check the rifle and skid through slushy mire to the track's end. The day before, the guys hired a front-end loader to plow two feet of snow and muck 20 miles to the ibex scarps—Turkey (pronounced TOOR-key-ah) isn't all desert. We wander miles past the track's end to shake the jet-lag and glass bezoar ibex.

Cheri and I scrape ourselves off the ceiling at the next dawn's call-to-prayer, scarf breakfast and make the trail's end as Sol peeks over a blade ridge, and after miring the Nissan, trek through crusty snow. Winds howl down canyon and great snowy plumes eddy off 10,000 foot crags. Cheri grins a "see, I told you we'd need winter gear" grin. I shrug that "OK, you're always right" shrug, but I've still got that feeling, so I don't mind it. Archaic man carved portals and subterranean houses into the soft volcanic tufa cliffs above, and we slog a prehistoric irrigation canal through the deepening snow. The guys feel we'll find ibex on exposed south-facing slopes three or four miles up canyon. I know they're right.

We spot ibex as we slog the snow, too, but none own scimitar headgear. Aygaun figures out he didn't buy bread for lunch, and hikes back to the pickup to drive into Yahyali for it. I suspect another reason, but no matter. Thigh-deep snow forces us to contour the slope above. Hasan spots ibex grazing a cliff ledge a mile up canyon. I can't make out any scimitars. The ranger points out two more, but if they own horns, they're daggers.

Guides tend not to take Cheri seriously. She stands 5'1" and weighs 100 pounds after supper. They look out for her, they humor her, but with her tiny 10 x 30 Zeiss binoc she slips in a pocket, well, that's so quaint.

"I see horns!" she hisses at me. I do take her seriously. I've seen her throw a round house that would flatten a 200-pound neighbor if it connected, shoot knots off a stump offhand with a .44 magnum revolver, and run a marathon for fun. She'd located my last argali, ibex, desert bighorn, brown bear, and half-a-score of other recent trophies, all with her cute little Zeiss binocular.

Hasan swings his Trinovid binocular in the direction she's looking, shrugs, and returns to the ibex up canyon. I can't spot anything with my Swarovski, either.

"See the ridgeline." She phrases it as a command, not a question.

"Got it," I answer.

"Follow it down to that big cedar," she commands.

"Which?" I see two cedars.

"The 'big' one, I said." She's getting irked. "Then straight down. You can't miss the horns." She says this like she's talking at someone with half a load.

One cedar is slightly larger, so I glass downward but all I see are dead branches, rock and snow. Nothing. I repeat. Hasan joins in again but loses interest. I'm losing it, too. The ranger takes a scan and then shrugs. I take a last scan and we stand to leave.

"Dammit, I SEE horns!" She's so sure, I take another look but think, *Don't involve everyone unless you're sure.* I haven't guts enough to say it yet, but when her conviction wavers, I'll pounce.

We've got a complicated jigsaw puzzle of a leopard in a tree. It took months to put it together. We labored and struggled and cussed, when suddenly it's there. *How can I be so dense?* I wondered. I swing the binoc across the slope one last time, and the fragments slip into place. Horns! Hasan senses my soaring adrenaline and he finds the horns, too. The ranger locates them and grunts satisfaction. Cheri grins her "I told you so" grin.

Hasan ranges it at 350 yards, but all we can see are horns. He wants me to shoot from where we sit when the ibex stands, but we can shorten the distance. In this day of thousand-yard rifles and robot riflescopes that do everything but pull the trigger, 300-yard shots are routine. But where and when I learned hunting, you didn't take them if you could help it, and I'm too stubborn to change.

I must talk Hasan into stalking closer. My credo, stalk as close as you can, then get closer. That's most of the fun of hunting anyway. The rest is technology and has little to do with bush skills, and even I can hold 7-inch groups all day at 300 yards on the range with an off-the-rack Remington.

Hell, this is Anatolia, after all, so make the most of it. All we see are horns, and absolutely no fur, so the ibex can't see us, either. The ranger and Cheri get comfortable to watch the show, and Hasan and I duck-walk through boulders, slink behind a low scarp and edge up a rockslide. We peer over from time to time, and the billy is still bedded. We crab higher, when Hasan sets his daypack on a boulder. I ease the gun across the pack and nod, OK, this works, and we settle down to wait.

We wait ten minutes, twenty, forty, when the ibex stands, pivots and walks down the slope behind the ridge and vaporizes. We don't see a hair. I growl but Hasan motions me to wait. Seems the ibex is gone, but I don't feel too bad. I've still got that feeling, after all. The horns stab above the ridge again and bounce back at us. Other ibex launch from wherever they'd bedded and a dozen horns puncture the skyline. I get the scope on what I think is the first ibex, but another as big stands, so I look him over, too. One skids down scree at us with horn bases so thick I swallow my gum. I settle the crosshairs solid on shoulder as he jogs quartering on, and touch the .300 Winchester magnum's trigger.

I'm stunned the billy doesn't fold, or I don't hear the slug slam muscle, but he doesn't and I don't. The goat pivots and bolts and horns bob over the skyline and are as gone as last week. The other ibex follow then veer off around the shoulder of the mountain.

Hasan shrugs. He doesn't know, either. Normally, I'll hear the bullet sock flesh like a glove against the heavy bag, but the gusty winds could have muffled it. I can't remember it flinch, but maybe I lost it in the recoil. On the other hand, the billy swapped ends and tore off. I've seen fatally hit beasts act the same. But they've done it when whiffed, too. I hate angst.

We scale talus, then finger-and-toe crumbly scarps until we teeter on the ledge. I'm angst-queasy, and we can't find blood. We wander down the ledge. Hasan's body language says he thinks I missed, and he scans across the canyon. Still no blood, I feel low as a slug, when I spot an oddity farther along the ledge. I know what it is. I sock Hasan and point and he grabs and crushes my hand. He folds his hands under his cheek to Cheri and the ranger 300 yards straight below to show the ibex is down.

Now, I've seen some things—guys fishing for 90-pound tiger fish in Angola with a live vervet monkey as bait, helling after a ten-foot polar bear on a dogsled on the polar icepack in full winter (we bagged it, too), and Charles DeGaulle shaking the Old Man's hand at a consulate shindig in Bordeaux as a kid. But I've never seen anyone do what Hasan did. He tied the feet of the ibex on one side together, tied those on the other side in similar fashion, used the legs as straps, and hefted the ibex onto his back. Guts and all. Now a big ibex might weigh 200 pounds. Okay, so maybe I could do it if I tried. But he side-hilled scree so steep loose boulders plummeted all the way to the bottom and edged along ledges with that ibex on his back. If he fell, he'd bounce a thousand feet down to the creek. He grunted it all the way to the bottom. Hasan stands maybe five-eight, and weighs a stocky 175. If he's not the Incredible Hulk, he's the toughest guide I've met.

Later at a lamb shish dinner in a pine-heated restaurant so small your teeth hit the wall if you smiled, Konakci cell phones Aygaun to offer me a deal on an Anatolian chamois hunt, since we've finished with the ibex so early. I'm not expecting it and I'm reluctant—after all, by the time we wrap things up here, drive to Kayseri, fly back to Istanbul, then fly to Trabzon on the Black Sea then drive into the hunting country, we won't get many hunting days. I feel so good about the ibex trophy, I should stand on it. You can't always draw a full house, I reason with myself.

We doddle at breakfast the next day, Konakci phones about the chamois hunt again—we must decide so he can arrange it. Cheri's always game for new geography, Aygaun wants the work, and Orhan says it's a quick hunt. I'm swayed.

We visit the 4000-year-old subterranean stone cities of Kapadoyka (Cappadoccia) before motoring into Kayseri and hopping a 737 red-eye to Istanbul and then Trabzon. I think of a B.B. King refrain, "The feeling's gone…" so I buy a blue glass eye charm. Conviction mists away.

Up north we rendezvous with guide Abdullah Erzijrum, Elevit mayor Naci Aydin, ranger Enver Yildrim, as well as Aygaun, Cheri and me. We caravan in two 4wd mini SUVs into the mountains past quaint wooden villages and 4-wheel-drive windy alpine roads past 13th century fairytale Zil Castle perched on a cliff above a piney rushing river, and eventually to the Kackar-Daglari National Park cabin where we overnight.

The new guys believe the heavy snow pushed the chamois down to the valley floor near Elevit, the tiny alpine village above. Inhabitants vacate the village in September. The guide and mayor also think the little 4wds will bust through the drifts to get there. Turns out, they've never hunted in March. Chamois hunting is normally a November and December road hunt during the rut when the little goats wander about the valley floors and the drill is spot a chamois and make a short stalk from the road, or shoot the trophy from the road itself.

The 4WDs mire in the drifts within a mile. I stroke my glass eye charm, shoulder the pack and rifle, and we slog knee-deep snow three miles to Naci's hut in Elevit. We spot chamois—2000 vertical feet up on the sheer peaks too steep for snow accumulation. So much for assumptions. I'm rubbing the glass eye charm so hard it blisters my thumb. The guys kill half a perfect hunting day washing dishes, and when they're ready to hunt, the fog rolls in and we can't see across the street, so they deal cards 'til supper. That leaves two days.

Everyone acts like we've got all the time in the world. We don't get out until 10 the next morn and climb through the forests and three-feet of snow toward where I'd glassed a chamois at 7 am while everyone sawed logs. Naci the mayor becomes the guide. We're back at the hut by noon. Naci and Aygaun are whipped. They spend the rest of the day playing cards. I fall asleep rubbing the glass eye charm. B.B. King croons, "The feeling's gone." in a dream.

I'm out glassing at dawn, but intentionally make noise enough to wake inhabitants of an ancient cemetery up the slope. The guys rise and we're out by 7:30. It's brutal slogging through three feet of wet snow up 60-degree slopes through dreadlock spruce. I'm an aerobics nut, and the snowy slog is tough on me, but Naci owns a watermelon-sized gut and Aygaun, though decades my junior, smokes like a chimney and gasps. It's cold in the timber, but the guys strip to essentials and sweat like spitted hams.

"Bee-Boop-Bee-Boop!" Abdullah is calling on the two-way. Naci shouts into it. Even at half a mile, the racket would wake a dead goat. The radio Boo-beeps! each time Naci releases the talk button. I put my fingers to lips—the glass eye charm won't help this. We edge up through trees again half a mile, when I notice a deaf chamois skyline on a scarp 300 yards out. The radio boo-beeps, the little goat stares and stares harder when Naci shouts into it. Then Aygaun and Naci shout back and forth and the chamois and pals bound up the cliffs like spring-loaded ping pong balls and put yards between us. At first, Naci sees no males. I've sometimes had trouble telling males from females, since both own horns, so I don't trust myself. I doubt Aygaun has seen chamois, so he's no help.

Naci shouts in his adrenaline intoxication and Aygaun translates that it's a King Kong billy. I get the crosshairs on the shoulder—no wobble, either—and begin to squeeze when Naci shouts at Aygaun and Aygaun translates that Naci thinks it's a female after all. I mutter "Dammit." The Three Stooges' hunt continues up the mountain. I get a prone shot in the snow as 200-pound Naci kneels across my calves shouting the Turk equivalent of "SHOOT! SHOOT!" The goat fires both afterburners because Naci hollers into the two-way to Abdullah behind the spotting scope two miles below who is telling us where the chamois are, as if we can't see them. The goat staggers over a near ridge and escapes, because Naci decides the avalanche channel is too dangerous though we'd climbed into hairier places. We get split up on the descent and I'm forced to jump 2 ½ stories off a ledge into a snow bank, fortunately don't hit bottom, and I skid two miles down the same avalanche chute Naci decided was too dangerous and make the bottoms first. We're back at the hut by lunch. And that's the bitter last nibble of that Turkish Delight.

Maybe not so bitter—the guys grin, hoot, laugh at anything, and always lend a hand. In spite of the screwy hunt, they're the best of company. Now that I've got things figured out, I'd hunt with them again.

Anyway, the ibex hunt—that first bite of Turkish Delight—was sweet as honeycomb.

No Respect

If life were fair, then chamois would teeter at the top of the mountain-hunter's peak of fame. Tell most North Americans you're bound for a chamois hunt, and you'll ogle adenoids at a yawn's deep end. I once called them "mountain jackalopes" when a chum bragged of a pending Swiss chamois chase. To borrow from Rodney Dangerfield, chamois "…get no respect."

Except in Europe. You'll find chamois culture festivals, chamois music festivals, towns named Chamois, chamois races, and Chamois Hotels. Chamois are Spaniard and Espacaza outfitter Jose Mallo's favorite game, bar none. Europeans hunters worth the name own a handful of chamois trophies, and even non-hunters sport chamois (*gamsbart*) tufted hats. I know guys that haven't missed a chamois hunting season in half a century and a Frenchman that owns 50 chamois trophies with their own trophy room. Convinced?

First, the inevitable biospeak. Chamois are native only to Europe and the Caucasus Mountains and Anatolia in southwest Asia. Only two species of chamois exist, including *Rupicapra pyrenaica's* three subspecies; all other chamois belong to the species *Rupicapra rupicapra*. Both the *CIC Caprinae Atlas of the World* and the *SCI Record Book of Trophy Animals* (ed. X) list ten varieties or subspecies of chamois, so that's a good place to start counting. Some of these are questionable, for example the geographical ranges of the Caucasian and Anatolian chamois varieties approach to within a few hundred miles of each other, so I suspect more detailed genetic studies will find these too closely related to list as separate subspecies. The Spanish chamois are probably a legitimate separate species, since molecular and other evidence shows the two species separated perhaps 60,000 years ago.

When acquaintances ask me about chamois, I tell them they're diminutive mountain goats, so they can get some idea. Truth is, they're more closely related to Asian serow and goral and North American mountain "goats" (these aren't goats, either) than they are to true goats, genus *Capra*, such as ibex.

Chamois ain't giants. Males range from 60 pounds up to 115, depending on variety; natch, females scale less. Males live the hermit life except during the November rut. Hunters bag about 75,000 of both sexes per year, but a hunt isn't a slam dunk. I know—I failed on both Caucasian and Anatolian chamois hunts. Those failures made me rethink that earlier quip, too—the one about "mountain jackalopes."

As I pound the keyboard a day before my "Timberline Reflections" deadline (I procrastinate like my undergrad students!), I'm ruminating on spending my declining years chasing the varieties of chamois I haven't yet bagged. Seems we hunters need goals, like the Grand Slam/Four North American Wild Sheep, or this collection or that one, and the more I ponder the more certain I am that I'll do it!

My first chamois hunt was an afterthought. I really lusted after a ram—a free-range mouflon. Since I booked the trip with Srdja Dimitrejevic's outfit anyway, why not score a chamois while at it? Croat pro hunter Dragan Matosic gathers Cheri and me at the Sarajevo airport and we sardine gear into his Russian Lada jeep, then motor deeper into Bosnia and pass shrapnel-pocked houses and roofless buildings, artifacts of the Balkan War. The December snow reminds me that Sarajevo hosted the winter olympics before that war, and I watched it on ABC's *Wide World of Sports* as a kid. As the jeep groans up out of the valley, I yank stocking cap over ears and scrape ice rime off side windows and gaze at snowy pine forest and distant Sarajevo far below with scores of new tile roofs. I'm vaguely depressed at the war damage and the roadside grave monuments to entire families, but that morphs into anticipation as we descend into calendar scene snow drifting through black pine forest.

We overnight at a tiny forest village at a mote-sized and quaint hotel and restaurant and dine with a local hunter on astonishing grub and local beer to die for. The man owns half a nose—another artifact of the war. When he exhales cigarette smoke, the effect is so astonishing my jaw drops.

We sight Dragan's Serbian .30/06 in the morning, and it's dead on, then jeep toward the chamois scarps. A combination of deepening snow and signs warning of land mines stop us dead. We scratch heads as the jeep idles. What to do?

"Ve go back," Dragan says. Alright, I think, I came for mouflon anyway. No big deal.

We skid back through our drifting tire tracks, pass the village, and slip and slide up onto the pass toward Sarajevo before the engine fries. Dragan and I were high school level mechanics, back in those wine-and-roses days before electronic car engines, but we know nothing about the new mechanics. We stagger through begrimed snow drifts to a miniscule road-side coffee shop at the top of the pass and Dragan phones Sarajevo for a wrecker. We sip hot wine and nibble pastries and wait. I still ain't worried, because I really came for that ram hunt. We huddle in the freon jeep as the wrecker tows it and skids its way into Sarajevo and deposits us at a hotel. While they're repairing the Russian jeep next day, we tour Sarajevo and see the standard tourist sites and best, sample victuals so savory we'll never visit Pizza Hut again.

I'm surprisingly relaxed, going with the flow. No chamois—no trophy fee. I really came for a mouflon anyway. Dragan's tense, though, on the phone more than any one should be. These aren't cell phones, either.

In the evening, he says, "Ve go Hrevatska." Hrevatska is Croatia. "Now, I tink, ve go." I assume we're aiming west after that mouflon, but an hour out into the cobalt night he says, "Ve get chamois license Hrevatska." Alright! I'm still going with that flow, and it may include a chamois after all.

We see the change as we coast down into Hrevatska, or Croatia, in the dawn. Border guards grin. Houses are no longer shrapnel pocked. The Adriatic slaps at limestone bluffs. The highway isn't cratered, and we couldn't find grimy snow if we tried. Dragan whistles to keep himself awake so he doesn't plow the Lada into a palm tree and I've got a hand cocked to grab the wheel just in case. Even in the dark, it seems like the French Riviera half a century ago, without the glitz and seething humanity.

Bosnian chamois have drifted onto the sheer Croatian limestone cliffs rocketing from the Adriatic in the past two decades, to the point they're more common than mouflon. Dragan isn't wasting time, either.

After breakfast at the Hotel Biokovo in Makarska, he says, "Ve go now." He means hunting, and we'll bag whatever we see, mouflon or chamois. We gather Biokovo Wildlife Reserve ranger Pero Saric, but we find few mouflon, so finger-and-toe high into those limestone scarps. We ogle chamois, too, including very good females; female chamois are considered trophies, but I'm biased and want a male. Males have slightly heavier horns, and I grew up hunting males—bucks, bulls, rams. Near the top of the range 2000 feet above the surf, a handful of chamois skid down a chute.

"You tchute beeg vun, yah?" Dragan say. Heck, yes. I'm struggling with the double set trigger on Dragan's 'ott-six and think I've got it figured, but I don't. I touch the trigger too soon and fire before I get the butt to cheek and powder limestone ten feet above the chamois, and that's it.

"Vhy you tchute tso bad?"

We spot other chamois that day, but blow the stalk, or the wind shifts or they eyeball us. The consolation is we dine in the pleasantly decrepit and antiquated luxury Hotel Biokovo—I half expect Humphrey Bogart to stride in—on five courses of the best calamari, oysters, crab, cheeses, pasta, salads, smoked fish and other exotica we've dined on so far, and sip astonishing Croatian wine. What chamois failure?

After a multi-course breakfast worth calories enough for a week, we're after chamois again. It's a brutal day, too. We motor to the trailhead and literally finger-and-toe the scree straight up, and at noon ogle a view of the Adriatic so spectacular I gasp, and I think I see Italy through the sea haze. We spot big nannies, and heck, they've got a record book section for females, but I've got that American male bias.

It's a long day and we stumble down the trail ten miles farther down the scarp, Pero arranged for a pal to pick us up there, when a chamois hops from behind a boulder. Even I know it's a billy.

"Tchute!" Dragan hisses. Pero is cool, and he nods toward the billy.

The chamois steps behind a dead pine 150 yards across the ravine, but I see an opening through the entwined branches and touch off. The chamois bolts at the shot but that sight picture was perfect and I know it's dead on its feet. Dragan and Pero know it, too.

"Die, dammit!" Dragan hisses as the chamois stumbles downslope and dives off a cliff and fetches up on a ledge. Pero climbs to the billy and lowers it down the sheer cliff with a climbing rope, then drops it into his pack and totes it down the trail. For those into the stats, the Balkan billy tapes 11 inches. What a birthday present! We celebrate at the Hotel Biokovo's restaurant that night on that hunter's ambrosia and that world-class Croatian wine, but Bogart doesn't show again.

You won't bag many chamois above the palms and surf, though. My 2012 hunt for alpine chamois in East Tyrol in Austria's Alps is more typical. It's December again and snow heaps along the runway in Lubljana, Slovenia. I shove hands deep in pockets as we scurry across the tarmac to the abandoned customs building. No one cares if you're coming or going, and what a pleasant change from official paranoia in JFK or anywhere else in the US.

Martin Neuper gathers us at the airport as planned, and with his pointy-toed black shoes and shiny leather jacket, I'd take him for local mafiosi rather than an outfitter. Our baggage remains in NY thanks to Delta Airlines efficiency. Air France functionaries, the only ones about, vow to get the baggage to us wherever we go, and wherever turns out a hotel in the Tyrolean Alps. It's even snowier there. Three days later, we do get the baggage, too.

In spite of the inauspicious start, our young (drat, I've forgotten his name!) guide outfits us, more or less, and we see chamois and shove through knee-deep snow into the conifer-forested Alps that first day. We bivouac at a Bavarian-style hotel and dine in the restaurant and quaff the local beer. Each village makes its own brand and when you ask for the last town's beer in the next village, they haven't a clue. The shrimp, pasta, fruits and fresh salad beats the ramen noodles and spam you get in typical American hunt camps, no contest.

Our young guide desserts us to guide a mountaineering expedition he'd already had booked, but fixes us with his pop's friend Benno. His dad tags along. Trouble is, they're both fond of schnapps. We spend the morning in a mountain hut beside a spruce-crackling wood stove sipping the stuff, too, occasionally glassing out the window at the astonishing alps. Under other conditions, it might be pleasant. I paid to hunt, though. But I gradually learn it's not as bad as it seems. It rained the night before and then froze, and navigating the ice-coated snow sounds like a HumVee caroming through a store window. I'm still pissed, though. I paid to hunt, not get snockered.

The ice melts toward midday and we climb to another hut and glass, spot a few smaller chamois, then skid back down the alp and motor elsewhere. Chamois wade the wet snow through forest high above, but none we want or none we can get to. Back to the hotel food and fine crisp sheets and that beer. This is hunting?

Same drill next day with about the same results, and ditto the day after. I savor the hunting, and so does Cheri. We both love mountain hiking, and when you can dry out in a hotel at the end of the day, we don't mind the wet snow, either. I'm content, though we're paying by the day.

On day four, we drive to the bottom of a logging road and trek up. As we climb, the snow deepens, no surprise, and we watch an avalanche rumble down the opposite canyon wall. None utter a word, because we know it could happen on our side, too. Two hours slogging up, and we spot chamois. I note good ones across the canyon, but it's a long shot, especially with an unfamiliar rented magnum, and I nix it. No one is sure how big it is, anyway. Benno spots a band upslope on our side and studies it. The rest of us hunker under spruce trees out of sight. After an hour, Benno says, "Goot!"

I rest the WSM across a pack on a boulder, get the sighting post on the shoulder as it steps behind a snag, and wait. Either the bugger is very far upslope, or it's tiny. I often forget how diminutive chamois are and think they're farther away than they are, too. Benno's range finder says just under 300 meters, and he tells me to hold dead on, so I do. When the chamois steps clear, I get the sight picture I want and touch off and know it's a goner. The chamois staggers to a cliff ledge, and I put another through the shoulder and it cartwheels into the ravine.

Supply and demand rule the world. So maybe it's best that many North Americans find chamois about as desirable as jackalopes. If they viewed them as one of the most desirable mountain trophies in the Northern Hemisphere, like bighorn or wapiti, for examples, demand would spiral into the stratosphere towing hunt prices along with it, thereby making it impossible for me to finish bagging all varieties of that handsome little "goat." Good thing that chamois "get no respect" in North America, after all. It's already too late to keep it a secret in Europe, though.

IN THE LAND OF VLAD

Crucifixes tacked to weathered oak doors and werewolf myths, Ceausescu the dictator that considered Drakula a national hero until he faced the firing squad for genocide, snow sifting through gloomy pine and barren beech forests, abandoned and begrimed Soviet-era factories. And not least is Vlad the Impaler, best known as Count Dracula, or Drakula the Turk-killer, Romania's most famous export.

Damned long way to go for a mountain jackalope, I'm thinking as I stagger off the Turkish Air jet and into the Bucharest airport. Though I've flown 21 hours on one leg before with endurance flights to places like Johannesburg, Shanghai and Moscow, I can't remember a worse flight: SLC to SFO to Istanbul to Bucharest. The thirteen hour non-stop leg from San Francisco to Istanbul is stuffed with Turk expatriates aiming home for the Xmas holiday, screaming toddlers, fat old ladies sleeping on the floor, and Cheri trying to keep me from socking someone. *Never again*, I promise myself. Seems I remembered that oath before.

I'm still shaking a severe case of jet lag as we motor out of a Romanian truck-stop hotel two dawns later just across the highway from the River Olt. We're crammed into a Balkan four-wheel drive: broker and PH Joe Jakab, and he's a large guy; Joe's man Friday, Christy; guide and driver Iulian; Cheri and me. I'm a guy that likes his space, but between the flight and this drive, I've never been more cramped. I'm hoping we don't find chamois. If it were up to me, I'd avoid them. I'm more jet-lagged than I like to be to shoot.

We slow in the pre-dawn dark at the village of Ciineni and gather our second guide, Radu Gheorghe, Gica for short. And then we aim up a muddy road and when it's light enough, I test-shoot the locally borrowed Winchester.

Then we're off again, into the Transylvanian Alps, itself part of the Carpathian Range. The sun is just stabbing into Boia canyon when Gica, from the backseat and sandwiched in a mass of flesh and camo, spots chamois through some miracle. Before I understand what's happening we're out of the vehicle and Gica sprints upslope and I'm following with the Winchester, and somehow in my jet-lag haze it occurs to me we're chasing Carpathian chamois. And through another miracle we get to within 60 yards in the thick woods. It's close enough for even me to tell it's not as large as I'd like, so I nix it, to my inward relief. Gica traces "95" in the leaf duff, meaning CIC points. Gold medal is 110, for a reference point. My pre-flight goal is simply a mature male, period. I care little for record books, even though I've a double handful of trophies that would score in the top ten, they tell me.

We motor up more logging roads, and spot more chamois. Though I've hunted four flavors of chamois before, I've never hunted them in the forests, like eastern whitetails. That afternoon we ogle still more of the 100-pound beasts, and one is good but no one, least of all me, can really tell how good and while we're trying to figure it out, like the Keystone Cops in the woods, they vaporize. Again, to my relief. Jet-lag is a serious matter, and it's fouled up my shot before. Part of me is still back over the Atlantic somewhere.

The day is largely a road-hunt, to my surprise. On previous chamois hunts about the planet, we walked, climbed, and trekked. Not that I'm complaining, you see, because I'm still jet-lagged and not overly ambitious about finding chamois just yet.

"Half my hunters shoot from the road," Joe says.

In the evening we walk up a small canyon, spot a brown bear and red stag, and then chamois. Some are good, I am told, and they decide I should shoot at one of them. Remember that jet-lag? We get the shooting sticks arranged with part of them down a steep slope and the other part on the level trail, and I have one boot two-feet lower than the other, and I'm chilled and shivering like a quakie leaf in a breeze, and I miss. I seldom miss, but I'm not surprised at this one.

Next day is a repeat. More road hunting with a few short walks up feeder canyons. The chamois we see are in the forest, and we don't see as many as the first day, either. In the afternoon, Iulian, Gica, Cheri and I scale a very steep and snowy logging trail a vertical 2000 feet and glass. We spot one chamois miles away in the crags, another brown bear, and that's it for the day.

Christy says, "Now they know you can walk, no more road hunting." We're at dinner in the truck-stop hotel. The food is okay by European standards, and the chilled Romanian pilsner surprisingly good. Those familiar to North American and Asian, and even African hunting, are used to tent camps or spartan log hovels and grub cooked on a fire. In Europe, no one camps. Tents are unheard of. I've made a score of European hunts, and have never seen a tent. Hotels and lodges are the rule, and you eat in restaurants or cafes. I'm getting old enough to sometimes appreciate it, if the hotel is clean and comfortable, but this one is not.

The following day, the third, is pretty much a repeat road hunt, except for the frozen rain and the wet snow. We shift across the river Olt, though, and motor up a logging canyon in frozen mud. Mostly wc drive, and we see little. We also take a few cursory and short "hikes" without results. We spot another brown bear and another stag and two bands of wild pigs. To my surprise, Iulian vaults from the 4 x 4 and opens fire, without results. Seems Eurasian pigs are taking over the country, are carrying diseases that infect other wildlife, and it's everyone's duty to kill as many as they can, they tell me. Later, the same scenario with the same results. The chamois season closes in two days, so I'm mildly concerned. The jet-lag is dissipating with the help of a Romanian beer and a fragment of Ambien each night, and I feel I can now shoot and connect.

Cheri decides to tour Dracula's castle on the fourth and only day she hasn't hunted right along with us, because she's afraid she might not get a chance otherwise. That day, we hunters cross the River Olt again, motor up the same canyon. Just to be sure, I double check the borrowed Winchester's sighting, and it's fine. We see boars, but they are gone before anyone can shoot. We glass another brown bear. The road is blocked by an avalanche, we talk loggers into clearing it with a front-end loader, and then motor on in the greasy, icy mud.

In mid-morning, we stop and abandon the 4 x 4, boulder-hop the creek, and trek up a steep feeder canyon. Gica, Iulian, me and Joe in that order.

Like I said, Joe is a very big guy. In a mile, Gica and Iulian spot chamois up the slope in the trees, but we wait for Joe to help evaluate the trophy. It's the next to the last day, so we can't act too picky, either. The chamois cooperate and stand and stare in the beech forest. Through the binocular, one seems a good male. To a large extent, chamois all look about the same to me. The guides think it's a worthy trophy from their body language, and that's good enough for me. Best to wait for Joe's judgement, though.

When Joe arrives, his opinion is to shoot, since time is short. No one is really sure how good the chamois is, but it's a mature male. The shot is horrid—the billy stands in a tangle of brush, it's a long ways, I'm trying to rest the rifle on an icy and snow-covered downed log about neck-high while skidding on a steep slope in a foot of snow. I have to ignore the branch tangle, since there's no way to pick a bullet flight path through it, pray to the red gods, grab a moment when my feet aren't sliding, and squeeze the trigger that's like the last turn of the key on a can of Russian sardines.

I pause and complain about the brush. "No way a slug is going through that."

Joe says, "Take the shot. It's all you got."

I lose the little goat in the recoil, but feel good about the release. The chamois drops in its tracks. I'm astonished because the branches are plenty thick enough to deflect a high-velocity 150 gr. bullet. That they don't, is another miracle.

Joe is more surprised than I am. "Damned *%#@!&$ good shot!!"

The guides pound my back and grin, because they worked for it. It's that best of all feelings, again. In spite of the hundreds of big game trophies I've collected, and the hundreds of congratulations, it's never the same and always new and the best high I know. Especially congrats from guides you respect, like Iulian and Gica.

The guides scale an icy scarp and fight up through the brush and snow, then spend most of an hour skidding the chamois down to where Joe and I stomp about in the creek bottom trying to stay warm and keeping an eye out for the bear we spotted hiking up. At least I stomp. And then we slide the goat down the creek to the jeep. We photograph, toast with a village-made Transylvanian brandy, and motor down-canyon and across the Olt River bridge to Gica's house, where Joe with surgeon precision skins the trophy and Iulian field butchers it. We toast with more brandy, and the neighbors cluster around and join the fun. Joe and I have no idea what they're saying, but all hunters speak the same language.

It's my practice to see some of the country on overseas hunts, either before or after the hunt itself. I've found it's best to tour first, because everything tends to be anticlimactic when compared to the hunting, but this time we tour after the shooting. We tour not only Romania, but Serbia, Bosnia, Montenegro, and Croatia—in Christy's speedy but tiny Audi, like those tours you see advertised on late night TV—five countries in five days. We see Dracula's defensive castle, though the trail is closed by angry bears; the Bridge on the River Drina, site of the Nobel-winning novel by Ivo Andric; bombed-out buildings from the Balkan Wars; snow everywhere that I'd hoped we'd avoid because I live at 6000 feet and am sick of it; stunning peaks and rivers including the Danube; and at last flee the snow at Budva in Montenegro on the Adriatic. We dine that night together and celebrate the hunt, and I turn the guys, Joe and Christy, loose so they can get home for the holidays. Cheri and I spend most of a week in a tiny hotel within the castle walls of the old town with a balcony over the sea. Best of all—no snow and it's no longer as frigid as a hooker's heart. The food is spectacular, like most of Europe, especially by American quick-food standards.

Then we hop a cab and motor to Dubrovnik in Croatia, where we stay in another small hotel within the old city walls and spend Xmas walking along the Adriatic Sea.

Don't Look

"Don't look." That's Espacaza outfitter Jose Mallo talking. I barely hear him because my heart slams like a stoked Buddy Rich on Slingerland snare drums. We—Jose, Cheri, two Gredos Reserve guides, and me—gape at three behemoth Gredos ibex across the creek. After the mountain deluge, calling it a creek is euphemism. It's torrent enough to drown you.

One ibex is easily top-ten class, probably top-five. Earlier, Jose and I discussed what class trophy I'd agree to shoot. I'm a college prof and writer, and spending much of a year's salary on a trophy fee is absurd. You could buy another hunt with King Kong's trophy fee or pay the year's taxidermy bill. Three or four inches of horn isn't worth it to me, and once it's tacked on the wall, who cares about an inch or three? Forgive me my sins, but I'm not much into record books, either.

In most of Europe, the larger the trophy animal, the more shekels you squander for the trophy fee. Logical, yes, but to those of us who learned hunting in democratic North America, where Joe Everyman can and does hunt the grandest trophy animal possible, the custom runs contrary to grain. I'd passed up the largest horns only once, on an east European red stag, and I wasn't yet at ease with that notion.

Let's patch in some back-story. When asked what I work at— that inevitable and unwelcome question—I seldom say writing magazine stories and books or teaching English and zoology at the university. What I do say is, "Hunt!" And that's what got us to Spain's Gredos Mountains in the first place.

As Cheri and I thumbed old Ovis magazine issues in wish-mode one winter day, Cheri said, "Let's do it!" She meant finishing my dozen varieties of native wild world goats, and for me, that meant no hybrids or feral beasts included. Now, I'd already scored all of North America's wild rams and the dozen species and subspecies of world sheep, all of them in absolutely unfenced native habitat, and all more or less accidental. A small handful of ibex, and Spain owned them, would finish that Capra collection, and that would finish the Triple Slam—12 world sheep, 12 world goats and the North American Grand Slam/Four North American Wild Sheep. Evidence to the contrary, collecting isn't my *forte*. If simply hunting for the adrenalin completes some collection or other, be it the spiral-horned antelope, Africa's dangerous game, or the dozen varieties of world rabbits, fine.

Over the decades, I'd collected some grand wild goats, too. A Methuselah 14-year-old Mongolian south Altai ibex with out-fitter Baasanhu Jantzen and Zorig as guides, jumps to mind. And an Azerbaijan 40-inch Dagestan tur in wilting August Caspian Sea winds; I never lusted after a frosted lager more. We collected an 11-inch Balkan chamois on the limestone scarps above the Adriatic Sea across the strait from Korkula Island, reputed to be Marco Polo's birthplace, with outfitter Srdja Dimitrijevic, too. We nearly froze on a December Gobi ibex hunt that after five days netted a spectacu-lar trophy on my birthday with famed guide Luya in 20-below zero temps; galloping Bactrian camels at the ger camp, and quaffing a celebratory bottle of Chinese wine as we toasted ourselves beside the dung-fired stove made that hunt memorable.

We reminisced about these hunts and more, a favored winter occupation. A recent hunt for spring Bezoar ibex in the dust storms of central Anatolia in the Aladaglar Range near the town of Yahyali with Safari Tours netted a grand 48-incher. We'll never forget a hunt with the Club Ibex outfit for western or Kuban tur during the 2008 Russia-Georgia War; we hunted half a dozen miles from one battle and because the local outfitter hadn't notified the army that we'd pack into the west Caucasus, a platoon of Russian army grunts, AKs at the ready, escorted us off the mountain and trucked us to a mili-tary base where we endured an all-night KGB interrogation. When they figured out we weren't CIA operatives, they turned us loose and we bagged a tur in the last hours of the expedition.

We hunted ibex and Marco Polo argali with famed outfitter and guide Yuri Matison and his guys Taktamat and Dovelot two decades ago, again in the freon gales of December, this time in Tajikistan. We scored a gargantuan 62-and-change x 17-inch ram on the second day. I managed one of the more marvelous shots of my career on an Afghanistan-bound ibex at more than 500 yards as it ping-ponged boulders. Indeed, when shots are that astonishing, we can't help but wonder how much luck had to do with it. I did everything but blow smoke from the barrel, for effect, of course.

When we reminisce, you and I eventually slap aside the cobwebs of memory and get to our very first hunt for mountain game, mine in November snows of central British Columbia with outfitter Cliff Eagle and Shuswap Native guide Herbie. For a wannabe teenage mountain man, the hunt was perfect and we put a 10-inch billy in the salt.

Heck, if I'm not hunting, my very favorite thing, bar none, is to retreat to my own clean, well-lighted place that houses most of my favorite trophies and reminisce, and plot that next hunt.

"Shoot the second ibex," Jose says, "and don't look."

The crosshairs of the 7mm magnum settle behind Number Two's shoulder. I pause and tell myself that the trophy fee for King Kong is three times more than for Number Two. I inhale, let most out in a long sigh, and touch off. Nothing happens. The ibex is maybe 175 yards away, the hold as solid as Rushmore. The fur should be on the ground, but the billy didn't flinch. I jack another round into the chamber and settle onto the stock and start to squeeze when something tells me to wait. "*Momento*," someone says. Three blinks later, the billy sways and topples. Old King Kong merely steps into the open and stares at his dead pal.

"Don't look," Jose repeats. I don't, either.

Epilogue:

Like I said, that creek could drown you, so we slog through the deluge back down to the jeeps and trek up the other side of the creek the next day to retrieve the trophy ibex. Without King Kong to compare him to, Number Two ibex is plenty terrific enough for me.

That dozen-goat collection and Triple Slam are history.

OSAMA'S LUCK

Give me luck any day. I mean it. Not to brag, but I've had my share of it—surviving a rattlesnake bite in the Utah wilderness, bagging a ten-foot-three-inch Tanzania lion, 40-inch Dagestan tur, ten-foot-four-inch polar bear, 63-inch Marco Polo argali, and others, too. So you gotta expect bad luck once in a while.

I should have known. Ten days before the trip, a student's virus flattened me and all but two of my summer semester writing students. And I never catch anything. Then, me owning a voice like Smoky Robinson, Cheri and I flew to Moscow. We killed five hours there then waded security in one of Moscow's airports with our pro-hunter Oleg Podzhykin; once through the indignities that stopped just short of body cavity searches, we winged three hours south to Stavropol. Another three hours racing at 130 kilometers-per in black night dodging unlit hay wagons and cows in a tiny Russian Lada sedan to our outfitter's house in the Russian Republic of Karachai-Cherkessia, where, when our hair quit standing on end, we managed two hours of sleep.

We were to jeep two hours farther south on dirt roads then packtrain into the Caucasus Mountains and camp a few miles north of Georgia's Abkhazia border. Oh, I forgot to mention the August 2008 Russia-Georgia war started weeks earlier, and they battled on the Russia and Abkhazia boundary a few miles south. No worry, though, because our hunt broker and organizer had assured me that, "Walt, the fighting is 400 miles away."

The local Karachai outfitter hasn't planned ahead and bought supplies, so he spends the next morning doing that. Late that afternoon when we finally drive the Uaz jeeps up the Abkhyz River Valley, the horses haven't been rounded up nor have they been shod. We wait into evening for this to happen. Then the Uaz jeeps can't ford the river's torrent to get to the place we want to hunt, and the outfitter hasn't phoned ahead to learn this (he knows everyone, and even the goatherds own cell phones), so we retreat to the mouth of another canyon where the outfitter assures us Kuban tur cavort on every scarp. It's midnight. We sleep in a hay shack. One day lost on an already lean schedule (I wouldn't know, but rumor has it most hunters collect their tur by the third day, so the organizer schedules five-day hunts). Okay, expeditions had started rough before but ended well, so I'm not hollerin' yet.

No surprise, but the outfitter doesn't round the horses up again until late morning. It's noon before they're packed and we trail out. Then we sit saddles three hours up trails so hairy that if a horse missteps we wouldn't quit bouncing for a thousand feet. Once, Cheri 50 yards behind me shouts, I pivot in the saddle in time to see her horse lunge and disappear and I'm out of the saddle bounding rocks to find what I'm certain is a bad wreck. Her saddle has slipped, but she's askew and still on the nag's back and it's on all fours. Lucky. We pitch tents in a glacial cirque a thousand feet above, and it's an hour before my heart slips out of my throat back to its usual place. I hate sitting a saddle animal when one of my feet dangles in space, and I hate it more when Cheri does it.

Before long a Russian helicopter gunship bristling rockets jackhammers above camp and disappears beyond the ridge. A moment later it hammers back over camp. Cheri ducks into the tent to grab a camera, and I hiss, "Don't!" because I dislike the look of those rockets. She sneaks a snapshot out the tent flap anyway. I get no respect.

Things settle, Oleg makes lunch—a tasty treat of milk, sugar and noodles (Cheri dumps it in the creek so as not to hurt his feelings)—and we ready ourselves to scale the cols above. I'm throwing the rifle over a shoulder when a soldier in complete battle dress stands from behind a boulder with AK at the ready. Within moments a dozen more do the same. We're surrounded. I'm no longer surprised at anything.

The platoon stalks into camp and Oleg and the outfitter explain. The Russian grunts keep the AKs handy. They want our passports, but the local outfitter kept them at his house in case the game warden wants them. It doesn't matter, though, because the local outfitter hasn't notified the army he'd pack into a war zone and doesn't have other documentation, either. He disappears back down the trail with two soldiers to straighten out the mess.

Two of the soldiers, kids really, try to converse with Cheri and me in their second-grade English, and Cheri gives all of them a hatful of American bubble gum. She's a big hit, and they become our fast friends while we wait. They're fascinated with my rifle, and take turns peering through the scope.

The outfitter doesn't straighten out the problem, and by radio the platoon is ordered to escort us off the mountain. We make it down at dark. At the bottom of the trail, a dozen more heavily armed soldiers mist out of the pines and join our procession. Apparently they'd expected bigger things. Our outfitter shows up and points at me, laughs, runs his hand down his face to indicate my beard, twirls a forefinger over his head to mean helicopter, searches his scant English, and says, "You! Osama bin Laden!" (Off course, this in the days before bin Laden was assassinated.) He slaps his thigh and doubles over in mirth. "They thought you are Osama," Oleg explains. We're escorted to a military base, and about midnight, hustled inside.

I'm peeved. We've lost another hunting day. We're escorted into what I take is the base commander's office, because it has two computers and a guy with stars on his shoulder is on the phone to Moscow, Oleg tells me, then we're taken to a larger lecture room. Oleg says, "Ve big news, efun in Moscow—foreigners in zee battle zone. KGB don't like thees." He grins. Big joke! I could strangle him. A woman serves tea and pastries, and the rest of our guys are escorted out and we're left alone an hour to think about it, I suppose.

When they filter back in, the outfitter and Oleg see the steam seeping out my ears and sit in the opposite corner. Uniformed soldiers and three KGB operatives in civvies with pistols stuck in waistbands enter. One agent, speaking fluent English, asks us to sign Russian documents. What choice do we have, after all? I disguise a question mark at the end of my signatures in case they ever get to the U.S. embassy or to the public. We have absolutely no idea what we're signing, and still don't. Two soldiers hand-copy the documents word-for-word and in triplicate. Apparently computers and carbon paper are scarce. This takes two hours.

The English-speaking agent questions us. He's very polite, as were the soldiers, so we hadn't felt threatened all day. Our passports, retrieved from the outfitter's house, fascinate him with their Namibia, Bosnia, Mongolia, China, Azerbaijan and other entries, and the illustrations on each page of the new edition. He's never seen American passports before. He writes down detailed information on what we do, where we live, where we were born, and if I'd ever been in the military, police or other armed force. He gives his notes to the two soldiers copying documents and they incorporate this into the forms. It's three in the morning.

The agent writes down more info while other agents question Oleg and the outfitter. Uniformed brass pace the room. We're informed that the outfitter hasn't secured proper documentation, but he is now buying the licenses and permits, and when that happens we will be free to leave. Free to leave? Cheri and I gape. The soldiers and agents have been so polite it hasn't crossed our minds we've been officially detained.

When we're released, finally, we jeep to that farm shack before dawn and grab a few hours' sleep. The outfitter doesn't radio our guys back up in the alpine camp with the horses until midmorning, so they don't show with our saddle mounts until afternoon. No surprise. No one here plans ahead. It's mid-afternoon when we ride into our camp and it's begun to rain, a daily occurrence. I'm anxious to climb the scarps; after all, we've been in the Caucasus three days and have yet to hunt, but the guide and outfitter explain they don't hunt in rain. Seems local tur hate inclement weather, too. The rain eases, Oleg and company knows I'm still boiling, so we scale a thousand feet up Peterbilt-size boulders that teeter when we step on them. An avalanche lets loose ten minutes after we pass the spot complete with Volkswagon-size boulders that make it all the way to the bottom two-hundred yards above camp. Oleg takes a bad dive that wrenches his back. We spot three female tur, and stagger back in the dark and rain over the scree and cliffs. We've managed three hours hunting in three days.

The next day we start at a reasonable time, not dawn, though, because that's expecting too much. Oleg's back is too sore to go. The weather cooperates and we scale into a higher basin, tight-rope its scarps, glass and glass more. We spot three tur. Distant avalanches let loose every few minutes with alarming explosions. I'd never been in more stunning country—a bit like Jasper or Banff but steeper, bigger and ten times the glaciers. It's also as treacherous a land as I've hunted, and I've hunted bad ones. The guides point out the Georgia border three miles south. The day is what you'd expect hunting mountain game. Great, except three female tur in a day's hunting make the pickings lean.

At dark we stagger our way back down the cliffs and boulders in an operatic Wagnerian thunderstorm complete with lightning blasting boulders off cliffs, cherry-sized hail that raise welts when we face into the wind, and the smell of brimstone. We duck each time lightning strikes so close there's no gap between the flash and thunder. I hop boulders like a pika and make it to camp twenty minutes before the guides, drenched even through the rain gear. Lucky again.

It's after ten of a rare cloudless morn before Oleg can get the guides up and going. Their togs are too damp, they protest. Finally, the guides and I scale the col into a basin and onto another col. We spot no tur after 30 minutes, so they shrug and turn for camp. On the way, the guides urge me to shoot a female chamois, the first we've seen, but I refuse. We're back for a late lunch. Before I know what's going on, they're tearing down the tents.

"No tur here. Ve go to another place," Oleg explains. But we've got only one hunting day left, and we won't get more hunting this day if we move camp. I'd prefer to ride it out here, hunt the evening and one more full day, but I don't make an issue of it. To top it off, in their wisdom two hobbled horses abandon us the night before and presumably take the trail down and out. We'll have to walk because we need the remaining horses to pack gear. Cheri and I trek out early.

I wanna go home, I have no faith in the move or guides, and to hell with tur.

It's midnight when we jeep to a stream and pitch the tents. One guide still trails horses to our camp. Oleg awakens the guides before sunup, because if he didn't we wouldn't start until noon. It's our earliest start yet, for one last day. He boils another of his noodles, sugar and milk specialties, but Cheri and I opt for oatmeal. I stuff American trail mix we brought from the States into my pack, because no telling if the guides would bring lunch. The day dawns clear and hope surges in my breast, like it does any hunting day. By nature, hunters are optimists.

The two guides and I sit horses two-thousand vertical feet and seven miles up a trailless ridge onto a plateau, where we hobble them. We shoulder packs and trek up another thousand feet, glass a basin north from the col, then tight-rope its blade-edge toward a snaggle-tooth peak. We spot tur far above, and one owns small horns. At this point late on the last day, I can't act picky. Once we get the guides afield, I'm impressed with their abilities. Getting them out, though, is the trick.

On the west side, the ridge slopes 75-degrees to a boulder field. Step on loose shingle and it's a fatal half-mile toboggan ride. On the east, you teeter a 400-foot sheer drop above a crevassed glacier. Lose a moment's concentration and they'd find you at the glacier terminus in four centuries. Either way, I don't look down.

The billy tur is sunning itself on the peak. We're miles away and the guides aren't worried he'll spot us. We snake to 350 yards after two hours tight-roping a 50-story plummet. Problem is, the ledge protects the tur's heart-lung area. The guides want me to try; I could aim for the liver. I decline, because it doesn't know we're here. With gestures, I argue for crawling closer. After all, we leave tomorrow and this is our only chance. We belly to another place, and another, until the tur should be 150 yards below. When we peer over the rocks, though, he's gone. The guides are sure he's seen us. I think he's stepped out of the sun and into the shadows beyond.

We hands-and-knee a boulder field and belly over the ridgeline to that 50-story drop. I gape. Now what? The guides lead, with too much enthusiasm, I think, onto a two-foot ledge. No big deal, unless you have a 500-foot drop at your heels. I'm still deciding whether or not I want a tur that bad, when the guides edge across. If they can do it, I try to convince myself, so can I. Testosterone dementia has gotten me into more trouble.

Okay, I tell myself, don't look down. I chant it. Watch that loose shingle. Jam your fingers into that crack. Grab that handhold! In the longest minutes of my life, I'm across and as giddy as I've ever been. Lucky again. The guys grin. We finger-and-toe up and it seems child's play after that ledge, but it isn't. One lapse would kill you. The guides expect the tur has retreated to this side of the col, but I'm too busy staying alive to care.

No tur. We climb back up the blade edge and glass down. Nothing. I'm wedged in a crevasse when the guide above kicks me in the head. "Vatter!" he hisses. So what? I wonder, we've seen water before and I'm not that thirsty anyway, when I realize he's using my name.

I spot the billy ping-ponging boulders straight away 200 meters out and get the crosshairs on its tail and drop it with a lucky shot.

We're up at dawn next day, the first time the guides have gotten up that early, because now we're aimed home. Nags on the way back to the barn. The road is worse in daylight. Oleg says, "Russians invent zis jeep because it vas cheaper zan fixing ze roads."

Later, I sneak a photo of the army base where we were interrogated out the jeep window as we clatter by. Later still, I realize I've completed the super and world slams, but I'm more thankful we're alive and we're not in a Russian gulag.

The tur I bagged won't make a ripple in record books, but any tur is a trophy. Better, we survived. Gimme luck any day.

Argali Angst

I teach university English and zoology, and last semester my human bio class opted to sweat their final exam at my house, mainly to slurp my infamous pronghorn stew, ogle aboriginal artifacts, and gawk at 200 or so big game trophies. Who says today's students are anti-hunting?

"What's your hardest trophy?" one pretty sophomore asked. I dreaded the question, and I've fielded it from cub scouts to octogenarian lady bird-watchers in sneakers, because it's nearly impossible to answer. I told her so, but she cooed, "If you had to choose."

She'd pinned me, as they always do, so I opted for the 10-foot-four-inch dogsled polar bear bagged on the 12th day on the icepack 100 miles off Ellesmere Island in full polar winter. Temps clawed to 31-below zero on a warm day; on a cold one they spiraled to 41-below. When pressed, I fingered my 63 x 17-inch Marco Polo argali from Tajikistan bagged with legendary Yuri Matison as number two, also taken in December extremes. After that, choices got tough, and included in the balloting, elephant; African lion-fair chase and no fences of course; 40-inch Dagestan tur; some fine ibex; and a Mongolian argali that took two expeditions, six camps, and a pickup load of angst to finally put in the salt.

I'd fantasized Mongolia since reading Roy Chapman Andrews' *End of the Earth* as a kid. Years later I fondled argali horns at a taxidermist shop. Then came magazine stories, videos, and a full-body argali mount in a Wyoming honky-tonk. I had to go.

Cheri and I stagger into the Ulaanbaatar air terminal after 26 straight hours in planes and airports in December temps cold enough to freeze the ears off a brass monkey, and meet outfitter Baasanhu Jantzen, all according to script. So far, so good.

Then things head to Siberia. Someone miscopied a numeral on the gun permit. My pet Remington stays in the airport.

"Iss okay," Baasanhu says. "You use my rifle."

Our driver speaks no English and he aims the Nissan out of the city in black December dawn and a coal haze so solid you can't see two car lengths. Pale orange headlights come at you in brown halos. The streets are soot-black icy and a bank thermometer flashes, "-30 C/-22F" through the bituminous smog. If you had to envision mankind's end, this would be it.

Central Gobi Desert, Mongolia, December

A few miles south of Ulaanbaatar, the crumbling blacktop turns to dirt. We motor all day into Gobi wastes, occasionally suck salt tea or gnaw horse-haunch by way of refreshment, until we make monastery ruins razed by Stalin's crew most of a century ago. As the Nissan idles in the gloaming, headlights flash then disappear in distant dunes. An hour later a head shoves through the Nissan window.

"My name ish Nara." Vodka fumes flood the Nissan. "I vill guide you," the face slurs. Fantasies shouldn't start this way.

We follow Nara and chums in a Russian Uaz jeep into the night and finally stop at gers pitched in a ravine. A ger is a Mongol yurt. Later I stagger out to pee in air so freon I'm certain I've *frozen* something.

The next dawn the Nissan tails the jeep deeper into the Gobi. Nara still guzzles the 100-proof vodka, but luckily the drivers don't. We grind to an island mountain range, debark, and file up a ravine. When we crest, 20 ibex graze across a canyon and gale winds blast us with buckshot gravel. I spot no good billies, but the target animal is argali, and I dislike getting sidetracked. Nara urges me to shoot one.

Later, I question Nara, "You sure there's argali here?" Not only haven't we seen sheep, we've seen no tracks. He nods, but looks uncomfortable. By next dawn, Nara's out of vodka, he staggers, he's got the shakes and a trophy case of DTs. When we gather the guide at his ger miles south, I question Nara again. He wants me to blast an ibex, but I insist we hunt argali. His face gets pea green and he staggers for the ger. He's gone an hour before I bang the Nissan's horn.

Three Mongols pile out of the ger and clamber into the Uaz. Our Nissan eats their Gobi dust until hours later when we clatter to a boulder jumble in the dunes. We spook a small argali ram. We cross-country to a far range and spot 30 argali including small rams, and my spirits soar. Argali at last!

"No goot," Nara says as we gnaw camel meat appetizer that night. "No big argali there." *How does he know?* I wonder. We've only hunted half the range. I assumed we'd go back the next day, so I protest. I hate angst. Baasanhu jeeps into camp with my rifle late that night. That's one less worry. Nara is upset over my insistence on hunting argali. I counter that that's what we'd come for. Baasanhu figures the twenty-below temps, winds fierce enough to scalp a yak and the tough country would make us content with a quick ibex and early ticket home. He didn't know we'd hunted colder climes, and Cheri is tougher than bull camel jerky. Baasanhu disappears to conference with Nara.

An hour later he proposes we give up on the argali this trip, journey to a range with larger ibex, and come back in the spring to a place with more and bigger argali and ibex. Fantasies don't work this way, but what's the choice? We clatter cross-country a day west and bivouac in famed guide Luya's camp, then grind south to mountains towering three-thousand feet above Gobi dunes. Nara's shaken off the DTs and becomes an exemplary escort. We hunt out of Luya's uncle's gers four days in blizzards, dust hurricanes, and twenty-below temps before one shot bags a grand Gobi ibex on my birthday. From there we motor back to Luya's Tsahir Mountain camp and glass the kind of argali rams that fuel fantasies. We'll return in May to hunt them.

Oshgog Range, Central Mongolia, next May

This trip, we've got the A-Team—famed guide Zorig and his renowned wife, skinner, cook and woman-Friday, Erka, and

Baasanhu himself. We'll rendezvous with equally famous guide Luya in the Oshgog Range. We motor west out of Ulaanbaatar in temperatures 70-degrees warmer than last December. Five of us and three weeks' gear and grub are sardined into the tiny Russian Uaz jeep. After last December, I obsess the argali like a Gobi wolf lusts after goitered gazelle chops. I can't even entertain the notion of another blown argali hunt.

We make Luya's Boombat Camp in late afternoon, ahead of schedule because Zorig drives like it's the Gobi 500. Within an hour Erka shoves into our ger with steaming water and a hot meal cooked on a tiny, sheep-dung stove. We scrub off airport grime and Gobi dust and sup. I'm cautiously optimistic, though so jet-lagged I eat soup with a fork and peel a t-shirt on backward.

We motor into predawn frost and a cobalt Mongol sky, and glass rams instantly. None are big enough. We move and spot more rams. In two hours, I count 40 rams and one ewe. My spirits soar like a Gobi lammergeier.

Later, Cheri glasses eight rams loping out of the Gobi flats. They cross the ravine that marks the boundary between so-called Hangay and Gobi argali ranges that Baasanhu and an American salesman arbitrarily decide upon years earlier. On one side of the ravine, you score them as Gobi argali; move them 50 feet west, and they become Hangay argali. The rams canter into the Oshgog hills and bed a mile west. One owns horns thick as a Michelin tire. Is he Gobi or Hangay?

After last December's bust, I'm more than content to bag the ram ASAP. Normally, I won't shoot opening day. I like dragging out my hunts, and getting my money's worth. We slalom down the knoll but the rams spot us a mile away and lope into distant mirages. No surprise there.

The gang shouts in guttural Mongol, to them it's merely conversation, gesture and deduce the rams ran north, and they seem to know where. Though I speak no Mongol, I understand them as if I do; all hunters speak the same language, and it isn't taught in a phrase book.

Hours later and miles north, we trudge up-slope in glaring midday sun. Luya leads, and he's alert as a falcon. I can't understand how he figures the rams would run here. If I were any more jet-lagged I'd doze, because it's the middle of the night back home. Luya crouches and scans, then duck-walks between boulders. I have no faith in the ploy, but shove one up the throat of the .300 Winchester magnum anyway. I've been wrong before.

Part of me doesn't want to shoot yet—I'm too fried. Another part wants the trophy ram as history. Above, Luya drops to knees. He bellies to a boulder, then motions. The same rams nap 100 yards across the gully. I slither into shooting prone, but though I run daily, I'm wheezing like a broken radiator and my heart bangs like Ringo on the drums in the old days. I'm as far away from shooting psyche-calm as you can get. Last year's blown hunt, five months' waiting anxiety, and jet-lag take their toll. I miss clean. Nobody muffs a hundred-yard prone shot.

All hunters know the feeling. It's worse than an IRS audit and your wife running off with her personal trainer, the same day. The guys know it, too, but they politely shrug it off.

We find the rams again, but they sail over distant ridges into the ether. I'm for retreating to the gers and a double scotch, but the guys won't have it. They're confident, even if I'm not.

Hours later, we spot the rams again, but they've seen us and lope over the ridge. No surprise, because that's the way the hunt's gone. We try to head them off as black cumulus boil from the North Hangay. Lightning stabs the Gobi, thunder booms and golf-ball raindrops crater the dust—sound effects courtesy of a Wagner opera. I expect instant immolation each time we sprint a ridge. Cheri and Zorig trek for the jeep in a sand blizzard. I don't expect much as we lean into the howling.

Later, I spot the rams single-filing right at us. Luya shoves the daypack ahead for a rifle rest. The magnum ram leads and the others caboose until they see us and skid to a stop. The big ram whirls and slams into the rams behind, they mill in confusion, then gallop upslope. I've got the crosshairs behind the ram's ribs as he quarters away and touch off. I think I hear the slug slam flesh in the maelstrom, but can't be sure. The ram doesn't flinch. I shoot again with precisely the same result. I slap trigger as they crest and they're gone. By now, that angst queasiness is too familiar.

The guys spot the rams cross a distant knoll, but I won't look. "The big ram is not with them," Baasanhu says. Dare I hope?

We follow tracks up the slope, but find no blood. I'm pessimistic, again. Not one blood spatter all the way up, and I become hopeless. When we cross I spot the ram sprawled on Gobi gravel. I'm so wired I yank Luya off his feet when I grab his shoulder and shake him like a dirty sock.

Epilogue: Jantzen outfits a stellar hunt, too. In the next weeks we cross-country 3000 kilometers through four ecosystems and bag trophy Altai ibex, gazelle and roe deer, and including December's Gobi ibex and that dream argali, that's five king kong trophies on my most productive of 19 Asian hunts.

I recall Andrews, too: "All this thrilled me to the core."

THE LONGEST SHEEP HUNT
PART I: ADDICTION

I've studied mountain man books since I turned eight, tomes like Guthrie's *The Big Sky*—they made a flic of it. And *The History of the Lewis and Clark Expedition, The Plainsmen of the Yellowstone*, and enough others to founder a dump truck. Long before that, Fess Parker in TV's Davy Crockett series became my hero and I got a birthday 'coon skin hat just like his, too. I knew I'd become a mountain man when I grew up. Mom tried to convince me of the dream's impracticality in the 20th century, but Dad grinned and bought me a .22. To complete my corruption, I thumbed dog-eared copies of *Outdoor Life* in barber shops and math class. I ogled those ads in back of the magazine that advertised forest ranger schooling and promised salaries of $150 a month and dreamed. Blame the Fates, but Jack O'Connor's hunts after whitetails in Mexico, but mostly his sheep hunting stories, finalized that corruption.

So I endured high school, and slogged through college and grad school aimed at work outdoors, and bossed fire crews for the USFS and researched waterfowl pathology for the U.S. Fish & Wildlife Service and studied wapiti behavior and ecology at Utah State University, but always really planned at becoming a hunting mountain man. Heck, my first wife thought I'd give up such boyish notions when socked with the responsibilities of a married man, and when I didn't she crunched the data and figured prospects might be better elsewhere, and I hoped they were.

Forward a decade. Grad school is behind, and that marriage and aimless solo sailing about the Caribbean and wandering lost Mayan ruins in the jungles of the south Yucatan, Indiana Jones-style. As I

239

squat across the smokey ceiba wood fire from a Lacondon Maya *brujo* sipping some jungle concoction that makes my feet numb and nose runny, I think in a too rare moment of clarity, *Why not*?! I couldn't find an answer.

The next year I bought a Montana combo hunting license, scraped the shekels together and paid the bills, and trekked into the Beartooth-Absaroka Wilderness north of Yellowstone Park, that first time afoot and solo toting a 70-pound pack and starting from the junction of the Lamar and Yellowstone Rivers in the Park and grunting up onto the Buffalo Plateau north of the boundary. This was June, when the rivers and streams ran high with meltwater, the elk grazed velvet-antlered, the bruins had thoroughly rubbed, and the bighorns followed the climbing snow line after the new green. I assumed on the part of the bighorns, because I didn't see any.

That combo license included elk, bear, deer, birds and fishing, and I bought one of those bighorn tags that you had to score on early or you might not. The state allowed for one or two rams to get bagged, three-quarters curl or better, and after the redshirts scored the ram, the state boys closed the season no matter how many nim-rods still scaled the crags. I planned to scout all summer and have rams pegged when hunting began in September. I fantasized a sway-backed, broom-horned Methuselah ram, and nothing less would do. And I did—scout all summer, that is. A state biologist said to look on Middle Ridge looming above the upper Hell Roaring drainage, so on my second trek I did. I pulled that ridge apart for five days with the binocular. A few picas, a marmot, and one shaggy cinnamon black bear, but otherwise nothing.

I kept at it, and toward late July, I stumbled into a USFS trail crew camp. Those boys had been repairing winter's ravages to the trail system for a month. They had ogled sheep in the Flood Creek and Deadman's geography, so I trekked east and burned two weeks dissecting that on-end topography with the binocular, dining on trout tricked with smokey dry flies supplemented with Uncle Ben's Instant rice and jerky, and punching holes in my belt.

I spied elk in the high basins, most of them mature bulls still in velvet. I pegged velvet-antlered magnum mule deer bucks, and ogled a handful of black bears. I'd have no trouble filling those tags. I found as many rams as I did five-pound gold nuggets, and back-packed three more times into other parts of the map in August and early September with the same results.

I shouldered a backpack heavy enough to fuse vertebrae and then lead a pet saddle horse subbing as a pack animal onto Buffalo Plateau from the north four days before the mid-September opening and overnighted with a guide primping his camp for the looming elk hunting dudes. Hungry enough for anything other than equine company, he donated those feed cakes for my mare, too much con-versation and whiskey that made my ears ring.

"Usually find sheep up on Middle Ridge," he told me. I'd heard that one before.

From my summer-long odyssey, one place seemed as good as another for rams. I still had no idea where to find one, but bands of elk bulls browsed Telephone and Hummingbird basins all summer, so I'd aim there first to put that elk fur in the salt and get on with the ram hunt. A single .270 130-grain Core-lokt slapped a 6 x 6 bull on the needle duff, but it took the best part of a week butchering and packing it back and forth to the truck and horse trailer and the trailhead farther north than I cared to think about. Of course I had to get the elk venison to the freezer back to civilization before I could resume that ram argosy, and after that phone call I dreaded, found that no one had yet bagged a ram and the hunt was still on.

Days later, I lead the packed-up mare back into the country through quadriceps-deep snow on the passes, detoured half a day for that elk loin I'd cached in a lodgepole pine, and wandered toward the Rainbow Lakes maybe a day's pack east. No rams there, either, but I salivated over a King Kong mule deer buck. To my surprise, I didn't give in and bag it though the season was on—I needed to get on with the ram hunt—and as far as I know, that buck sired many more magnum-antlered deer. Then the mare and I forded Buffalo Fork and trailed up into the lodgepole pines onto south Buffalo Plateau and its golden dead-grass meadows surrounded by looming pine forests and coliseum basins and wapiti music on the wind, and we didn't find the rams there, either. I aimed down into aptly monikered Hell Roaring

Creek, hooked cutthroat trout on gray hackles and grilled them over creekside driftwood fires and slid the pink flesh from the fine bones and almost didn't mind that I hadn't ogled rams. I'd engulfed the last of that elk loin, too, medium-rare.

Up Hell Roaring, I whiffed pine wood smoke now and again on the trail all morning, and then stepped into a clearing and a USFS cabin built before the 20th century, its windows and door heavily barricaded with wicked spiked steel bear protection. A ranger stepped out the door. He put on his Gabby Hayes Stetson and looked like one of those old ads in *Outdoor Life* or a cover of *National Sportsman*. He even wore a red-and-black Mackinaw wool shirt.

"Seed bighorns up on Middle Ridge last week," he said, "or mebbee the week afore?" He even talked like Gabby Hayes. We sipped bourbon-laced coffee next to the 1895 wood-burning kitchen range. Seems I'd heard that story before, too, and went on snipe chases because of it.

"I'll look that way, then," I said, and spent that night and gorged on baked chicken, cinnamon biscuits, canned spinach and slugged back a shot or three of his whiskey. The Forest Service fed its boys well. He passed it down the line, too, and my mare munched all the USFS horse cakes she desired, with the Forest Service pack string as company. Next dawn, she frisked like a colt and toted her load with more gung-ho than a Marine.

Two days later I'd once again clawed atop Middle Ridge. No sheep, no sheep tracks, not even an elk or bear track. Another snipe hunt. I wondered if all the woods bums were in cahoots and they recognized a greenhorn when they saw one. Then I aimed east again, through the Rainbow Lakes geography—no rams—then into that Deadman country again, spotting nothing but a grizzly and yearling cub, a few buck mule deer, and a black bear in a distant basin for all that effort, and hunkered out a blizzard that kept me tent-bound for three days with the mare excavating for whatever greens she could find. I told myself that any nimrod could enjoy a camp in a sky painted with a billion stars and a warm breeze freighted with pine scent and coyotes hollering down the ridge, but it took a special breed of hairy-chested mountain man to enjoy the banshee scream of storm wind through the pine snags and the whip of tent fabric and the pelt of snow pellets and temps that would frighten a boreal owl. I told myself that the first night, but by the third I longed for those gin-clear skies and temperate pine-scented breezes.

When the squall roared east and the sky cleared and thermometer plummeted to single digits, you could see the nag's ribs. I glassed again, first from this summit, then that col, then another crag. No surprise, no rams—same old story, but I glassed a mountain goat, the first one I'd seen. Days later, one wandered into camp on a sunny morn intent on the salty grass where I'd peed and couldn't be dissuaded, either. I took apart the geography so thoroughly with the glass that I learned where every pica stashed its hay pile. A grand bull elk harried his harem through camp one day, and the mare paid them scant attention. She'd become a trail-hardened vet. The elk hunt had been going for weeks now, and the pack string traffic had turned the trails into muck that would bog a coot, and the bulls had beat it south into the Park. I kept as far from the main greasy trails and the redshirts as I could get, too, this in those days before hunter orange. The mare's company was enough for me, but I listened for her bell in the night though she was tethered with a stout rope to graze, because I feared she might make off toward a two-mile distant whinny and equine company and a common lust for grain. I suspected she wasn't as fond of my company as I was of hers, because I always started our conversations. Some of them lasted long into the night.

As I stared into the deadfall fire one night, in one of those two few moments of clarity, I realized I was living that boyhood fantasy. The mare tied to lodgepole snag too big to drag off if she scented near bear, nickered as if in agreement. I'd chased rams for so many months I'd lost track in wilderness where the real mountain men had wandered, and I did it their way. Except I had those maps. And a compass. I resolved on that moment not to use them again, those mountain men hadn't, so I stuffed them to the bottom of my pack, just beneath the wool britches so soiled they could stand by themselves. I thought of burning them, but you never knew. The maps, that is, not the britches. The maps hadn't helped me get onto rams anyhow.

Next day I aimed where my nose pointed, this time northeast toward geography I hadn't yet wandered into. The country became higher and more bluffed-up and I glassed more mountain goats. I kept to those USFS trails, mostly, because too much of these wilds stood on end and if you got off the trails you fought through the deadfall jungles you shouldn't try to work a horse through. I tried one day, and the mare's feet shot from under her and she pinwheeled downslope and crashed into deadfall so hard it would register on seismographs in Helena and got herself stuck as solid as a peg in a too small hole. It took most of a day sweating in the sub-freezing temps sawing her out with a backpack saw and rolling the log sections downslope, but other than missing a divot or two of hide, she looked none the worse for the fun. After that, I left her tethered or hobbled off the trail where she could graze. If I bivvied over night, she'd survive, and bear scent no longer fazed her, much.

On one of those forays, I spidered near-vertical walls toward an on-end hanging basin. I found a set of matching shed moose antlers, Boone and Crocket class, too, pondered how the bull had climbed there, and lashed them onto the pack. I continued on, into that canyon head—and gazed at three gold nugget rams and choked on my day-old gum. Trouble was, they loafed on rock outcrops surrounded by lodgepole pine dreadlocks six hundred yards across the gorge.

I tried to remember how many months I'd fought through these wilds searching for rams. *Take yer time, boy,* I told myself, *and don't screw it up.* Easier said than done, because my knees knocked and I gasped to catch my breath. I owned text-book ram fever, the kind you read about in the old magazines but never quite believe. I tried to get rational, and told myself to watch the rams and collect myself— *Take a deep breath, pal.* I took a deep breath. Those sheep weren't going anywhere soon, and they hadn't spotted me yet. After anyhow 40 minutes, I slid downslope through the pines to the creek, shed the pack and clawed up through the forest toward the rams. I studied where I stepped, tried not to gasp so the rams would hear me, and took an hour to cover maybe 200 yards. I couldn't think of a thing I did wrong. When I'd scaled to what I figured was their altitude on the 65 degree forested slope, I searched for one of those rock spires I remembered about 100 yards east of them. I found it, crossed fingers it was the right one, double-checked the wind, fingered and toed up it, and there they were! They bedded and chewed cuds 60 yards off and all stared in different directions, one right at me. He stood when my head popped above the boulder, and I jacked a round up the throat of the Remington and the crosshairs settled naturally behind his shoulder. The ram wasn't spooked, just alerted at what could have been a pica or whistler. The ram owned a three-quarter curl, or I thought. The other two rams, still chewing cuds and dreaming of hot ewes, paid me no attention. They seemed all the same size. I checked the safety and lay the Remington on the scree and eased up the binocular. Probably a legal three-quarter ram, but certainly nothing like my broomed Methuselah fantasy. What to do?

I watched the rams an hour in the cold, then two, until I couldn't feel my toes. I hadn't realized I had a decision to make. Bag the ram, butcher it, pack it down to the mare miles below, and find my way back to familiar geography and a trail I recognized that would aim me back to the rig at the trailhead. It might take most of a week. But I couldn't see any way to hang that head on the wall so it could compete with my old mature ram fantasy. I was worn out after the months in the wilds, and the butchery and pack work didn't look pleasant. I spidered down the rock spire, shouldered the rifle and caromed downslope to the pack, shouldered it and aimed back down toward the mare. I'd camp off the trail and decide what next. On the way down I paused on a ridge and glassed those rams again a mile up canyon and still chewing cuds at peace with the world.

I hooked a brace of cutthroat trout for supper and pondered the next move and talked to the mare at the edge of the firelight. After a long talk in which the mare and I weighed the pros and cons, we decided to aim west again in the general direction of a trail which might take us back to the rig and the trailhead, and hunt rams along the way. The elk hunters had returned to TV football, and the ridges and passes were snowed up and it might be tough getting a horse through some of them. It would become impossible with the next storm and I wasn't leaving without my mare. And that's what we did. We found no rams in the Deadman geography, none over in the

Rainbow country, and none along Buffalo Fork or north up the trail to the trailhead. I was right, too, it took most of a week.

It wasn't quite finished, though. No one had yet bagged a ram and the season was still open, maybe for weeks yet. The mule deer hunt was on, too, but I guessed the bears might be in hibernation. I'd truck the mare home to Utah because of the late season threat. She took the last of those trails with wooden legs even though she knew she was aimed home. I'd come back with a backpack. I did, too, and bagged a mule deer buck south of Big Timber in November snows, but not one like I'd spied in the wilderness to the south, trekked into country easterly from where I'd spent those months, and didn't find another ram, either.

In all, I spent five months off and on trekking through the wilds. When it was over, I could still fantasize that king kong Methuselah bighorn ram on that fantasy wall. I wasn't finished stalking rams in spite of the failure. Or was it a failure? Heck, I'd become a mountain man of sorts, and I'd become a sheep hunter and not only a sheep dreamer.

Epilogue: In later years I pulled off more than 20 sheep hunts around the planet, but that first months' long odyssey through the Yellowstone geography remains the most memorable. Yep, I've bagged bighorns since, but that fantasy Methuselah ram with its broomed horns still hangs on that fantasy wall. It'll have to do for now. Those bonus points keep adding up, though.

THE LONGEST SHEEP HUNT
PART II: THE TREK

"You got grub 'nuff?" bush pilot Joe Firmin hollered over the idling Cessna 185. "That skimpy pile ain't lastin' two days. You got fixin's for a hungry camp, you ask me. See ya in a month."

Joe snapped the side window shut and I stepped clear and he shoved the throttle forward and the mustard-colored Arctic Circle Air Cessna '185 clattered down the beach of grapefruit-sized rocks. Just before it lunged into the air, I heard a pop like a 9mm pistol shot as the tail wheel blew, and then he sprung airborne. The '185 clawed for altitude to clear the black spruce downriver and then circled and flew over and waggled wings and I punched a fist up. In a moment he'd disappeared into the leaden Arctic skies to the south aimed at Ft. Yukon, and I stood on the beach and pondered my token pile of gear and grub—backpack stuffed with tent, bedroll, clothes, a small bag of rice and one of tea, sugar, and one day's dehydrated grub. I planned to kill my meat. I hoped.

I felt the lump in the throat with the sudden and full realization that the nearest hospital and pavement were 250 miles southwest in Fairbanks, the nearest humanity ten days' tough trekking to the fly-in-only Gwitchin Athabascan cluster of shacks optimistically named Arctic Village. This in those glorious and grand days before GPS, cell phones and eternal connectivity. I didn't carry a two-way radio, either. *Too heavy*, I told myself. I'd feel like I was cheating if I had one. I was on my own, and that's the way I wanted it.

I didn't go into this thing blind. I'd camped a month and hunted from this beach the season before and scored a double-shovel caribou with a 57-inch beam, a 65-inch moose, ptarmigan, and any number of two-pound grayling from the eddy in front of camp. I could do it again.

I only wanted caribou this time around. Last season I'd bagged a king-kong moose three miles downriver and took a week at two trips a day to get most of it back to camp. I say most of it, because the bears found it. I wasn't carrying the .270 because I didn't need the extra weight on one of those packing trips, when I came face-to-face with a fat black bear with a jaw-full of moose meat neatly wrapped in a cheesecloth game bag. He choked a growl, stepped off the game trail and into the belt-tangle poplar and disappeared, clutching the meat. I didn't argue. It's only a black bear, I reasoned, so I still didn't carry that 10-pound rifle. A fool greenhorn move, too. That dusk I burst into the flood channel where I'd hung the boned-out quarters in white game bags from the willows. In the gloaming, they looked like ghosts flitting through the gloom. As I grunted a meat-laden pack frame onto my back, *G-R-R-OAR-R-R!* blasted from the willow shadows. I left the pack hanging in the air and backed away, fast. When I rounded a bend in the channel, I sprinted the three miles to camp and didn't look back, either. After that, I didn't take a pee break without that chamber-loaded .270. Next morning, seven-inch, long-clawed grizzly tracks wandered through the hanging game bags, and the bear wasn't just looking.

This season, I'd avoid moose-hungry bears. I didn't want the pack work, anyhow. Caribou would suit me fine. Beside, that ADF&G boy in Ft. Yukon that measured the moose antlers last season said, "You'll never git a bigger north of the Arctic Circle."

The caribou showed three days later. A band of a dozen bulls, most big enough for any record bible, crossed the rapid 400 yards downriver. I sprinted after them, forded the belly-deep riffles, and chased them toward the Old Crow barrens in the Yukon Territories, but didn't catch up. I got back to camp soaked and shivering like a willow leaf in a wind, and tossed deadfall spruce onto the coals and stood naked in the heat of a six-foot blaze while my clothes dried.

Next afternoon maybe that many more crossed the same riffle, and they got away, too, but I wasn't fool enough to chase them across the river again. The caribou migrated out of the Brooks Range peaks to the northwest aimed at the rutting grounds hundreds of miles southeast in the Ogilvie Mountains in the Yukon Territories. The riffle downstream was shallow enough they used it year in and year out. Next afternoon I killed my caribou out of a herd of a dozen, all sky-scraping, big-antlered bulls. With the fat bull meat, the winey blueberries thick as gnats and sweet as cane and maybe fermented because I felt buzzed after a plate of them, or grayling I'd land on smoke-colored dry flies if I wanted dietary change, I wouldn't go hungry. The tundra grew edible mushrooms, and I could shoot the head off a ptarmigan if I craved fowl. Life couldn't get better.

So I'm sipping breakfast tea out of my lucky blue porcelain camp cup watching two fat caribou loin chops sizzle over the coals as Sol claws above the Old Crow barrens to the southeast, when it hits me.

You've got more than three weeks before pick-up! You're not one of those Abercrombie & Fitch cheechakos that fish eight hours a day, and even if you had a scattergun you'd shoot more ptarmigan than you could eat in a year, and you didn't buy a moose tag.

Now, leisure is perfect, but in moderation. Three weeks of enforced relaxation looked grim. I'd read my last book. Whittling wouldn't last long, either. I already talked to myself. ("It's OK to talk to yourself," my Circle City Gwitchin neighbor Neil Roberts said, "but you better worry if you answer yourself back.")

From the battered topo map, nothing was named along the Colleen River upstream of Strangle Woman Creek two days' trekking south. That meant no one had explored the geography. Any time man gets someplace, he names it, and he's vain enough to make sure it gets on the maps, too. A bush feast of caribou steaks, instant rice with mushrooms and caribou-blood gravy, blueberries and tea made for a grand wilderness evening. I dozed off to wolves telegraphing each other across the barrens.

That restlessness returned at breakfast, so I spread out the map remnant on the beach gravel and studied it. I had only the Colleen River drainage portion of the topo map, because I'd ripped off the west section with the next river drainage on it—the Sheenjek—to use for something important last season. Not too complicated, though, just aim upriver. I'd leave the map fragment behind after one last look. No map meant surprises—I grinned at the idea. I wouldn't wait for the dawn, either, so I shoved my camp into the pack, added caribou backstraps wrapped in cheesecloth, patted the Buck belt knife on my hip, grabbed the wallet of flies and the fly rod, shouldered the Model 700, and trekked north. I wasn't worried about grub—1983 was a bumper year for blueberries, grayling finned in every eddy and I flushed ptarmigan every other hour on the trail. Weather couldn't be better, either.

I must feel like the guys in the Lewis & Clark Expedition when they started out. Optimistic. Pumped. Except I'm trekking solo, and that makes it simpler. I don't notice the first miles through belt-tangle poplar scrub, across hip-deep muskegs, along gravel flood plains still blushing with wilting fireweed, over and under ice-out brush jams. I pass big-clawed grizzly and saucer-sized wolf tracks in the mud, caribou droppings and tracks, and moose scrapes and rubs. It's September. Willow and poplar leaves shimmer gold and start to drop, and the blueberry and low-bush cranberry leaves flame crimson. From time to time, I break into a wide grin, the kind everyone makes when they just feel too grand not to. I have no destination on any given day, so I camp on sandy river beaches, atop pingo frost heaves, or on glacial ridges called eskers. I never know what I'll find because I have no map.

When the sun hangs a finger above the southwest bluff, I find a mouldering cabin in a thick forest of dwarf spruce. The roof has collapsed and completely rotted away, 10-foot spruce trees grow from the floor, but the walls of the 10 by 15 foot cabin still stand. I worry a double-crossed Russian Orthodox icon from under the caribou moss and rotting timbers. Propped against the wall, it stands belt high. The place feels threatening in the gloaming, gray and black lichens climb the rotting log walls, and rusting utensils I kick from under the tundra carpet look older than anything I've seen. Maybe from the Hudson Bay days when Ft. Yukon more than a hundred miles south was a trapping hub—mid-1800s, maybe. I half-expect a grinning, moss-stained human skull.

I push on, out of the dank woods and into the belt-tangle scrub and across a big flood plain and jump cow moose feeding in wilting peavine, and to a sand beach back in the protected willows where I pitch the first camp while a boreal owl circles above the willow-wood campfire for reasons only he understands. Later I step out into the dusk and onto the beach, rifle handy. Mist rises from the silent river and a pale wolf gazes from the opposite bank, too innocent to have experience with man. It stares a moment, then vaporizes into the dwarf birch.

I scarf as many caribou steaks for breakfast as I can hold—*better to carry it in your belly than on your back*, I reason—and push on, north along the river, the cottonwoods becoming rare and turning to scrub, the black spruce infrequent and the trees seldom over 10-feet now, the country open and the foothills steepen. Bands of caribou migrate down the glacier eskers, always southeast. Fresh wolf and grizzly tracks meander along the river bank. Then one day the river forks and I follow the left branch toward what I hope is the Brooks Range divide, beyond which water drains north into the Arctic Ocean and where I'll eyeball the Arctic Coastal Plain on a clear day. The Porcupine Caribou Herd calve on the Plain in the spring, and the grizzlies, wolves, eagles, wolverines, foxes and other beasts beeline to the carnage to gorge on caribou veal.

I labor up over the tundra and tussocks with the pack when a pair of wolves join me a hundred yards across the ravine. They parallel me for miles, and stop when I rest, and continue when I do. I yip at them and they yip back. Maybe I'd been too long on the trail, but I swear one wags its tail.

Days later, I cross a ridge and descend into a protected valley, a waist-deep brook meandering through the timber, and beaver dams like beads slow the stream before it disappears beyond the shoulder of a bluff. The place feels like Utah with cottonwoods and willows again. I gnaw a cold caribou steak and downstream watch a rolly-polly mama grizzly grunt a cottonwood deadfall down the slope toward a wide beaver dam. Two yearling cubs follow. She shoves the log into the water and pounces on it, swats it with a haymaker I hear two hundred yards upstream, ducks underwater and then shoves the log under, and the cubs join the fun. I munch blueberries and watch for an hour and they're still at it when I climb out of what I name Camelot Valley and aim through the hip-deep dwarf birch scrub. I camp beside another brook and hook half a dozen grayling in the time it takes to cast to them and feast on willow-blackened fish.

I push on, northwest, upward, and the river becomes a creek. The country becomes barren of trees or brush except in stream bottoms. Caribou migrate in the distance, fewer now because the season is advanced, and very light wolves ghost after them. I spy maybe four grizzlies a day grazing the fermenting berries, and never a contrail or the drone of a bush plane. Whenever I cross through creek-bottom brush, I chamber-load the .270.

Maybe ten days after I'd started the trek—who's keeping track?—I angle up toward a ridge that should be the divide; beyond I'll see the Arctic Ocean Coastal Plain if I am right, and I've got my doubts, and if the air is clear enough, I'll ogle the Arctic Ocean beyond. At the ridge, though, I glass only more mountains rolling to the horizon. I angle farther to what I think is northwest, because I don't carry a compass, into a broad tundra basin, and up and beyond and climb another slope and far beyond, the late sun mirrors off the tiny headwaters of what should be the Sheenjek River, if I remember that section of the map I'd seen a year ago. I angle to what I think is due north because I want to see the Coastal Plain, and before sundown, I do, and in sea haze and distance I spot the Arctic Ocean. Maybe. Next day I aim southwest again toward what should be the headwaters of the Sheenjek River. Downslope, white spots people the rain-dark slate scree. Through the 10x binocular, they're Dall rams. Not a trophy among them, if you are an experienced ram hunter, but I'm not. My sheep hunting experience so far is one unsuccessful bighorn try. I don't have a tag, anyhow. I aim down to those headwaters and camp on a gravel beach and hook grayling for supper and glass distant mountain sheep on both sides of the headwaters.

The next day I'm trekking west again, then south into mysterious gray limestone gorges thick with half-billion-year-old marine fossils I can't begin to identify, and I scale nameless peaks. Nothing is named in this drainage upstream of Last Lake, the last lake north in the watershed. The last place you can land a float plane, they tell me back at the Gwitchin village of Circle on the Yukon River where I own a cabin.

I shove on, out of tea and rice, sugar and caribou, surviving now on blueberries and grayling, but I've never lived better. I see more rams, with only the odd ewe and lamb. The caribou have come and gone, their trails scouring the scree slopes and the tundra barrens. Snow dusts the peaks and ice lingers in the bogs and ponds. I shoot two ptarmigan with the .270 for supper, and eat bones and guts, too.

Then southeast now, crossing the Sheenjek many miles downriver. I carry the pack and rifle on my head as I lunge across the brisket-deep surging current, then build a quick driftwood fire on the other side to warm up and dry my clothes. I wander down to Last Lake, and wonder if it is big enough for a float plane, because I'm thinking a year ahead. *Getting in, no problem, but you'd struggle taking off with any kind of load*, I think. And then I climb east up a big canyon that aims toward those Colleen headwaters again. And I pass more rams. I know I'll come back.

Three days taking my time up the canyon east and over into the tundra hills of the Colleen drainage again and I spot something odd on a pingo in the distance, and detour to investigate. It's two rough-hewn, square-in-cross-section, belly-high posts with a carved cone on top. They'd been hewn with a stone axe, from what I can tell, and whoever did it spent some time. I kick something yellow-brown from under the tundra, and it's a lemming-chewed human femur. I snap photos, then angle into the upper Colleen drainage.

A day later I'm astonished and disappointed at a human more than a mile north standing on a bluff of Canadian Shield rock. He's the tallest thing on the tundra and stands out like a beacon. Nothing grows to give perspective, and the tallest plants are stunted willows no more than four inches tall. He's stocky and apparently he's studying me, too, because he isn't moving. I drop into a ravine and aim his way to get a better look with the binocular. When I belly to ridge line, he's still there, maybe a quarter mile off. Something's odd with this guy, but why worry? I've got a rifle, after all. I continue in his direction and he continues to stare. He doesn't seem to have a gun. I drop out of sight into a long ravine that should angle to within a few yards of him. I chamber-load the .270 in case. In case of what? I wasn't taught to meet strangers with a loaded gun, but there's something strange here. *You've been in the bush too long, Chum,* I tell myself. I climb out of the ravine and I'm face-to-face with the guy, a rock human effigy the Inuit built to haze caribou in the direction of a waiting hunter. My blood pressure returns to normal and I kick about the tundra and find a mouldering harpoon point carved of bone or antler, perhaps used to hunt caribou, and rock circles used to anchor caribou hide tents in wind. I want more than anything to take the harpoon point with me, but it's illegal.

A day downriver I discover a fossil mammoth tusk poking from the river bank. I can't free it, and couldn't tote it downriver anyhow. By now it's on the bottom of the river where it has fallen after the erosion did its work, buried again.

I trek downriver, through the wolves and bears and the winey smell of overripe blueberries, living on dried mushrooms and grayling, making anyhow ten tough miles on a good day through muskegs and tussocks and across sloughs. I'm pushing my time limit—I've lost track of it—but I hope I've a day or three before Joe's pickup flight. I'm a lean guy anyway, but with weeks of fish-and-berry diet, I punch another hole in my belt. That afternoon I kill three ptarmigan with one .270 slug; they line themselves up down the caribou trail, one behind the other and another behind that, and I touch off. The 130 grain Core-lokt spoils meat, but I eat all but feathers, heads and feet. I dream that night of big ram horns and a fat hamburger, with tomato, onions, pickles, and a plate of greasy, heart attack french fries.

Joe's '185 roars over the beach willows two days later, swings to face into the upstream wind and clatters onto the rock beach and taxis up in front of camp. In minutes I stuff the gear into the pack and haul the two remaining caribou quarters to the Cessna. "Sorry I'm a day light," he says. I hadn't realized it.

"You'll need a Ft. Yukon beer to keep those britches on yer hips," Joe says by way of greeting. "Mebbee two. Let's call this place Hungry Camp. Look good on maps."

The Cessna clatters over the rocks and leaps into the air when it seems we're already out of beach, and then we're winging south toward Ft. Yukon over endless tundra and black spruce.

"Every been to Last Lake?" I holler over the engine noise. Joe nods negative. "Wanna go?"

"You buy, I'll fly."

THE LONGEST SHEEP HUNT
PART III: PURSUIT

This fixation dates back to my very first bighorn sheep hunt in the geography just north of Yellowstone back in the early '80s, and it started in June with scouting and didn't end until November without a ram, all of this solo and out of a backpack or off a packhorse. I ogled legal rams, but I'd obsessed on a broomed grandfather ram, so I didn't shoot.

Then I'd trekked solo through the Arctic wilderness of the upper Colleen and Sheenjek River drainages in the most remote geography on the continent for a month, just wandering but with an eye to finding my very own sheep pasture. I didn't see another human. I bagged a grand caribou that season, lived off bull steaks, blueberries, grayling and ptarmigan, and never lived better. I located plenty of sheep, too. This before cell phones, GPS and eternal connectivity, and I carried no radio. Talk about the days of wine and roses.

"Catch this," Joe Firmin hollered and tossed me the mooring line to the '206 float plane. I double wrapped it around spruce shin-tangle on the bank and he hopped ashore. He eyed my backpack and midget inflatable raft. "You floatin' to Ft. Yukon in thet!? Solo? An' no radio? Mebbe six weeks an' three hunert river miles, an' b'fore ice-up?" He shook his head and hopped back onto the pontoon, then said, "Your ma raise any more fool children?" then climbed into the cockpit. I shoved him off, he thumbs-upped through the Plexiglas and fired the engine.

In minutes he'd taxied the Cessna to the far end of Last Lake and shoved full throttle, aimed right at me. I stood my ground at the opposite end of the tiny lake and he roared over at ten feet elevation, the tie-line streaming lake water all over my gear.

"He did that on purpose," I said to no one, then, "Talkin' to yerself already. Tsk, tsk," and shook my head.

I grinned and feigned grabbing for the rifle when he aimed back at me so low I ducked, and then he disappeared downriver, south. I felt that familiar catch in the throat with the sudden understanding that I was stranded alone in the Pleistocene again with the nearest pavement hundreds of miles south. The difference was, I had to get myself out this time. No pick-up flight. I had no time frame because I planned to hunt until I bagged a ram, so no one expected me. Heck, no one even knew I was here except Joe.

"Git to it," I told myself, and wondered if once I got used to solitude again, I'd quit this dialogue with myself. "OK, OK," my alter ego answered.

I shouldered the pack and trekked toward the river a mile across tussock bogs, then returned for the inflatable boat, then for the 30 gallon steel drums I'd store the gear and inflatable in to keep them safe from grizzlies, maybe. I inflated the boat and ferried everything across the Sheenjek River, deflated the boat and shoved gear into the barrels, fastened lids, and aimed up a big nameless canyon westerly on my second sheep hunt. I grinned big at that osprey winging upriver.

I slog the tussocks up the mile-broad, U-shaped glacial valley I'd trekked the season before, wondering if I'll acclimate to the 70-lb. backpack, 10-lb. Model 700, and bric-a-brac dangling from my neck and pack.

"You better hope for no grizz, 'cause you aint movin' quick in this getup," I say to myself. "It's too early to talk to yourself," I tell me, just to keep the dialogue going.

The season before while searching for my very own wild sheep pasture, I'd ogled perhaps the most northerly sheep on the planet, but no real trophy. This time, I loosely plan to trek a big loop, hit the divide to the next drainage west paralleling the Sheenjek, then trek south all the way to the southerly edge of the Brooks Range, then east down Old Woman's Creek back to the Sheenjek River, then north along the river back to my cache. When I make the cache upriver, I'll float downriver in the eight-foot raft hundreds of river miles to Ft. Yukon and its fly-in-only civilization. *Screw-up, and you freeze in the coldest winter on the planet*, I realize. I must get out before ice-up and that might mean late-September. Then I'll charter a flight back to my cabin up the Yukon River at Circle and cut the winter's firewood.

Summer means mosquito season, and they seethe over light trekking britches turning them pale gray, they're that thick. It's no trick to inhale a mouthful of arthropod protein if I'm careless. I wear long britches, parka, gloves and a stocking cap, and slather Cutter's on anything left bare.

I doze in the nighttime twilight—it doesn't get dark this far north in August—to the whining and pinging. They're gone with the morning frost.

Then it's into a gorge thick with half-billion-year-old marine fossils I couldn't identify last season, but I'd studied up over the year. Here's a six-inch snail—a gastropod; a bivalve clam the size of a grapefruit; and an asconoid sponge maybe 600 million years old, from the beginning of the Cambrian Explosion. I still can't identify most of the strange marine fossils, but I make sketches in my journal. Then it's westerly again, and I glass small rams with a few ewes and lambs for good measure. Bull caribou skyline windy sawtooth ridges to escape bot and warble flies. Blueberries are scarce this high, but I munch tart handfuls when I find them.

"Keeps off the scurvy, "I joke at myself. "Glass for those rams," my serious alter ego scolds.

A squall swirls over the divide from the Arctic Ocean and I hole up in the 3-lb. tent and read paperbacks I avoid at home—Pushkin, Donne, and *War and Peace*. Honest. I doze and listen to ice pellets drumming tent fabric, talk to my alter ego, and write in the journal. I'm content enough, because I'm in no hurry, though when the snow and rain continue into the third day, I get antsy. Then the weather breaks and I trek west, then south. The first day out I spot maybe 40 sheep, but no trophy rams. I see another grizzly, and then another scavenging a caribou carcass. The caribou hug the windy skyline but when the bot or warble flies find them, they sprint in their panic down the blade-sharp scree and injure feet and legs, and wolves and bears score the cripples. Grizzlies are common enough, too, so I chamber-load the Remington when I trail through willow brush in the creek bottoms. "No use takin' chances," I tell me.

Two more days trekking south, and I find a band of full-curl rams, the best I've seen, but they're skimpy in heft, so I trek on and glass nine wolves file down the drainage. Two are pale as a palomino and one is black. I glass moose in the high basins to escape the flies and mosquitos, too, and once a wolverine. It sometimes freezes at night, and the wildflowers are wilting.

In the next nameless drainage south, something tells me this is the place, so I skid the talus down onto a flat bench with a spring gurgling from the scree and blueberries and cranberries growing in profusion. "Sheep Valhalla," I joke at myself, and pitch the tent.

I fill plastic jugs with spring water and pack in willow deadfall firewood. Thrice bull caribou cavort through camp in astonishment, a curious red fox circles the tent, and a grizzly chews a shed moose antler downstream. None of them have scented or seen a human before. The place feels plenty lucky. The sun's out, and my duds could stand by themselves, so I scrub them in the creek. The camp resembles an explosion in a skid-row laundry with the clothes spread on dwarf birch to dry.

Very early next morning—remember it doesn't get dark yet this far north—I shoulder the .270 and wander up the nameless drainage. I find only young rams, so I aim over a blade-ridge to another creek, then still-hunt down in the direction of another nameless stream that dumps into the drainage near camp. I glass sheep, too, and a grizzly and a wolf and hundreds of scattered caribou, and a cow and calf moose. All hug the high basins and ridges because the ravenous mosquito and fly hordes would suck them dry in the river bottoms. As I wander into the camp maybe 15 hours later, in the perpetual night-time twilight and I carry no timepiece, it occurs to me that I haven't seen a real trophy though I've glassed plenty of rams.

"What about that?" I ask myself. I'm still carrying on a dialogue with my alter ego. "If you're gonna score a ram, you may have to settle," I answer myself.

A few grayling fought the riffles up the nameless creek from the Sheenjek River far below, and I score three with the tiny fly rod for supper, and after a dish of Uncle Ben's instant rice, chocolate pudding with blueberries, and tea, I doze, then scale the ram scree again. "A guy could hunt 24 hours a day, 'cause it never gets dark," I say to myself. My alter ego grunts assent.

At mid-day, I guess at it from the angle of the sun, I hunker in Sol's heat on the spongy tundra, scarf two granola bars and nap. Later, I ridge-hop and glass sheep, but no trophy, then swing east and north toward the camp and I'm an hour out when I ogle two rams cross-canyon in the verdant tundra. I study them through the 10x binocular. One is bigger than any I've seen, but not as large as I want.

"You've been bush-whackin' two weeks, and he's the best you've spotted, Pal," I tell myself, and then wait for a retort but I don't have one. Instead, I watch the rams. Maybe an hour later, I say to myself, "Let's get closer."

I duckwalk and belly over the bluff, skid the scree into the creek bottom, and ease downstream out of their line of sight, then climb the tundra slope where the rams are bedded and sidehill toward them. I take my time. I'm ambivalent about bagging one. When I belly across a scree saddle, they're 50 yards below. I glass, think, glass more. I use another hour doing that, because they haven't a clue I'm in their bedroom. A sow grizzly and yearling cub wander downstream two-hundred yards below.

Yup, the ram's bigger than anything you've seen so far, I think. He won't make a ripple in any record book, that's sure. Those horns haven't much heft. I've been out weeks and he's the best I've seen, no question. He's got a full curl. *Ram chops beat grilled grayling any day. Those horns would look grand in your Yukon River cabin, too.* I'm talking myself into it. *Put the fur on the ground, and you can trek to the river and take your time floating out to Ft. Yukon. Just fish, float, shoot ptarmigan and camp. A holiday.*

I put the crosshairs behind the larger ram's shoulder and press the trigger. The rest is anticlimax—he drops, skids four yards and that's it. Maybe 36-37-inches, I note when I walk up, and then the alter ego chimes, "You did it, and about time, too!" I quarter the ram, excise the backstraps and pile meat on the spongy tundra then shove the loin strips into my pockets. I'll pack out the meat next day.

Late next morning, I climb from camp and leave the Remington because I don't need extra weight packing meat. Another fool cheechako move. When I gaze across the ravine, the ram quarters and head are downslope in the creek covered with mud. I know what happened, alright, but I'm not leaving the head, even if the rifle is in camp and I've got to wrestle the grizzly to get it. I skid downslope, grab what's left of the head, note the muddy long-clawed grizz tracks, sprint up the slope but have second thoughts and skid back down and grasp a chewed hind quarter and a chunk of haunch and sling them over my shoulder and get the hell out. I don't breathe normal until I'm within arm's reach of the .270.

EPILOGUE

I lounge around the lucky sheep camp and gorge on exquisite ram steaks, read, nap and enjoy the unusual sunny weather. Caribou migrate southeast toward the Ogilvies in the Yukon Territories and I see scores a day, mostly bulls. I spot the odd moose, and on a hike a cow with calf flattens ears, growls and charges with deadly intent and only my banshee screaming and arm-windmilling make her veer off. I've learned my lesson, again, and the Remington becomes a permanent companion. Wolves wander into camp and once steal a leftover broiled hunk of sheep haunch. That fox becomes daily company, too. Grizzlies keep their distance, lucky enough. White sheep people the browning tundra slopes up-canyon. When I finish off the ram meat, I shoulder the pack and aim downstream, camp late that night at its confluence with the Sheenjek River, and next day trek maybe 13 hours upriver to the cache, camp again, then float out.

I'm taking my time floating downstream, because the weather holds though the leaves have dropped. I fly-fish for grayling as I float, keeping only enough for supper, and score as many ptarmigan as I can eat. Caribou ford the river, and three times bull moose browse along the shore, and they're rutty, too. Twice I grunt-call bulls into swimming to the boat, for fun, and the last one is so reluctant to leave I shoot into the water to make him change his mind. Spruce tree "sweepers"—trees whose roots have been undermined and fallen onto the surface of the river and can scuttle a boat—line the banks in the slower river downstream, and only vigorous oar work avoids them. Ice lingers in the quiet water, and I wear all my clothes as I float. From time to time, grizzlies wander the banks, but they're no trouble. Then one day the Sheenjek spits me into the larger Porcupine River, where I camp, and late the next day I paddle into the slough behind Ft. Yukon at its confluence with the Yukon River.

Author's Note: If this sounds familiar, you've seen a very condensed version of the story earlier in the book. Apologies.

Author's Note: A very condensed version of this expedition appeared in an earlier story published in another magazine.

A Mongolian Jaunt

When it was wet, we bore the wet together,
When it was cold, we bore the cold together.

Genghis Khan

PROLOGUE

Sometimes you get what you wish for, I thought as the Nissan jolted the last hundred kilometers of Gobi Desert, aimed at the capital Ulaanbaatar. I'd fantasized Mongolia and the Gobi since I was a kid and first read Roy Chapman Andrews' *Ends of the Earth.* I still remember that quote: "Gobi! All this thrilled me to the core."

But December's argali expedition did not thrill me to the core, because we didn't hunt argali, for reasons that remain murky. Instead, we fingered-and-toed isolated Gobi peaks in 20-below temps and maelstroms that would pluck a lammergeier. And we scored a grand Gobi ibex, too. But when you journey half way around the planet for argali sheep, and fail, everything else is mere consolation. I couldn't fully appreciate the Mongol nomad hospitality in any ger we happened upon because of that argali preoccupation, either. Nor did I enjoy sipping fermented mare's milk and listening to Mongol throat-singing warmed beside a dung-fire as gales shrieked outside the ger felt, or gnawing camel haunch on a Gobi scarp.

"You must return in the spring," outfitter Baasanhu Jantzen said. "For the argali." We agreed on price, but I doubted I'd come back.

*****

Cheri and I return the following May, five months later. It's tough to give up a fantasy. Baasanhu, guide and driver Zorig (rural Mongols normally own only one name) and Zorig's wife, cook and woman-Friday Erdensetsag (Erka for short) collect us at the airport. All five of us sardine into a Russian Uaz jeep already crammed with weeks' of gear and grub. We aim south into the Gobi, and within 30 minutes leave the last pavement behind. That workhorse of Asia, the Russian Uaz jeep, becomes our Conestoga on a roadless and often trackless ramble through eight provinces, four ecosystems and 3000 kilometers of Mongolian wilds.

We make the first camp in the Hangay Range after a day clattering over washboard dirt trails. I envy Zorig's kidney belt. Luya welcomes us to his gers; he'd guided us to the Gobi ibex last December. Before long, Erka shoves into Cheri and my ger with steaming mutton cooked on a sheep dung-fired stove. I'm so jet-lagged I doze over the soup. The next day we finally score that argali ("Jet Lag Argali," *Sports Afield*, Dec. 2007). I unwind for the first time in five months. The pressure is off. With the argali ram in the salt, I no longer own a care. If I bag another trophy, fine, if not, also fine.

Two dawns later we jeep cross-country southwest and lunch at Orog Lake, a verdant oasis amid dusty gravel dunes as far as we see. White gers dot the emerald grasses like vanilla ice cream scoops. Hundreds of goats, sheep, horses and camels graze the shores. Then the Uaz probes south toward the east Gov' Altaj until we find a rocky nomad trail through it, and then drop onto another of the Gobi's endless arid gravel plains. Four-inch dust devils swirl inside the jeep as we clatter cross-country. Half-an-inch of gray dust covers everyone except for our ghost-white eye sockets when we remove sunglasses to blow off the dirt. Our next target on this argosy is Altai ibex, two days' cross-country battering southwest.

Zorig and Baasan believe we're aimed right. In the afternoon we stop for directions at a ger in a trailless canyon still clogged with winter overflow ice. I don't care if we're lost; after all, I've scored that argali, and grin each time I think about it. The nomad's wife serves cold horse knuckle, odd bread fried over the ubiquitous dung-fired stove, and salt tea. The nomad points us in the right direction. No roadmaps or road signs exist, because no roads exist. A good sense of direction and a map drawn in sand with a finger gets you where you want to get. The trail leads into the Edren scarps. Zorig is certain big ibex wander the cliffs to the south because no one has hunted there. As we descend a bluffed canyon into the setting sun, we eye a village far out on the gravel plain.

"We sleep there tonight," Baasan says. Erka grins. Zorig motors to a tumbledown USAID adobe midwifery. "Here, the nomads have babies." Before the gear is unloaded, Erka shoves into Cheri's and my room with a steaming dinner cooked on a Coleman in their room. The building has no toilets, so we are pointed to a village outhouse. It's overflowing, so like everyone else in the place, we use an alley. We're told two nomads died of bubonic plague last summer. We're happy to flee the midwifery next dawn, and I fervently hope its voracious bedbugs weren't plague-toting fleas.

We spot foxes and consider stalking distant gazelle that day, then jolt down another rocky canyon and out onto another gravel plain. A long mountain reclines in the distance.

"Eej Khairkhan," Zorig tells us. I ask the meaning but he feigns ignorance. Khairkhan has a sense of the sacred to it, and it's used to avoid a real name, because the gods anger if anyone speaks their names.

"The Sacred Mountain," Baasan adds. "Women pilgrimage and circle the mountain to get pregnant."

We leave the dirt track at Eej Khairkhan and motor cross-country toward distant mountains, drive into another canyon and across over-flow ice that if it collapses would plummet us eight-feet to the creek bed beneath. Through the Red Gods' favor, we survive the ice and lunch with another nomad family. I'm amazed at the hospitality, and though poor as Gobi gravel, they give us what they have without any expectations of payment. It's the Mongol way. Zorig talks with them at length, and apparently they'd earlier agreed upon something. We're off into the afternoon, and the jeep grinds up-canyon and three hours later onto a high plateau with 15-foot snow drifts on the leeward side of the 11,000-foot cols of the south Altai Range.

Zorig audibly sighs when he sees two white gers hunkering between distant snowfields. Apparently, those nomads had erected the gers for us. We stow gear, and Erka serves another hot dinner at short notice. Cheri and I share a ger, and the gang get the other one. We scope ibex in the evening, and in the sand-hazy distance gaze into China.

Great 60-inch argali and ancient ibex skulls litter the high plateau. "Dzug," Zorig explains. A brutal winter exterminated the argali. Pleistocene ibex still wander this isolated geography, though. Since the argali perished, no one hunts ibex here.

We find bands of grand ibex in a gorge the following morning, scope them and plot. Two or three might tape 43-inches.

"There!" Cheri says. "Standing in the sun." As she often does, she's found King Kong. It might measure 45-inches. The billy doesn't move for an hour while other ibex feed about him, and then it beds down. "He's old."

We watch the ibex another hour, and three hours later we're edging down on them. We've got too many ibex eyes to account for, and some of them spot us and sprint toward Inner Mongolia. Others ogle us, too. We stalk onto Methuselah trying to avoid a young stud that wants to battle his way up in the hierarchy. King Kong is ancient, and through binocs we spot its hips and ribs shadowing through the bleached winter coat. The old ibex leaves the billy band and limps toward where we hunker in the rocks 600 yards away. We duck-walk into a ravine, and snake across it and onto a blade-ridge. Then we hands-and-knee to further lessen the distance. Stalking as close as possible, and then some, pumps my adrenaline like nothing else. Blasting a beast at half a mile lowers hunting to mere technology. But we can get no closer.

"Two-hundred-ninety meters," Zorig says. He's got a range-finder. Where I grew up, a 300-yard shot was a long one and you didn't take them if you could get closer. We can't get closer, so I prop the pack across a boulder, hold the .300 magnum's crosshairs below back line, and the ibex drops without a twitch. Zorig tapes the horns in camp—45-inches, but more important, it owns 14 annular horn rings. It has only four teeth in its head, and it would not survive another winter. I like to get them like that.

We take a day off from the Uaz's cross-country battering. Cheri and I hike and photograph, Erka fleshes hides and boils skulls, and Zorig and Baasan tinker with the Uaz and other gear. A day to unwind after bagging a grand trophy, be it in Mongolia or Tanzania, suits me.

We sandwich into the jeep again the next dawn and descend a gorge pointed north. Over-flow ice, that is water that forced itself onto the solidly frozen stream the winter before and itself froze, blocks a fork of the canyon. I sigh in relief as we take another fork, because we can't be lucky enough to survive two over-ice drives without mishap. We break out of the canyons between bouldered outcrops pimpling a plain. We scale the outcrops and glass for black-tailed goitered gazelle. Hard-freezing nights at 11,000 feet have become 80-degree heat in five hours. We motor off the rocks and into the dust whirl-winds and heat mirages north again. We're running low on gas, and we must make Tsogt, a tiny west Gobi village, before we run out. At that, we're not sure we can buy gas there.

The Uaz climbs another rocky range, descends, and the village dances far out in the heat mirages. In the village, Zorig goes door-to-door before he finds someone that can operate the manual Robinson Crusoe-affair pump.

We get on our way again into the west Gobi dust. We overnight with another nomad on the plain at a bog. I hope the ravenous mos-quitoes don't carry malaria. Baasan trades ibex blood he collected from my ibex for camel milk chilled in a spring. Cold tastes good, but it can't touch the snow-bank chilled Chinese wine at the Altai camp.

We're off again, north toward the city of Altay. Though it's a sizable town, air or dirt road is the only access. Late that afternoon we spot gazelle so far out in the heat mirages we're not sure they're real. We finally decide they are, and we slip out of the Uaz and hide in a gully, while Zorig drives the track toward Altay to give the gazelle something else to think about. The distant gazelle drift our way until an hour later they graze within range. They spot us squatting in the shallow gully and sprint straight away. A .300 slug up the stern drops the grand gazelle in its track. I hadn't planned on one, so it's another bonus, and the best meat we'll eat.

Then it's back in the Uaz and we reach Altay city long after dark. We'll stay in a hotel, and we look forward to the luxury. We shouldn't have, because the shower doesn't work, the electricity is spotty, the sheets could stand by themselves, and rooms reek of urine, sweat and tobacco. We're scheduled to fly to Ulaanbaatar the next day, but Mongolian Air schedules are flexible at best and often non-existent. The plane does not show the next day, or the one after, nor the one after that. No one knows when a plane will appear. We want out of the filthy hotel, so we look into driving, which should take three days minimum to Ulaan. Zorig feels ill and will stay in Altay with his Uaz, so Baasan books us a "bus," a Uaz van. Cheri and I have used them throughout Asia from Azerbaijan to the Russian Far East, and we're keen on it. We climb aboard but we stop at every block and pick up more and more Mongols aiming for the big city until we have maybe twenty bodies crammed into the van. Now, I'm not spoiled, and I've endured all sorts of trials. I could suffer it a day, but not three. I raise hell, yank my gear off, and tell Baasanhu to rent us a jeep. He's of the same mind. We raise a minor ruckus, a cop shows up, and Erka stops Baasan from slugging him. The cop vaporizes when he learns we're American; he does not want an international incident. To make a very long story shorter, Zorig lends us his Uaz, we find a driver that will return the Uaz to Altay, and we jolt toward Ulaanbaatar.

A day and a half of dirt roads and eateries so tiny and primitive five of us absorb all seats, and hotels I blow the electricity out of by flicking on a tiny water heater later, Baasan says, "We've still got days. You want to shoot roebuck, or catch taimen?" Part of me looks forward to showering off embedded Gobi grit and sleeping in beds with sheets sans bedbugs in Ulaanbaatar, but I've got to deal with that other part, too.

"Let's go for roebuck," I say. Cheri glares because it all happens so quick, but then she grins at the prospect of more fun, and the next dawn we turn off the dirt road to Ulaan and aim north toward Siberia. We collect a local guide, and then motor into pine-and-birch forested valleys, and May-green wheat fields and mud-greasy roads. It's impossible to grasp that only a few hundred miles south gravel wastes stretch as far as you see.

We bivouac at a house in a farming village called "Happy Valley." The house is cramped, but the people are hospitable like all but city Mongols, and I'm developing a fondness for goat and mutton. We spot four does in two days; we should have gone fishing. Erka, Baasan, Cheri and I figure to hunt one more day, then motor for Ulaanbaatar in the evening if we don't score a roebuck. We find nothing that morning, return to the village for lunch, then drive into a more remote part of the valley. The geography looks just like mule deer country in Utah or Montana.

We're weary of weeks of living together in cramped settings over 3000 kilometers of dirt track. Cheri opts to wait in the Uaz while we hunt. The local guide walks off alone. I stalk in the opposite direction. Baasan and the roe deer expert glass from a ridge. I climb to the opposite side for the solitude, a quality we've had little of in past weeks. The sun drops and I binoc squawking and courting flocks of black grouse up the canyon. I'm content to sit a mile from the nearest human.

As the light goes, first one, then another, and another roe deer mist out of brush. Most lick exposed clay ledges, and all lack antlers. No one is keen on my bagging game at this point, because we'd have to skin, salt and butcher, which means we wouldn't leave for the big city until the following day. I'm not hot to bag a buck either, but I'm reveling in the breeze and the canyon that looks precisely like a place I've bagged mule deer bucks in Utah.

Heck, if this were Magpie Canyon, Utah in October, a mule deer buck would walk out of that thicket 300 yards up-canyon, I more than half believe. I glance at a doe across the draw as the light fades and the last sun burnishes the ridge. When I look back at that spot, a roebuck steps into the open. Sheesh, I tell myself. I don't really want to shoot it. I glass the buck forty minutes in lingering dusk, and each time I look, the antlers get better. It owns all three points on each side, a wide-spread, and the beams stretch on forever. I'm now watching the buck through the riflescope, but can't decide. Everyone wants to get back to Ulaan tonight, but those antlers. The crosshairs steady on the shoulder, and I touch the trigger. When the local guide shows up half an hour later, he's ecstatic, because his payment is the meat. I'm pretty happy, too.

We make Ulaanbaatar the next day, ending the second of two expeditions with a 3000-kilometer cross-country argosy through the best game ranges of Mongolia. Ending, too, with five grand trophies. But it's not only horns. It's fermented mare's milk, dung-fired stoves, an-inch of Gobi grit in your ears, and Zorig snoring in the next ger.

To quote Andrews again, "All this thrilled me to the core."

BLACK CATS, BROKEN
MIRRORS AND SIXES

I intentionally walk under the ladder over the sidewalk in front of the Japanese restaurant. Sam goes out of his way to walk around it.

Once inside, Sam says, "It's not that I'm superstitious. Hell, I'm an academic and biologist, after all. But why take the chance?"

Sure, I think and sip my Kirin beer and ponder the menu. He knows I'm not buying it. I make it a point to walk under all ladders, maybe to prove something to myself. I don't mention that it makes the skin on the back of my neck crawl, perhaps because the act may offend the Fates and awaken spirits that live within the inverted triangle, but no one could call me superstitious. Certainly not. I smirk at Sam's caveat and bask in my questionable objective superiority.

It snuck up on me. Things like this usually do. I honestly can't say when it started. No doubt decades ago, perhaps in my adolescent shooting days. I remember once crossing my fingers at a shooting competition.

Even in later years, I wasn't aware of it. Back then, I annually charter a bush flight into the remote Arctic, and Roger Dowding's Cessna 185 lands on a remote river bar and spits me and gear onto the gravel, then roars off into the southern leaden skies. The routine: I inflate the raft, load duffel into the boat, and shove into the current. Most of a day later, I row into a nameless creek mouth, off-load gear and store it and the deflated boat in 30-gallon steel drums I'd cached in earlier years against grizzlies, hoist the 70 lb. backpack and rifle and aim up a nameless drainage into the sheep peaks. I camp in the crags until I score a ram, then trek back to the cache and float down-river for another month hunting caribou, moose and ptarmigan and hooking grayling on tiny, smoke-colored flies. Most years I see no other human. Elysium.

I score my first Dall's ram two seasons earlier. In no hurry to return to the river and begin the second phase of the expedition back to civilization, I linger in the peaks, gorging on ram chops so I won't have to pack them out, hiking and photographing. One fair morn, while attempting to shave with a scalpel-sharp Buck belt knife, a backpacking mirror slips from my fingers and shatters into at least 13 pieces. While fleshing the cape later that afternoon, I lacerate my thumb with the belt knife. I don't see a link.

Another rare sunny morning and another year, with horns and meat already in camp, I climb into a basin and note white spots against the emerald tundra a mile away and stalk them, for fun. I close, ease around bungalow-sized glacial erratics and come face to face with three rams. One owns the horns of ram hunter's fantasy. Forty-six inches. Fifteen-inch bases. One horn is broken back six-inches, but who cares? While I'm a neophyte ram hunter with only a pair of rams to my credit, any fool knows this is King Kong. I barely note that one of the other two rams owns an unusually wide spread. Alas, my ram is in the salt, so of course I can't shoot. But through the next year, King Kong peoples my day and night dreams.

Same drill next season, but my objective is focused—the magnum broken-horned ram. I hunt four days and pass up decent rams without ogling King Kong, before bad luck and the weather closes. This far north of the Arctic Circle, it won't lift until next June, eight months away. I must put a ram in the salt and sprint down to the river and speed out to Ft. Yukon two hundred river miles away before the river freezes and I'm stranded. This in those glorious days before cell phones, and I carry no two-way radio, and I intend to float all the way to Ft. Yukon so can't expect help from a bush pilot rendez-vous and search if I don't show up. No one expects me, either.

Remember that old, wide-spread ram that hung out with King Kong? I bag that 11-year-old ram with a 31-inch tip-to-tip spread two days later, on day six, bone the meat, break camp and aim down to the river. I wet my feet in the river a day later and shove into the current, the mush ice congealing in the quiet water along shore. Ten days later, I bust and paddle my way up the frozen slough behind Ft. Yukon. I don't breathe easy until the '185 banks onto the gravel strip at Circle up the Yukon River and I finally kindle a fire in my cabin.

Same drill next season, only this year Cheri accompanies me. After the float downstream, and the trek to my now familiar camp site in the ram crags, we hunt King Kong five days with no luck. By then, I've more or less given up on the old boy. The geriatric ram has almost certainly died in his dotage—he'd be 15-years old—perhaps in a slide off an icy ledge in the brutal Arctic winter or from the wolves we see every day. On the sixth day, I score a magnum 39-inch ram with a luxurious cape, and the following day we pack the meat into camp, bone it, and the day after aim down-canyon toward the cache on the river to begin a leisurely float downstream.

When we drop below timberline, a black lynx steps out of the spruce timber onto the caribou trail, stares a moment from 15 yards, then crosses the path. I've seen only three live, wild lynx in all my years in the Far North bush, so they are rare, but I've never heard of a black melanistic lynx, ever. Even the old trappers had never seen one. Later that day a shoelace on one boot catches a lace hook on the other and I pitch on my face. Cheri guffaws when she learns nothing is injured but my ego. I don't see any connection here, either, but it occurs to me that both Napoleon and Hitler owned an inordinate fear of black cats.

We make the river cache in the evening, inflate the raft and shove into the current next day to hunt caribou, moose and ptarmigan. We take six weeks to float the meat-laden inflatable into Ft. Yukon, and except for two or three snow flurries, the weather holds, in spite of the black cat stepping across the trail.

Next season, I'm in the Arctic sheep crags, solo again. I'm still hoping against hope to find King Kong, enough to pass up a handful of decent rams in the first days of the hunt. Since Cheri and two friends will fly onto the river below, I must hurry to rendezvous with them. On the fourth and fifth days, I ogle no rams at all. I must meet the gang below, but I'm not leaving without a ram. I hunt hard the sixth day, and as I slog a shale basin and ease around a bend in late afternoon, there he is! I'm not about to get picky at this point, and the ram faces away and all sheep horns look big from behind, but I guess that he bests any ram I've bagged. I ease back around the bend and out of sight, scale the black musical shale rock as quietly as humanly possible, then snake across the crest. The ram beds at less than a hundred yards quartering away, and another ram nearly as good beds just above. One shot from the 7mm/08 behind the shoulder, and the big ram lunges to his feet, staggers three steps and collapses. As luck would have it, it's the biggest ram I've bagged to date, and for those into the stats, the lemon-colored horns own 11 annular rings and tape a shake over 40-inches with 15-inch bases.

That same season, I put a fine Stone's sheep in the salt in the Folding Mountain geography above the Toad River in British Columbia. We start out with bad luck—ours is the first hunt of the season, and the green horses without saddle in ten months accept no human discipline without severe protest. We throw every nag in our string to get a saddle on it, one catapults my duffle into the creek, and I stand clear of the rodeo and let the wranglers and guides fight the nags. Once on the trail one horse skids in the muck all the way to the creek bottom. Later, my saddle nag throws me when I'm not paying attention. Good luck—I land in the shin-tangle that cushions the sudden stop. Still, I'm mad enough, mostly at my stupidity, to use a Louisville slugger on the beast. Guide Ralph Kitchen saves me the trouble with a green spruce limb nearly as big. We spend most of six days weathered in the leaky tent with a foul Labrador dog, but on the fifth day the clouds unravel themselves on the crags and we see sun for the first time.

On the sixth day, I score the chestnut-horned, very dark pelage, full curl ram with one long shot. By that time, it finally registers that I'd bagged four rams in a row on the sixth day of the hunt. Still, I'm the practical biologist and college professor, so I chalk it up it to coincidence. The fact that I think about it at all, though, makes me wonder.

Lest we assume this tome is about Dall's sheep, there's that small handful of leopards. Of course the first is always most important, and this one is. I'd made the safari mainly for a Spots trophy. We spread baits over half of Zimbabwe—a scrawny goat bought from a local n'dbele, haunches of sable and kudu I bagged, an impala. Then we hunker in grass blinds where we see tracks—first in this one, then in another and then in a third, a fourth and a fifth. Once PH Russell Tarr and I doze in a blind in the Zim dark, while Cheri clasps our wrists so she can yank if we snore, when all of us nearly missile through the blind covering. A leopard with a sense of humor stalks just behind the blind and roars from five yards. On day six, without luck so far, we aim south to the Bubye River, and to shorten a long story, build a hurried blind—the sixth of the hunt, by the way—and finally score a 7-foot one-inch cat on a culled impala that same day.

Then there was that Spots on a topi bait along the Msima River in Tanzania. We had cats feeding on two baits, but we'd climb into the one where a leopard with big feet visited each night. To stay legal, and with a government game scout along just in case we considered otherwise, we had to shoot in daylight. The tom only comes in the dark. We visit the bait each day, peel back the meat dried to biltong by the equatorial sun, with hopes the cat will feed more easily and becomes so comfortable with the predictable grub supply that he sneaks in early. Three hours before dark each day we climb into the blind built of acacia woven with long grasses and endure fiery tsetse bites. For five days we exit the blind in the sudden dark of an equatorial night and eat a silent supper watching the Bohor reedbuck and hippos in the Msima marsh by camp in the lantern light.

The cat slipped on day six. He came just before dark. The sun had set, and on the equator that means darkness in minutes. Cheri is the only one awake and she elbows PH Larry Richards and me in the ribs when she hears the crunch and slurp of a feeding leopard. The .375 already rests on the portal woven into the grass blind lined up on the bait, and it takes a moment to slip onto the stock and slide the safety and squeeze the trigger, and that is that.

In other years, I score two Cape buffalo, several very big mule deer, a Gobi ibex, my largest Wyoming public lands pronghorn, a

58-inch East African kudu, and other trophy animals, all on day six of the hunt. Biologist and academic be damned, I could no longer ignore it. "Six" is significant.

It seems my gradual decades-long acceptance of my superstition wasn't solely limited to the number "6." Cheri began to look for a small rock that somehow reminded her of the next animal we hunted for. I dutifully put it in my pocket as per her orders, and went on with the hunt without paying much attention. At the end of the successful hunt, she collects the "bull" or "ram" rock and puts it on a windowsill reserved just for that purpose. We have dozens of them now, and I've begun to believe. Before a hunt, the search for that talisman has become a routine as certain as checking the zero on the rifle.

Other nimrods are even more superstitious. Dax Willems knocks twice on the fuselage each time he boards a bush plane, and the practice not so gradually expanded to include airliners. I find myself doing the same if I follow him aboard. Peter Spear wears a threadbare balaclava on hunts and has for decades. One African PH whom I'm sure would prefer to remain anonymous, arranges the six pills he must take at breakfast in a perfect circle, making the final adjustments to the circle with a fork, before sweeping them into a waiting palm and swallowing the mess with a gulp of coffee. One male Austrian outfitter must wear a cleaned and pressed black scarf on the first day of the hunt; the vain fool offsets it with makeup, including rouge and mascara. Russian outfitter and guide Yuri Chernyshchevic hopes to have three things go wrong before a hunt in the belief that bad luck comes in threes, and once he gets those out of the way the hunt will be successful.

In Mongolia in 2007, Cheri bought me a leather key fob with a heroic carved argali head, in celebration of the magnum ram I'd just scored. I had the number "6" carved into the off-side, after all of those day-six kills. These years later, I still carry that leather key fob, but both the argali image and the number six have been worn smooth from rubbing it for luck each day. I don't mention that to Sam, though.

Author's Note: This essay was written before the Wild Sheep Foundation (WSF) was formed out of the old Foundation for North American Wild Sheep. I wrote this for *Sports Afield* magazine, and it got me into a pissing match with what is now called the Grand Slam Club/Ovis, or maybe the other way around. To *Sports Afield's* credit, they included the prose duel in their magazine.

THE SUPER WORLD SLAM CAPER

In a 1948 *True* magazine article, Grancel Fitz started the hunt "slam" business when he branded the bagging of all four North American sheep with the Grand Slam moniker. Jack O'Connor in numerous magazine articles and books popularized the term, and he lived to rue it, too. As he said, "Some of the boom in sheep hunting may well be laid to my doorstep. I hope that when I arrive at the Pearly Gates, old St. Peter does not hold it against me."

I'm with O'Connor—I don't approve of "slams." This from a guy that owns the Grand Slam of North American sheep, the so-called bear slam and a handful of other "slams." In my defense, I got them all accidentally—that is, I wasn't aiming to get them and they came about as a result of simply hunting as much as I could. To me, setting a hunting slam as a goal—"like buying a can of corn," as O'Connor put it—defeats the purpose and benefits of hunting. So why am I "working" on my super/world/triple sheep slams (since completed—author's note)? I can't give a rational answer. I could mention it would help sell my hunting books; or it would make the multi-millionaire/European royalty club a bit less exclusive if a poor college prof and outdoor scribe could get admitted—reverse snob appeal; or maybe it's as petty as bragging-rights. I dunno.

Today, the Foundation of North American Wild Sheep (FNAWS, and now renamed the Wild Sheep Foundation—WSF) has its grand slam of North American sheep (FNAWS), the International Sheep Hunters Association (ISHA no longer exists) has the super slam of wild sheep and the capra slam of wild goats. The

Grand Slam Club/Ovis claims the world slam of sheep, the grand slam and the capra slam. FNAWS's and GSC/O's Grand Slam includes bighorn, desert bighorn, Stone and Dall sheep. ISHA's Super Slam of twelve sheep requires at least six native old world sheep; it allows fenced sheep if fences don't interfere with the animal's movement, including animals restrained behind a fence and often non-endemic, as does GSC/O's World Slam. For either of the latter, a guy intent on getting his name in the archives can jet to a Texas ranch and slaughter several fenced sheep and collect a portion of his world/super slam in days. (Please save the hate mail; I know high-fence shooting can be tough—martinis back at the ranch might be too dry) The new kid in the arena is the O'Connor Conservancy (OC—now defunct); it's just getting off the ground and has a better idea—it won't allow high-fence sheep in its slam at all. To further roil the pond, as I write this GSC/O is suing ISHA and FNAWS over intellectual property rights of the various "slam" terms, this in spite of the fact that Fitz originated the term as applied to sheep and O'Connor popularized it.

More complications—OC and ISHA allow some sheep subspecies and not others; they include both the Rocky Mountain bighorn (Ovis canadensis canadensis) and desert bighorn subspecies (Ovis canadensis var.), yet exclude the California bighorn (O. c. californiana) if you've got an O. c. canadensis in your collection. GSC/O's world slam allows both O. c. canadensis and O. c. californiana. ISHA, OC and GSC/O seem even muddier on snow sheep subspecies, Ovis nivicola, allowed in their slams. GSC/O allows both the Tajikistan Marco Polo sheep (Ovis ammon poli) and the Kyrgyzstan Hume argali (Ovis ammon humei) in its world slam, while ISHA and OC allow only one or the other. The two or three subspecies, depending on who you talk to, of Mongolia argali are equally confusing. If you can figure why some organizations allow multiple subspecies of the same species of wild sheep and not others, you've got more gray stuff between the ears than I have. Baffled? Me too. To further confuse matters, the organizations allow either two or three tur subspecies, a wild goat found only in the Caucasus Mountains, in their slam collections. Too, ISHA and OC function under FNAWS's umbrella;

GSC/O is on its own. The above organizations contribute to wildlife conservation projects, and I support them. In many places, sheep populations would not exist without FNAWS and other organization-sponsored sheep reintroduction projects, though some of these are of questionable value.

With the super/world/triple slams, arguably the most prestigious accomplishments in hunting, and given human nature (the owning is more important than the getting), shenanigans inevitably enter the picture. I know a handful of Super/World/triple slammers—church-going family men, community pillars—with questionable world slams. One well-known slammer shot a Mongolian argali across the hood of a Russian Uaz jeep, collected his Okhotsk snow sheep from a helicopter, and guides tracked down and killed a sheep he wounded; add these to the high-fenced sheep, and his slam is questionable. Of ten world/super slammers, nine have high-fenced sheep in their collections. Half admit to killing at least one wild sheep from snowmobiles, ATVs, jeeps or 'copters. Locating sheep from aircraft before the hunt is common practice. No organizations approve of unethical hunting, but it's impossible to keep slam scams out of the picture when getting your name in the archives becomes the critical part of hunting. Still, some hunters have collected twelve world sheep completely fair chase (me).

By the end of the year, and with more luck that is usually my mettle, I may be only one sheep away from the World Slam (two from ISHA's Super Slam—I've since collected both, by the way). No ram will have been taken behind any kind of fence or from any motor vehicle. So why do it? Maybe this quote from *Danse Macabre* helps: "He is a fool who injures himself by amassing things. And no one knows why people cannot help but do it." Human nature again, but let me explain.

I became a sheep nut decades before ever owning a tag and about the time my voice solved its adolescent squeak. I blame Jack O'Connor's sheep stories in the old *Outdoor Life*. More than three decades later, I finally drew a desert bighorn tag in Utah and self-guided my way to the Grand Slam of North American wild sheep (now also called the Four North American Wild Sheep or FNAWS—

accidentally; see "The Accidental Slam," *Sports Afield*, Oct. 2006). At the time, I'd collected fifteen world sheep (numbers, not subspecies) and hadn't thought of seriously securing the Grand Slam, let alone the World Slam or Triple Slam (12 wild world sheep, 12 wild world goats, and the Grand Slam—no worries, I'm confused too). From my first unsuccessful sheep hunt, it took 22-years of tough hunting to complete my Grand Slam. I waste no sympathy on those 60-day wonders that roar from camp to camp and collect their slams in a single season; they can't understand what they've missed. Some, however, become dedicated sheep hunters and learn.

My first sheep hunt was a do-it-yourself affair in one of south Montana's open areas (in these, the drill is you hunt until a pre-determined number of sheep hit the ground, at which time the season is closed). I horse-packed and backpacked alone five glorious weeks in the Beartooth-Absaroka Wilderness, slew elk, deer and birds, fished, and passed up ¾ curl rams, the only sheep I saw. I didn't suffer insomnia because my crosshairs never settled on a ram. I had too much fun trekking timberline basins and sleeping in a tent in the Yellowstone wilderness to consider the hunt a bust.

Then, I built a log house and moved to the banks of the Yukon River and two years after began hunting Dall sheep in the most remote country on the continent. Over the next decade, I did pretty well, too.

In 1988 I connected on my first Stone sheep in the Toad River country of British Columbia with guide Ralph Kitchen and the Folding Mountain outfit, and had compiled two of the four varieties required for the Grand Slam, though that statistic hadn't crossed my mind. In the early 1990s I scored on a California bighorn ram in southwest British Columbia west of the Fraser River with guide Ken Olynyk and outfitter Layton Bryson; I still didn't think in terms of slam. And then I lucked out on that Utah desert bighorn sheep (Luck?! I had max bonus points and had for years), and surprise, surprise—two Grand Slam plaques materialized on my walls—one from FNAWS and the other from GSC/O. Was I corrupted?

Almost all world slammers collect the four sheep required for the Grand Slam first and then move on to the Super/World/Triple

Slam. At this point, I'm not sure I knew either existed, and if I did, I couldn't have cared less. Cheri and I traveled to the Russian Far East in the early '90s on an abortive bear hunt in Kamchatka booked through a big East Coast agency; the hunt was a bust, but we contacted Olga Parfenova, hunt organizer for Tor Company in the city of Khabarovsk. The following August she pieced together a hunt in the Dzhugdzhur range in the central part of the province and after six days of not seeing a ram, I collected two fine Okhotsk snow sheep. Bagging two rams was entirely legal.

A year or two later, we hunted another RFE province. We spotted rams every day and made three stalks that failed for one reason and another. On the sixth day, we found six rams a mile away, made a circuitous sneak so we'd stalk them downhill and upwind. My guide, Vladimir Plaschenko, motioned me on without him—one always stalks more quietly than two—and I eased within 25-yards and collected a 40-inch ram with 15-inch bases, and my first top-ten-class Asian sheep. Another ram just as large hung around until Vladimir arrived, and we thought seriously of collecting it, too, but though I've done it, I dislike the killing of two trophies at the same time because it waters down the heady elation of the first trophy. Keep in mind, though, that Jack O'Connor killed two Stone rams on at least one hunt. After some agonizing, I let the second ram go, to Vladimir's disappointment. The Super/World Slam hadn't crossed my mind, and listing the trophy in a record book was more trouble than it was worth (I'd have to rent a moving van and truck my top-ten trophies to a SCI Master Measurer in another city). By the way, both subspecies of snow sheep would count for the GSC/O slam, but only one toward either the ISHA or OC slams. I think.

Sheep hunts aren't always successful, either in North America or Asia. A year or three later, I escorted a handful of hunters for a ram and bear combination spring hunt on the west coast of the Sea of Okhotsk in the Russian Far East. I wasn't looking for a ram, but the other three hunters were. Two shot at small rams, but none scored. Three killed bears. I'd arranged this hunt through Olga, too, and her new boss was Spartak Company. Yuri Chernychevich was our outfitter; for half-a-dozen reasons, at least two involving vodka, we got out of the village of Okhotsk five days late and managed only two full hunting days. Fortunately, I haven't made many sheep hunts like that.

Wes Vining, then owner of the old Hunting Connection hunt brokerage, arranged my next Asian sheep hunt. Remember, I'd grown up reading Jack O'Connor, and from time-to-time he'd mention Marco Polo sheep as the Holy Grail of sheep hunting, indeed, all hunting, though to my knowledge he never scored one. As a kid, I'd watched Lowell Thomas's narration of the Klineburger brothers's *Great Shikar* film into Afghanistan after Marco Polo sheep. Ovis ammon poli became my Grail, too, though collecting one would be like a high school nerd getting a date with a cheerleader—too wonderful. Wes, bless his heart, offered Cheri and me the hunt at reduced cost—a cancellation hunt in December. Best of all, we'd hunt with Yuri Matison, owner of Badakshan Expeditions and the guide that put most of the top-ten heads in the record book, including the world record. How could I get so lucky?!

I'd have been ecstatic just to collect a good ram—that is, anything over 55-inches around the curl. In the Tajik Pamirs, weather is extreme in December. Base camp stood at 13,000 feet and we hunted to 16,000. Cheri and I both run and were in excellent condition. No matter, we still had a tough time gulping enough oxygen. The first dawn we edged over a 14,000-foot col and gazed into a tremendous basin. Six-hundred sheep grazed, rutted and bedded. At least three rams would tape over 60-inches—the hunter's equivalent of winning the lotto. Taktamat and I unsuccessfully stalked the brute of the trio; in snow camo anoraks, wc showed like pimples on the home-coming queen's nose whenever we crossed a slope blown free of snow. Later, Yuri, Dovelat and I chased the rams while Cheri and Taktamat watched. I kept up with the guides without problem, but gasping in the sere, freon air freeze-burned my bronchi and I developed a cough that lasted a year. It could have been worse, thanks to the bronchial anti-inflammatory I'd brought. Hunters die at extreme altitudes stalking Marco Polo sheep.

Somehow, ice got into the .300 magnum's safety. When we eased up on the magnum ram at 200-meters, I couldn't free the safety. The ram vaporized into the next cirque. We'd slalomed into a canyon seething with six hundred sheep and had scored zero—something like diving into a barrel of honeyed Turkish dates and ending up sucking your thumb. You bet I felt the altitude and exhaustion on the walk back.

Yuri felt sure he knew where the ram and his ewes had gone. We bee-lined there the next dawn, first over frozen marshes, then up bouldered river beds and along yak trails and finally, we slogged up near-vertical scree to a high col. Winds wailed and ten-story snow curtains ghosted across the canyons. Using the blowing snow as cover in the barren terrain, we crawled to within 450 yards of the sheep. I wore three layers of head gear, and when I tried to shove them out of my eyes as I lay prone on the blade-ridge, I accidentally shed all three. The 20-below-zero wind howled at 40 knots and my ears burned then went numb in less time than it takes to tell about it. After praying to the Red Gods, crossing my toes and spitting downwind, I guesstimated range, bullet drop, wind velocity and direction, and hoped. I was lucky and we collected a very near 63-inch by near-17-inch ram (for those further interested in stats, Yuri green-scored the ram at 228 1/2 SCI points, enough to put it in the top five in the year 2000 when I bagged it). My birthday, the end of the hunting season, and the magnum ram were reasons enough for a three-day bacchanal with the guys all the way back to Moscow. Whew! I have a full-body mount of the ram and it's one of my most valued possessions—right after the winter dogsled 10-foot polar bear and just ahead of the 10-foot Tanzanian lion.

I booked my Trans-Caspian urial hunt through Vance Corrigan's Hunting Consultants with outfitter Vladimir Treshchov's National Hunting Service (Vance has globe-trotted world sheep pastures for more than four decades and helped with facts for this article). Treshchov was head honcho for all hunting in the former Soviet Union and knew the intricacies, political and otherwise, in manipulating his way through former Soviet bloc countries. His functionaries—drivers, cooks, skinners, guides—worked for the Turkmenistan government, and without them we couldn't have navigated the ten or so roadblocks to the Badkhyz Reserve near both the Afghanistan and Iranian borders. The place was lousy with urial, Persian goitered gazelle, onagers and a variety of other exotic wildlife. I passed a dozen exceptional trophies the first day because I didn't want to end the hunt too soon, but killed a stunning, full-curl, 35 by 12 1/2-inch ram the second dawn, and we spent the rest of the hunt stalking gazelle. The Badhkyz was the gentlest sheep country I'd hunted.

ISHA and OC allow two tur, a wild goat, genus Capra, in their super slams. GSC/O allows all three tur—the Kuban, Mid-Caucasus and the Eastern or Dagestan—in its slam. Illogical, perhaps, but the on-end terrain of the Caucasus Mountains makes tur hunting more physically challenging than most sheep hunts.

In 2006, I arranged an expedition for five of us with Turkish outfitter Orhan Konakci's Safari Tours for Dagestan tur in Azerbaijan. I couldn't have been happier or luckier. Of all the Asian hunts I've made, Konakci's outfit was one of the most efficient and productive (on a subsequent Anatolian chamois hunt, just the opposite was true). First, we hunted Eurasian boar in Anatolia and all of us got shooting and I collected a 10-inch, top-ten boar; then we hustled to the eastern Caucasus. We spotted seventy to eighty tur a day and all three hunters killed nice tur. I got lucky again. Bulgarian professional hunter Erdogan Avci green-scored my king kong tur at number two SCI, and it measured 40 inches with 13-plus inch bases (in-camp, green measurements, of course). I haven't got this officially scored, either, because I guess I'm not concerned enough with the archives. I do like the sound of "top-ten," though.

The Caucasus is steep. One world-slammer characterized the tur country as the "graduate school of mountain hunting." I like steep country, and so does Cheri. On the third evening, I spotted a brontosaurus of a tur a mile down the ridge. It was late, the sun plummeted to the west ridges, but we slalomed down scree, spidered down cliffs and eased up on a single tur bedded across a gorge. It wasn't the magnum tur we'd spotted, but it was good, the light was going, and one shot put the fur on the ground. More tur climbed from the bottoms, including the behemoth billy. Both the outfitter, Arif, and Erdogan commanded: "CHUTE!" One shot spined it. It's legal to shoot two animals for the added trophy fee in Azerbaijan, too, though I wouldn't have if I'd gotten the big one first.

As mentioned, sheep hunts don't always work as planned. In December 2006, Cheri and I flew to Mongolia to hunt Gobi argali with outfitter Baasanhu Jantzen. I'd fantasized about sheep hunting in Mongolia for two decades, but fantasy seldom matches reality, and it sure didn't in Mongolia. To shorten a long story, our interpreter loved vodka, no trophy rams existed the single day we hunted a two-mile range of volcanic hills, and local ibex would set no records. After a conference with Baasanhu, we agreed to jeep a day to another place with bigger ibex, give up the argali sheep hunt and return next season for the argali. I wasn't happy; after all, we'd traveled half-way around the world to collect an argali, but what can you do? Baasanhu held the full house—my hunt fees and fantasy. After six days hunting ibex, I finally scored on the only trophy we found, but an ibex is a disappointment when you came to hunt argali, especially at thrice the going rate for ibex. Five months later, though, I collected a magnum 50 by 19 inch Hangay argali (green measurement, as most of my measurements are because I refuse to tape them once they get home), an Altai ibex so ancient he'd watched Chenggis Khan, and exceptional gazelle and roe buck. Jantzen redeemed himself, though my wallet is much lighter than originally planned.

Trophy sheep are the tangible part of the super/world/triple slam equation, but intangibles are just as important: photographing fresh snow leopard tracks in the Pamirs; wandering south Asian villages that haven't changed in millennia; sipping fermented mare's mile in a Mongol ger while men "throat-sing" songs centuries old; galloping two-humped Bactrian camels across Gobi dunes; or giving your lunch to half-starved religious pilgrims on the trails of the Caucasus. Game trophies eventually fade into the wall, but you always have the memories and the places. And that's why I do it.

That Ol' Man

Merle Haggard crooned lost love from the honky-tonk juke-box, and a pink neon Budweiser light made the beer in the mug look like strawberry soda pop. The bartender chewed a toothpick, and someone clicked pool balls and swore in the back gloom.

"Thet ol' man's camped on t' south rim 'cross Sheepherd Crick 'gin this season," the younger cowpuncher said to the older. They sat in the first booth of the Shooting Star Tavern nursing a pitcher of 3.2% Utah beer. "Pushed some heifers out thet way last week and he wuz cookin' sompin on a campfire."

I sat in the next booth nursing my own beer. I'd hunted Sheepherd Canyon geography off and on for the best part of four decades and had seen no other camps for two decades now. Hunters didn't camp anymore, because they drove in and out in a day.

"Al'ays camps in thet timber patch that licks up onto the flat," the other cowhand said.

Hell, I thought, *that's my camp. They can't mean me. "Old man"?* Okay, my temples had grayed and I'd shaved my beard the year before because I noticed with astonishment how gray it had gotten in a photograph. But I grunted a buck out on my back most seasons, cut firewood and jogged. "Who they calling 'old'?! Damned punks."

"Thet ol' timer's gonna git a heart attack huntin' like thet off by hisself."

"Old Timer?!"

That first year, Jaques sat the big bay gelding and said in his Basque accent, "Seed 'im down dat bald ridge in dem heaffy oaks."

286

(Had it really been three years, now?) He'd bumped the buck pushing his sheep herd through the canyon the day before. "Berry beeg. You shoot dat buck." He lifted the bota of homemade chokecherry wine he always toted from the saddle horn and I took a long squirt. It warmed my ears. We'd shared that wine and too many campfires since my first deer hunt in the country before I got legal back in LBJ days.

The next black pre-dawn I wormed from the tent and shouldered the .270 and trekked across the high plateau, then dropped down the ridge as the light came and scanned across the big ravine that was almost a canyon, hoping to jump the buck from that oak scrub tangle and shoot across the ravine. I kept out of sight on the distant side of the ridge, snaking over now and then to glass. When the sun hemorrhaged onto the 9,500-foot Wasatch Range twenty miles west, I hands-and-kneed across the ridgeline and hunkered under a wind-twisted fir and glassed the oaks. The leaves had fallen, but the entwined oaks were so tangled you couldn't see into them.

Nothing had shown in two hours, so I slalomed into the ravine and still-hunted up into the dreadlock oak scrub with a fool's optimism, and slid my feet through the autumn-dead leaves rather than lift them and set them down and make more noise. Chickadees searched the tree bark and the autumn sun filtered through the bare oak branches. Something upslope blasted like a steam valve and I hurdled deadfall and fought out of the oak jungle as it splintered uphill like a D7 'dozer. I stumbled into the open just as a magnum buck broke from the tangle and pivoted to stare from 30 yards, then the buck bounded over the ridgeline and I couldn't get the crosshairs right and pull off.

My gawd, I thought, *my gawd!*

Later I thought, *That spread!* Thirty-seven inches anyway. *And that mass, my gawd!* And that was the last of him that season.

I scouted a week before the following hunt. As I hunkered in fir shin-tangle, he minced out of a maple thicket in the dusk to browse in the evergreen chaparral. I stared transfixed through the 10x binocular until full dark and wished hunting season was open, and thought, *at least a yard of spread with that cheater point. Six-inch brow tines. Circumferences bigger 'n my wrist.* I stalked away from the long ravine in black dark so not to spook him.

It had snowed that eve of the opener. I kicked the snow from the tent and drank the tea and warmed myself beside the fir dead-fall fire in the pre-dawn dark, and remembered the buck with that Pleistocene span of antlers. I slogged across the flat again the two miles to the rim, then hunkered in shin-tangle and waited as the east horizon lightened off toward the Guildersleeve. When the light came, the buck stood at the edge of that oak tangle and stared from 600 yards, then misted into the dreadlock brush. You couldn't mistake that buck in a century.

I'd wrangled the time to hunt, had put the university classes I taught into the testing center, and managed a full work week and two weekends. I found his tracks, too, but hunted six days without another glimpse.

By late afternoon of the last day, I'd still-hunted up the two-mile draw to its head. As I bent to examine a track, I glanced up as two grand bucks bounded over the skyline and vaporized into Cottonwood Creek. No question, one was my buck with that cheater on the right antler, and the other a taker, too. And that was that for the season.

Old Jaques died that winter on the sheep wintering range out on the Promontory alone in his trailer sheep camp. I like to think he took a last squirt from the *bota* as he felt the juniper wood heat from that tiny stove. Hell, I'd miss his camp hunkered out on the point across Sheepherd Canyon and the tang of that chokecherry wine and that Basque accent he hadn't changed in the decades I'd known him.

I scouted two weekends before the next hunt. The buck's tracks skirted that maple thicket, and he'd mangled a spruce sapling with those antlers then trailed up onto the ridge and browsed forbs and serviceberry, but I didn't spot him.

I scouted the next weekend, on Sunday, and paid respects to the Red Gods and to Jaques in the familiar pre-dawn black and the glow of the deadfall fire, then stumbled across that big mesa from camp as a gory sun bled onto the Wasatch to the west, and glassed the long ravine. He browsed along the dry creek 500 yards down-slope, and he edged closer to the brush tangle until he misted into it before the sun hit ridgeline. Too far for a shot even if the season was open.

So, he's still here, I thought later and poked at the fir embers at the campfire on the eve of opening day and sipped Scotch whiskey from the blue metal cup. *It's been two years now since you've seen him. Two years you've hunted him. This is the third season.* And later, you haven't even had a chance.

I knew the landmarks in the dark, now, the aspen stand I skirted at that gully head, the ten-ton boulder I'd named Ishmael always hunched alone out on the plateau, the fir shin-tangle I stumbled through in the pre-dawn black before the mesa dropped off into the long ravines. Starlight was enough to find them, because I'd made that black-dark trek often enough.

An hour after sunrise, I spotted him bedded in the maples a canyon south. My slope was so open he'd nail me the moment I stepped across the ridgeline, and at more than 500 yards he was too far for even a Hail Mary shot in the brush. As I watched, two horse-back hunters crossed his slope down the ridge and brushed toward the tangled maples. I hoped they'd spook him toward me. As they neared, the buck rested his chin along the ground and became invisible. One hunter rode thirty yards above the buck and the other that much below, but the buck wouldn't budge. When they'd ridden over the canyon rim again, the buck raised his head and listened to make sure they'd gone.

Later that hunt, the buck stepped out of the maple and oak tangle in the last of the light and browsed, too far for a shot in the dim. He re-taught me an old lesson: Mature bucks feed only at night during the hunting season. I glassed two minutes until full dark, then trudged to the camp.

Sure, the light was bad, but the antlers looked thin, and that fourth point lost four inches of length, and the same with the cheater, I thought. "He's passed his prime," I told myself and fired the kindling and guessed his age at maybe nine. "Hell, he's an old man." I didn't spot him again that season, but killed a mature buck near the camp on the last day.

Is it really the fourth season now? I half-wondered as I poked at the campfire the eve of the next opening day. Could it really have been that long? I hadn't seen the buck in a day of scouting, nor found the big tracks. *Is he still alive?* I wondered. I hadn't scouted much, either. *Didn't want to leave scent around*, I rationalized, but maybe I'd gotten tired, or those punk cowhands were right. Each season my hair showed more gray in the self-portrait hero photos I took if I shot some hapless meat buck when it became clear I wouldn't bag Him, again.

In the dawn I trudged the flat one more time toward the long ravines in five-inches of new snow. "Good tracking snow," I whispered to myself as I skirted that quakie stand and hiked to that reliable old boulder Ishmael hunkered alone out on the flat and then patted him and said hello. I settled into the shin-tangle at the ravine head and watched the light come, first the faint gold band east toward the Gildersleeve ridges, then it bled into the cobalt sky and onto the high Wasatch peaks. The shadows became stunted fir and sagebrush clumps, and I shivered in the dawn chill.

I slid down-slope and cleared the ridgeline and any chance of the buck sky-lining me, and saw the big tracks. *Within the last two hours*, I thought, because the powdery snow hadn't yet sifted into the prints. Fresh snow and big tracks had always meant a shot at something, but I wanted a shot at Him. I squatted in the sagebrush on the trail and waited for more light, then took to the trail again to walk off the chill. The spoor said the buck browsed the serviceberry and dried forbs in very early morning, so he shouldn't go far. *Unless he senses me somehow.*

I'd trailed enough old bucks to know they button-hooked downwind of their back trail and bedded to scent or spot following danger. This buck wasn't thinking of bedding, at least as of two hours ago. A buck meant to bed down only if his backtrail meandered as he explored bedding sites. These tracks led from serviceberry to frost-dried forbs as the buck browsed with purpose in the predawn black.

The sun had just gilded the peaks of the Wasatch, when I sensed something at the edge of true vision across the shadowed canyon. Through the binocular, the buck minced out of a maple thicket and turned broadside and stared from 350 yards. He should have picked me up somehow. I frantically searched for a rifle rest, but found only wobbly three-foot oak scrub. On the steep slope, shooting prone wasn't an option, either. A sitting shot was the only way to clear sagebrush.

I noted that cheater point off the right antler, fought that buck fever and lowered the crosshairs and when they settled half-a-foot above back-line, touched off the .270. The slug *whoomphed* into buckskin and the buck whirled and bounded cross-slope then angled up toward ridgeline. He's not hit bad enough, I thought, because badly wounded deer never go up, but then the great antlers sagged and the buck dived into the powdered snow.

"Sorry, old fella," I said when I swallowed the lump and fondled the antlers. "You've gotten corny-sentimental, old man," I told myself aloud. No, they weren't that more-than-a-yard-wide rack with beams as big as a man's wrist they'd been two years earlier in his prime, but they still spread 35-inches. I skidded the buck on the snow up the ridge and cleared the rim onto the plateau by midday, then slid the buck to the cattle trail and trudged back to the camp for Ol' Blue, my battered Toyota truck. Without the slick powder snow, I'd have had to quarter him and pack the meat on my back. Later, grunting the Sumo buck into the truck bed was tougher than I'd believed and after, I sat on a boulder too long to catch my breath. This ended it. Jacques first, and now the old buck.

When I'd caught my breath, I tied the buck off in the bed so the antlers hung over the tailgate, then drove across the big mesa and farther and passed the cow camp in the dusk and those buckaroos gawking from the aspen-pole corral. One had some gray at the temples, now.

Damned punks, I thought and imagined their conversation: "Never seed no buck like thet up here," one wrangler said to the other.

"Me neither. Thet ol' man's got some hard bark on 'im, too," the other said.

I aimed the pickup down the old timber trail and into Magpie Canyon, and later forded the South Fork River and then up onto the blacktop and later still parked at the Shooting Star Tavern so the buck showed in the truck bed to good avail, and ordered a burger and beer and sat at a booth with my back to the door to hear the comments when people walked in. Some customers figured it out and bought me beers until they covered the table, but I was too tired to drink them. I was too tired to tell them about it, too.

STORIES OF ASIA AND EUROPE

"Hunting," I answer when they ask about my favorite thing. Sure, it's changed—tacking another trophy on the wall is no longer that important. Getting away from the halls of academia, the computer screen and, yes, people, is. Leaky wall tents in alpine basins, waking in the night to the bell mare beyond the tent canvas, and ear-numbing cold is, too. My next favorite thing, I realize lately, is telling stories—in university lecture halls, at the odd hunting chapter convention, to pals with single-malts in their fists. I even get paid for it from magazines and book publishers, meager though that is.

As a result, I get questions. Some are tough, like "Why do you shoot animals?" Others aren't: "What's your favorite country?" For the second time this year, someone asked, "What's the best hunting—Asia or Europe?" Four of us, hunters all, sat in my own "clean, well-lighted place" (after the title of a Hemingway short story). Ice clinked in his Scotch glass, and the dinner party barreled on in another part of the house.

My habit is to tell a story when asked a question, and let the audience connect the dots.

"Well," I began. That's always a good start. I talked of my first Asian sheep hunt two decades ago, of winging from SLC to Anchorage, and the next day hopping an Alaskan Air flight west to Magadan in the Russian Far East, and then south to Khabarovsk city. The next dawn we winged north again in a Russian turbo-prop that thunderstorms forced down at the fishing village of Ayan on the Sea of Okhotsk. When weather cleared the following day, we winged into the interior of the territory to the village of Nelkan. From there we hammered and shuddered in a Soviet surplus helicopter into an anonymous Dzhugdzhur basin. Riding those 'copters is equivalent to a petrifying amusement park ride, except you could die. We found no rams, so we shouldered backpacks and trekked east toward the Okhotsk surf. In the end, we bagged two grand rams, and we earned them, too.

What kind of answer is that? the guys wonder. I see it in their eyes. They gaze at those snow sheep mounts. I add that the hunt was so good, I booked another snow sheep expedition for the next season that scored a 40-inch ram on my best of a dozen Russian trips. In Russia, you never know. Any hunt can turn into either a disaster or a diamond.

I took a sip and segued into another story, this one of chasing urial on the rolling hills of the Bahdkyz in Turkmenistan on the Iran and Afghanistan borders, of refusing to bag a 38" ram on the first morning because it was just too early in the hunt. I like to drag the hunts out, to get my money's worth, and to absorb the country. I didn't sleep that night, either, because of that decision. No sane sheep hunter passes up a ram like that, first day or no. Perhaps because of that sleepless night, I slap a magazine-cover ram in the salt the following dawn. I still don't regret that decision, I think. The next day temps plummeted and snow shrieked down from the Hindu Kush turning the Persian goitered gazelle hunt, a two-hour proposition, into four days of greasy roads, zero visibility, shrieking ground blizzards, and food poisoning. Would I do it again? You bet, *sans* the food poisoning.

The guys gaze at the full-body trans-Caspian urial mount. Ice clinks in glasses, and that's my cue. I tell of the Tajikistan Marco Polo ram hunt with famed outfitter and guide Yuri Matison and his guys in the 20-something-below temps of December that scored my top mountain game trophy, not to mention a grand ibex, frost-bite, and a three-day celebratory bacchanal over three countries all the way to Moscow. I'd do that one again, too.

Then without transition I'm telling of Mongolia, and an argali hunt in December in 20-below temps, blizzards, and dust cyclones.

The ordeal netted no argali, but I scored Gobi ibex and the epiphany that despite the argali bust, I hunted in my new favorite Asian country. The next spring, outfitter Baasanhu Jantzen talked us back for that argali, and on the 3000-kilometer cross-country argosy in a Russian Uaz jeep, we added black-tailed gazelle, Altai ibex, and a grand roe deer. As important, we sampled fermented mare's milk, listened to millennia-old Mongol throat-singing in remote nomad gers, and dined on camel haunch.

And we scored a 40-inch Dagestan tur on an Azerbaijan Caucasus pack hunt in the steepest geography on the planet, magnum bezoar ibex in Anatolia in the dust storms of spring, and other expeditions. That hunt in the west Caucasus after Kuban tur during the Russia-Georgia war earned us an army escort to a Russian military base and an all-night KGB interrogation, and in the very last moments, a tur. Technically, that was a European hunt, but I think of it as Asian. I wouldn't change a thing, though that tur could have been larger.

"What about Europe?" that pal asks. I pause to reboot, and slurp. Ice clinks again in those glasses.

"Well," I start again. "Europe's more cushy, more predictable. No 20-below blizzards, no dust cyclones, no frostbite or food poisoning. I can't imagine not scoring game. Guides know just where to find the trophy, too. You don't feel the tension of Asian hunts, but that tension makes the hunt memorable."

I tell of the Croatian two-day chamois hunt that scored a 10-inch billy, and the first-morning mouflon on the Peljesac Peninsula, of the five-course meals and the best food on the planet as the Adriatic lapped at our bayside hotel. Srdja Dimitrejevic arranged the efficient, predictable hunt. No complaints, either. Then I slide into the two-night, moonlight boar hunt in the Balkans that netted a top-10 class Eurasian boar. Smooth.

I lapse for a moment into a French chamois hunt when I was a kid when the Old Man, a career army officer, was stationed at Bordeaux. I'm rolling, now, because the stories don't pack as much substance and I'm breezing through them. When I lecture on campus, I worry if topics pass too fast and my captive audience doesn't ask questions. No one questions, but two guys freshen their single-malts.

We settle back into chairs. "Go on," someone says, so I do. Before long I'm telling of my last European hunt with Jose Mallo of Espacaza in Spain. Again, we hunted in December. I've got a month off between semesters each December, so invariably Cheri and I aim for another sheep or goat hunt.

We stepped off the flight in Madrid and Jose collected us even before we got the luggage. I liked that efficiency; it gave me faith in the hunt. Before we knew it, we motored south and in two hours made a country posada off the cover of *Architectural Digest* run by a Brit couple in the orchards of the Gredos Mountain foothills. Food was terriff (if Sinatra used the word, why not?). The next dawn we collected our guides, two reserve game wardens, and trekked into a deluge and the Gredos. In late morning, soaked in spite of raingear, the guides got us on to three grand Gredos ibex. One is top-five class, and the guides estimate the trophy fee at $10,000, far out of my price range; in most of Europe, the bigger the trophy, the higher the trophy fee. I'd grown up hunting for the largest animal you find, so ignoring the best horns rips against my fabric. "Don't look at it," Jose counsels. I forced myself to ignore King Kong, and killed number-two with one shot. It's across the rain-swollen creek, and we'd have to swim it, so we hiked back down and returned on the other side the next day. The second-largest ibex is 13-years-old, and now that we haven't got King Kong to compare him to, I'm ecstatic. We're done, so we motored at 130 klicks per hour to Madrid, and the next morning Jose's guide Carlos whisked us east for Beceite ibex. We "camped" at another designer posada made from a hundreds-year-old stone farmhouse on a knoll at the base of the Beceite Mountains. We spotted ibex from the room, too. We drove out to hunt even before we unpacked. The guys wasted no time. Ibex rutted in the orchards along the road, and we glassed a handful of real trophies, until finally Joaquin Sabater, the local guide and mayor of Bel, pointed. Carlos wanted me to shoot, from a paved road, yet. I refused. I wasn't shooting from any road, and it was just too early in the hunt. The next day, though, we all drove to the top of the Beceites and foot-hunted down and about mid-afternoon Joaquin eyed a grand, dozen-year-old billy we put it in the salt, though it wasn't the largest we'd seen. Carlos wanted to rush us back to Madrid, but I put my foot down. Cheri and I needed a day to hike, rewind, and photograph, and it cost us dollars, too.

"Got it." That buddy clinked ice in his glass. Like I said, I tell stories. You connect the dots.

Four-of-a-Kind Bruins

It was early March, full winter on the polar icepak. The thermometer lashed to the dogsled upstander read thirty-six-degrees below zero. "Don't even take a squat without that gun," guide Jaypatee Akeeagok said as I was about to shove through the tent flap to answer nature's call, that is, if I could manage in four layers of clothes beneath half-cured caribou parka and pants. "We're in real bear country now. Anything that moves on the icepack is meat to *Nanook*." A hundred miles of dogsled Arctic Ocean icepack west of Grise Fiord on Ellesmere Island, the northernmost community on North America, we'd spotted fresh polar bear tracks.

"Eat men." The assistant, Pauloosie Attagootak, grinned. I figured they were funning the greenhorn, but they slept fully clothed on their stomachs facing the tent flap with the guns just outside, and staked the sled dogs in a rectangle around the tent to warn of bears in the night. We stowed rifles outside because moisture inside would condense and they'd flash-freeze when we took them out again.

The drill was to scale icebergs frozen into icepack and glass. We spotted two to five bears a day as we mushed west beyond Cape Storm. We took three-hours to pitch camp each sundown and three each dawn to break it. In my clumsy caribou clothes, a slip off a three-story iceberg meant a dead cheechako. I worried more Jaypatee might fall; if he did, we wouldn't make it back to Grise Fiord, because Pauloosie couldn't handle the savage Greenland husky sled dogs. Pauloosie kept a seal-hide whip handy when Jaypatee dumped frozen caribou chunks on the ice at the evening dog feeding frenzy.

"Don't get near those dogs," Jaypatee had warned before we mushed away from Grise Fiord. While we hunted, sled dogs killed a girl in a village just south, if you doubt the dog danger.

"I think maybe eight-and-a-half-foot *nanuk*," Jaypatee said days later when he slalomed down from an iceberg.

"Big enough?" I shook my head no, and he shrugged. We didn't see another bear worth considering in the next week. Periodically we'd jog behind the dogsled to warm up with our mittened hands grasping the upstanders. I ran twice as often as the guides. One afternoon, I stumbled and slurred my speech. The guides recognized early stage hypothermia and hustled up and heated the tent.

Another afternoon, Pauloosie said, "Storm tonight I think." He squinted at the thin clouds. "Mebbee camp soon."

We camped on the lee of an iceberg the size of destroyer and sawed packed snow into blocks and stacked them igloo-style around the double-wall tent. Later you couldn't see your feet in the blowing ground blizzard.

Jaypatee heated forty-below flashlight batteries on the Coleman stove in the tent and radioed Grise Fiord. Winds shrieked through the village at fifty knots and had stranded Inuit hunters on the Baffin Bay icepack.

We broke camp each dawn and mushed three hours, heated fresh-water iceberg chunks for soup, mushed another three hours and stopped for lunch, and then sledded until sundown. Eleven days into the hunt we found tracks the size of watermelons.

"Big *Nanuk*." Pauloosie grinned. "Eat men."

Later we found the same magnum tracks a day or two fresher. Jaypatee climbed an iceberg and glassed, then skidded down. "*Nanuq*!" he said. "It's big, too. Are you cold?" I was, but reached for the .375 in the soft case.

Jay whipped the exhausted dogs into a trot then a gallop and we bounced over the broken ice. I shivered in fits. A mile on, the dogs caught the bear's scent and doubled their sprints. We white-knuckled the lashings with mittened hands. To my astonishment, Jay slashed the leather fan-harness and the berserker huskies sprinted until they bayed the bear.

While the dogs feigned and *Nanuk* lunged and swatted in a millennia's old dance, Jaypatee peeled the bulky parka over my head. I maneuvered for a shot, careful not to hit a darting dog or let the bullet shoot through and kill a dog on the offside. I no longer felt the cold and paid no attention when my bare thumb sizzled against the minus-forty-degree rifle barrel as it would against white-hot steel. When I pressed the trigger, three-hundred grains of metal slammed shoulder and the bear threw wild haymakers like a prize-fighter out on his feet. A clincher finished it.

My hand went numb and the feeling only returned after long minutes hammering it against my thigh. Later, my thumb blackened from the freeze-burn on the rifle barrel and my ear lobe suffered frostbite.

"*Eskimo*' means 'eaters of raw meat,'" Pauloosie said. He tossed back a chunk of raw caribou, grinned and lobbed me one. I gulped the frozen 'bou and grinned back. "Now you're Eskimo."

The first time I chased grizzlies, I was an improvident punk 17-year-old college freshman that saved a year's wages from a factory job. Cliff Eagle owned an outfit in BC's Cariboo country. I had the time of my life—a horse rolled over me on an icy trail, I surfed avalanches after mountain goats, nearly froze, and bagged game.

"Seed fresh black bear tracks on the log road," Eagle said the dawn after Charley and I'd packed back to the Crooked Lake base camp from an unlucky moose hunt. "Use the hounds," he told Charley, a revered Shuswap hunter. Eagle referred to the four new black-and-tan and never-tried hounds he'd just freighted in from Vancouver.

The hounds missiled along scent like they knew what they were doing. The long-clawed tracks belonged to a grizzly, though. We sat horses through the Chinook-wet snow until the chase trailed into an old burn thick with blowdowns no horse could navigate, then we hoofed it. Three ridges north, the dogs bawled like they'd bayed every bear in the Cariboo. As we neared, a dog slinked up and shuddered. A moment later, a second hound cowered up, then silence. When we backtrailed them, we found a dead hound and no grizzly. The surviving dogs wanted no part of the scent.

I've had other fun with grizzlies. Once on the Colleen River I hauled moose meat three miles upriver to my camp when deep growling rattled my fillings. I backed away. Quick. I wasn't toting a rifle, either. Another time I scaled a no-name drainage to grunt out a ram carcass. It had vaporized, and it didn't take a quadratic equation to figure it out.

On one float-hunt, I scrambled up a Sheenjek River bluff and wandered between close-growing spruce searching for a tent site. Branches splintered and I pivoted to face a quarter-ton of bristling bruin blasting at me. Cheri in the raft shouted something and I sprinted three steps and soared off the bluff onto the raft while the baffled bear skidded to a momentary stop. Cheri leaned into the oars and a moment later the boat caught the current as the bear searched the bluff for us.

Another season I'd killed a caribou and when I trekked up to pack it out the next dawn, an ugly, black-faced mama grizz and a two-year-old cub nearly as large splintered from willow doghair straight at me. My finger tightened on trigger when she stopped, growled, rucked fur and made racket enough for an Irish football stadium. The kid rucked right alongside her, but they let me back over the ridge. I let them keep the meat.

Early another autumn as I picked blueberries a hundred miles north of the Arctic Circle, Grizz made a no-mistake charge faster than a quarter horse on steroids. I shot down at it from mere feet, with fatal results. I owned a bear tag that season, too.

I bagged another grizzly with similar drama, but most grizzly hunts are routine. Most pals took their grizzlies with long shots, spot-and-stalks or similarly tame methods.

Still, grizzlies are more apt to charge unprovoked than any beast I've hunted, including elephants, cape buffalos, lions, polar bears or hippos. Grizzlies mauled three pals: Barry Gilbert, a research fellow at Utah State University while I was a grad student there was very badly mauled in Yellowstone; the post office mistress in my then home village of Circle, Alaska was mauled on a camping trip on the Yukon; and Charley, one of my Shuswap guides, surprised a bear that ripped off his scalp. Most grizzlies go for the head, so protect it if you wrestle one. Don't get me wrong, I love watching grizzlies, but it's fine if I never hunt another. Their fish-fed coastal cousins, on the other hand, are another matter.

"There he is again!" I sputtered.

"Gawdawighty!" Scrom gasped. "If that aint themotherofall-bears I'll eat it raw with a spoon. You git a chance, you shoot that calf-eating illicit son of an immoral cow whale!" I didn't need instructions, because we'd stalked the bear all day.

Cheri and I were on the last day of a fourteen-day hunt with R & R Guide Service outfitter Rob Jones and guide Scott "Scrom" Ruttum on Alaska's Nushagak River. We froze, because four-hundred yards below, the coastal brown bear stared right at us. Don't let anyone tell you bears can't see. The breeze blew wrong, and if we stayed put, the bear would smell us. We dragged gear on hands and knees then sprinted downhill to where the bear couldn't scent us.

The Mulchatna caribou herd migrated into the valley the day before, and they calved everywhere we glassed. Wolves, eagles, foxes, wolverines and bears dined on hundreds of hapless calves. An hour earlier we'd watched "our" garage-sized brown bear kill and eat two caribou, then disappear into black spruce timber.

When we relocated the bear, we shed gear and crabbed toward the Pleistocene relic. The bear cat-footed into an alder patch and stampeded caribou. The brute ran down and swatted another calf into the afterlife, then ripped it apart. We circled downwind and weaseled within a hundred yards. My heart pounded a conga rhythm, though I'd stalked hundreds of bruins. The bear faced away as it munched, and I wondered if the .375 grain Sierra A-frame soft-point would range forward into the chest. I didn't chance it.

After what seemed a weekend, the bear stood broadside in the shin-tangle, and the cross hairs settled on a shoulder as big as a wine keg. I started to squeeze. The bear pivoted to face us—odd humps on the tundra a few gallops away—and pegged us as more caribou venison. It took another step toward us, the crosshairs settled where the spruce-trunk neck swelled into chest, and I pressed. A fistful of hair exploded into sun beyond and I knew I had the bear, but it sprinted through shin-tangle.

"Shoot," Scrom hissed from behind, "Shoot!"

I was certain Bruin was dead and didn't know it, but I swung through the galloping bear and when the crosshairs passed high through the flank, touched off. Half a ton of brown bear cart-wheeled to a stop on the tundra.

"Gawdamighty," Scrom exhaled.

The first shot, little more technical than swigging a jug, entered the base of the throat and angled back through chest, lungs and heart and exited the flank. The bear didn't know it was dead. Though the second shot wasn't needed, it was the kind you'd always remember. I did all but blow smoke from the barrel.

Scrom is a drinking man, and he'd hauled a six-pack in his backpack. We toasted the Red Gods, the king kong bear, the best of hunts.

"To Cheri," Rob toasted. Cheri had spotted the bruin. In the high latitudes, it doesn't get dark during the May bear season. When we'd staggered back to camp in the dusky wee morning hours, we cracked a bottle of R & R whiskey and celebrated two weeks of chasing brown bears. I prefer hunting coastal brown bears—I've hunted them in North America, Kamchatka and the Russian Far East along the Sea of Okhotsk—because they're so damned big.

"If you don't shoot," top Utah houndsman and outfitter Wade Lemon hollered, "I'm gonna." It was the evening of the last day of the hunt and we'd chased black bears a week through rugged Manti country in central Utah. The eleventh hour bruin was no king kong, but I didn't have time to act picky. At that moment sixteen bear hounds of various races from at least three packs bawled with such enthusiasm they registered on seismographs at the state university two-hundred miles north.

I'd hunted black bears with traditional methods—spot-and-stalk on autumn berry pastures, ambushing on salmon streams or moose carcasses, blundering into them—but hunts somehow lacked adrenaline. Except, maybe, a Canadian hound hunt as a kid. The bear raced into an old burn, climbed a dead fir rotted and broken off, and slid down into the upper hollow of the snag thirty-feet above the ground. Fur stuck through a knothole and we poured enough lead into the snag the bear would set off metal detectors from a quarter mile. No question bruin was dead, the question was how to get it down. We returned the next day with a crosscut saw and felled the snag. So I booked a hound hunt with Wade Lemon.

The first day we surprised a magnum cherry-coke-colored bear from an elk carcass. Lemon's hounds bayed the bear, we spurred the horses upslope, and when I eased into the dreadlock jackspruce with the Model 94, I spotted a single patch of that fur through the tangle. Hounds bayed and darted and I wasn't one-hundred percent the fur didn't belong to a dog, so I didn't shoot. To my regret. The bear pistoned over the mountain and we followed, noting a record-class track in mud, down the east slope and into cliffs until we gave it up that night with less than half the dogs. Some didn't turn up in towns far below until after the hunt, either.

Wade Lemon is a likeable guy, and he has friends. Plenty own hounds, too. Two days into the hunt we added three packs with as many owners and so much enthusiasm, bears didn't stand a chance. We hounded bears, but the bears won. They had even more enthusiasm, apparently. Events didn't look any better the last day. One pack treed a tom lion, and Wade rode off to help pull the hounds. We took other packs east, and jumped a bear, but it and probably a second bear galloped back and forth under the timbered rimrocks and befuddled the dogs. Hounds trailed to and fro and back again all afternoon, until a hound or two sleuthed the tracks and finally, before the sun dropped out toward Nevada, hounds bawled "treed."

Sixteen hounds bawled more racket in the ravine than a Titan rocket booster. You had to shout into the next guy's ear to get heard. The brown color phase bear stood on a branch twenty-five feet up a big Doug fir as I watched with my hands covering my ears.

"Shoot that thing," Lemon hollered. "Right behind the ear."

I did.

Years after, the late Bill Dodgson, former SCI Hunter of the Year and fine fellow, pointed it out to me. "You must have a bear slam."

Cheez, I figured, I never thought it.

The Horned Grail

First, let's splice in some backstory. In those days I'd annually expedition into Arctic wilderness hundreds of miles from anything that could be called civilization, even by Far North standards, all this in that wine-and-roses epoch before cell phones and the technology explosion. Earlier years I'd solo two-months each season, but this time my favorite prof from graduate school days at the University of Utah, Flo Krall, expeditioned with me. Famed (heck, he flew Cheryl Tiegs and other notables and appeared in *National Geographic* specials) Arctic bush pilot and good friend Roger Dowding gathered us at my cabin on the Yukon and winged us three hours north to a river bar at the headwaters of the Sheenjek, we floated a day downriver from there, cached the gear and then trekked up into a nameless canyon 15 miles to my favorite sheep haunt. I glassed a ram on a scree slope and hurriedly pitched the two trekking tents, shouldered the rifle and leaned into the wet-snow blizzard. To shorten the story, I bagged the ram with a single .270 Core-lokt and my sheep hunting and meat worries ended for the season.

One sunny morning, one canyon south, and three days later, I stalked a distant band of white sheep. For fun. After I'd duck-walked a mile as Flo watched with the binocular, I sidled through bunga-low-sized glacier erratic limestone boulders smack into the three rams.

At the time, I'd bagged only two rams, so no one would call me an expert, but I'd studied Dall's sheep heads throughout the Far North including the NWT and the Yukon and knew a big one when I saw it. Eyeball-to-eyeball at long spitting distance, one ram owned horns far grander than those ram mounts I'd lusted after in the taverns and sports stores, and that included top tenners.

The ram had broken back the right horn to a mere 40-inches, but the left flared out, pinched in to nearly touch the cheek, flared again and then soared up and dipped downwards again—close enough to a curl-and-a-half to call it that. I guesstimated 46-inches on the curl anyway. Maybe 16 on the base. Thirteen or 14 annular growth rings. That broken horn added character, and reality.

I made the following hunt next season.

Nobody knows what's in those mountains. Maybe too many bears live there. No hunters go that way. Gwitchin caribou hunter, Strangle Woman Creek, 1983.

Each expedition, I recalled that Gwitchin quote. He got it right, too. Nobody knew what they'd find in those mountains.

Pavement, hospitals and M*A*S*H reruns were far away now, in miles 400 to the south, in mindset 30,000 in the future. I'd stood on a tiny river bar littered with Pre-Cambrian gravel beside tangled duffel long after Roger Dowding's bush Cessna climbed then disappeared into the Arctic skies to the south, noticing again the surprising din of primeval silence and then feeling the familiar lump in the throat with the sudden and full understanding that I would not see or hear—I carried no radio—another human for at least eight weeks, if I was lucky and made no mistakes, and never if I screwed up.

Gradually apprehension disappeared, as it always did when I made this kind of expedition, replaced by the comfortable feel of solitude but not loneliness (wolf, caribou and grizzly tracks crisscrossed the beach). But I had immediate concerns: Where could I camp where I'd find enough firewood? Was the big ram still alive? Keeping dry, well-fed and alive was enough to think about, and they made petty the concerns of that other time.

As I pumped the inflatable boat, the memory of that broken-horned ram drifted up through river bottom mists, and in a dream state he stood on a high shale fin silhouetted against a swirling blizzard, one horn broken back half a foot and the other pinching in close and then flaring out and down like a grand argali.

Eventually the days ran together—I no longer cared if it was Tuesday or Sunday, August or September, 1984 or the Paleolithic—until all I knew was that I'd floated a day downriver, cached raft and gear in steel drums I'd brought in earlier years to protect them from grizzlies, and trekked up, first through muskeg bogs in the bottoms then through the stunted spruce forests and Arctic birch and rushing streams and dwarf willow and fractured glaciers, to the frost-shattered limestone and alpine tundra into the highest country that hid much of each day in the clouds. I couldn't remember how many days it took to reach the bare limestone peaks once the bottom of a tropical sea, witness the fossil sponges and corals fifty million years older than the first vertebrates. I plodded upward, deeper into country where no civilized man had walked, toward the ram's canyon. Wolves trotted alongside, forty yards off, barking and howling in curiosity, predatory brotherhood or something else. I fingered-and-toed up a steep canyon thick with migrating caribou and gazed into a prehistoric park.

A thousand caribou browsed the already browning tundra between patches of early snow, and lower down two wolves ghosted like quicksilver beads across the tundra and through dwarf birch and into a milling then fleeing band of caribou as the wolves cut out a big bull crippled from the glass-sharp scree. The bull whirled and rushed, searching with still-velveted antlers for his tormentors, a last act of desperation because within moments the wolves tore into thin underbelly as the downed bull held his head as if to bellow in rage. In minutes a dark grizzly rushed from nowhere and chased the wolves from the kill and in more moments the undiscouraged wolves ran a lame yearling to ground and the ravens followed. Farther up that nameless peak I named Dark Mountain—still the modern man, I could not yet fathom that all things need not be named, that would come later, and I could not yet discipline myself not to label—a ram band grazed dirty white against the black shale rock.

I pitched the tiny tent beside a garrulous stream, scrounged willow twigs from the knee-high scrub and kindled a fire as the sun dipped behind the looming mountain and the air chilled. In spite of the techno-age sleeping bag and a wonder parka you could shove into a pocket, I belonged as I never had any place, and I understood all over that this was one reason I took the risk.

I stalked a ram band next dawn, straining fingers-and-toes up a seventy-degree avalanche chute a thousand feet, then over a rocky bench, and a dozen rams clattered about the cliffs like fat white insects on a dark wall. At least two went 40 inches around the curl, but they weren't the grail, the broken-horned ram, and I felt no temptation.

I didn't find him, but grizzlies, caribou, wolves, sheep and even moose wandered everywhere, like a *National Geographic* wall poster. I half-expected *Smilodon* to stalk out of the swirling mists. Wolves visited my camps, barking and howling from very close, too innocent to own experience with man. Once, two wolves, one very light and the other quite black, came in the twilight that passes for night (until September, when true night comes and gets longer and longer until by November there is no daylight), and gazed as I boiled rice and grayling over willow wood coals, yipping like frustrated pets. I wished I owned meat enough to toss them, and I understood how primitive man had domesticated them. And without electronic stimulation, I had time to understand what I already knew but had forgotten back there.

I stalked and passed up rams often, living on rice, berries and grayling snagged with a nymph on a hand-held leader, and never lived better. Time meant nothing. Once I bluffed wolves off their caribou kill and thieved a hindquarter. Weeks passed, and out of rice and caribou haunch, above creeks and fish, I acknowledged I would not find the grail. I killed a lesser ram, a fine one by other standards, and trekked back down canyons and lived on the meat, climbed over passes and across fractured glaciers and howled in answer to wolves, until, as I staggered into a chasm, I glassed a ram on a ridge just as mists boiled over the divide and swallowed him. Was one horn really broken? Had the other really flared that much? Did I imagine the whole damned thing?

I turned away from that place and time that seem a fantasy now, toward something that became more and more real with each step toward the cache. I drifted out, then, on the Sheenjek River current aiming at its confluence with the Porcupine River a week downriver and then farther downstream from there to that Great Brown God, the Yukon River, and the fly-in Gwitchin village those Hudson Bay trappers named Fort Yukon that represented it and where I could no longer hide from it. The expedition wasn't quite over, but the justification for it, the search for the ram grail, was. I floated and hunted caribou and moose—winter meat—and fly-fished for two-pound grayling and wing-shot ptarmigan. I lingered at familiar camps along the now homey wilderness river and lounged away nights atop frost-heave hills called pingos as the mush ice congealed in the river, and stared at the always alien aurora shimmering and coiling, and tried to figure how the grand and dramatic aurora could remain so silent.

I'd spend more seasons chasing the horned grail despite the understanding that wolves had probably pulled him down in his dotage or he'd slipped from an icy ledge to feed the ravens when the snow melted. I was, after all, a modern man and had to own a concrete reason to justify going back, to make valid the risk. I couldn't even say to myself, let alone civilized men, that it was really the always inexplicable aurora, and the need to belong, to really go home and belong. I couldn't explain it in a way anyone could understand that it was the gory poetry of wolves killing caribou or the gooseflesh-raising wail of Arctic loons. I couldn't tell how it was the very blonde grizzly facing me down over a caribou I'd killed and that I'd never, ever feel so intensely mortal as at that warning growl.

So there must be a reason, a concrete grail to quest for. Without that, it's merely abstraction. The grail may change—in later years it became a 63-inch Marco Polo ram, a snow leopard photo, a ten-foot polar bear—but the true reasons for it never do.

THE DIRTY DOZEN

As I neared the end of collecting twelve varieties of world sheep, what I call my Dirty Dozen, I wrote an article exploring the why of it (*Sports Afield*, Sept. 2007). The theme was that hunting shouldn't become mere collecting, "…like buying a can of corn," as Jack O'Connor put it, because it lowers hunting to the status of acquiring, and too often, buying, that collection. The owning, and the status and certificates with it, shouldn't become more important than Canadian sunsets and memories of leaky wall tents in frigid timberline basins, Mongolian dust storms so fierce they'd scalp a camel, and Pamir blizzards that freeze the breath in your throat.

Yes, I know—I've bagged the four varieties of North American sheep, the twelve of world sheep, the twelve world goats, and own at least some of the apt certificates; I've managed Africa's dangerous game, North America's four bear species, and other collections, all more or less accidentally. But after a tough day lecturing university students, or worse, clacking away at the keyboard, I stagger to my own clean, well-lighted place and gaze at my big game mounts but especially the world sheep and goats taken in unfenced wilds in native habitat. Awards or certificates never cross my mind. Instead, I reminisce galloping Bactrian camels across Gobi dunes, sharing my lunch with half-starved religious pilgrims staggering the trails of the Caucasus, and awakening in a Utah cave with a rattler coiled six-inches from my nose. I remember that 15,000 foot Pamir blade ridge in a shrieking December gale that tried to hurl us into a thousand-foot gorge; it ended with grand Marco Polo ram, too. And I recall hunkering around a sheep-dung fire in a Mongol ger while blizzards raged, or gawking from the backpack tent on a do-it-yourselfer and stalking a 46-inch Dall ram (I couldn't shoot, either, because I'd already collected a ram!). And the guides—Hasan hefting a Bezoar ibex on his back and grunting it down the scarps to the valley floor, guts and all, or Vladimir emptying the blood from his rubber boot but refusing to quit stalking snow sheep.

My rule is never to shoot a high-fenced animal (or low-fenced, for that matter), no matter how far away the fence or how challenging the terrain. I once passed up a heck of a bargain on a Konya sheep hunt in Turkey because of this rule; ditto a Texas shoot and a South African rhino. I won't shoot a non-native ram, either; the sheep or goat must be native to that place. If you have different standards, though, fine; democracy can't function without tolerance of the other guy.

When I wrote that magazine article, I had two to go for my dirty dozen world sheep. So Cheri and I arranged a mouflon and chamois hunt with Srdja Dimitrijevic of International Safaris, in Croatia. Now, I'm aware of the mouflon reintroduction and introduction myths often passing as history. One or another might be right. But we couldn't get another sheep hunt for my December break, and beside, Cheri was weary of holidays swaddled in extreme-weather gear and hunched in twenty-below gales. Hotels and five-course meals along the Adriatic seemed like cheating on a sheep hunt, though. Cheri saw no problem with it.

First, we hunted chamois a day's drive north of Sarajevo in Bosnia, but the weather chased us out and on the retreat, our prohunter Dragan's vehicle electronics fried. Before the weather got tough, though, we found millennia-old rock art rams pecked into boulders near the Croatia and Bosnia border. Absolutely native mouflon roamed nearby desert ranges in Armenia and Turkey today. Mouflon must have lived there for primitive man to carve them. If the glyphs were indeed urial, they ranged farther, in Iran or Turkmenistan (where I bagged a king kong Transcaspian urial). Later we spent nights at Makarska, Croatia. Hotel Biokovo's logo was a heroic ram the concierge assured me was a copy of one painted in a nearby Balkan cave.

Circumstantial evidence suggested, at least, that mouflon were/ are native to Croatia. In any case, after roaming Croatia from south of Dubrovnik to north of Split, no fences even existed. Rabid hunt brokers and rumor has it that Croatia owned the only completely unfenced European mouflon herd. As mentioned, the weather chased us out of Bosnia, so no luck with the chamois there. We hunted them in Croatia, and after two days finger-and-toeing the limestone scarps 2000 feet above the Adriatic Sea, we shuffled down the trail one evening, when the park ranger dropped to belly. My one shot collected an 11-inch-plus chamois.

We shifted our mouflon "camp" farther down the coast to the Peljesac Peninsula and another hotel on the sea. Mladin Binic was the park ranger and our local guide. Late that morning we jumped ewes and a wide-horned ram. I caught Mladin's and Dragan's adrenaline rush, so we clawed through tangled brush up the backside of the ridge to head them off. When we peeked over, the ewes eyeballed us and ping-ponged through boulders. When the ram burst from dreadlock brush, I rested Dragan's .30/06 across a branch, steadied the crosshairs at the base of the ram's tail as he bounded straight away, and touched off. The ram dropped in his track. That meant only one to go for the planet's dirty dozen sheep, though that thought was a hemisphere away.

At the SCI convention that winter I bargained a hunt for western, or Kuban tur with Sergei Shushanov's Russian Hunting Agency, in the Russian republic of Karachai-Cherkessia. Though technically more of a goat, tur are allowed in the planet's dozen-sheep collections, and with good reason: They're found only in the roughest, nastiest, on-end geography in the galaxy—the Caucasus. I'd bagged a 40-inch Dagestan tur two years before in Azerbaijan on a hoot of a hunt, and I wanted another tur.

The Russia-Georgia War broke out days before we departed. Sergei Shushanov assured me, "Walt, the war if 400 miles away." When we landed in Stavropol, unlit military helicopters hammered overhead every two minutes on their way south to the war. The drive in a Pleistocene relic Lada sedan dodging unlit haywagons and cattle on potholed roads in the black of night at 110 klicks per hour was adventure enough, but we were in for more. We chased down horses and shoed them much of one day, and used up another packing into the peaks. We managed a day of hunting before the Fates stepped in. It was noon before I got the guys up and going, when a 'copter gunship bristling rockets and guns hammered over camp.

Hours later, first one, then another, and finally a dozen Russian soldiers jack-in-the-box from behind glacial boulders, AKs at the ready. We're surrounded. Oleg Podzhykin, outfitter and translator, and the local guide and outfitter, conferenced with them. The local guide disappeared down the mountain with two grunts while the other soldiers kept an eye on us. They're kids, really, and they practiced their English while we entertained them with tales of America. Cheri made great friends with a hatful of American bubble gum while they checked out my Remington.

By dusk, they're radioed to escort us off the mountain. Hours later we're met by our guide and another dozen grunts. The guide laughed, ran his hand down his face to indicate my beard, twirled a finger above his head to indicate helicopter, pointed at me and said, "You! Osama bin Laden!" and doubled over in mirth. Apparently that helicopter over camp thought I was Osama. Big joke. Lucky the 'copter didn't blast us into molecules. We were trucked to an army base south of Stavropol, hustled inside, and the pistols-in-waistband KGB operatives dressed in civvies interrogated us all night. Apparently, the local guide hadn't gotten permission to enter a war zone, and one battle took place just four miles south on the Abkhazia border. It's dawn when the guide was finger-printed and got his documentation, the KGB was interrogated-out, and we were set free.

We made camp in late morning, hunted three hours, and then yanked the camp. Apparently, no big tur lived there. We moved camp that night, then sat horses the next dawn into the scarps and climbed from there. To make another adventure short, I bagged a tur late that last afternoon and completed my dirty dozen collection with a single shot. The tur wasn't big, but what can you do? Oleg gets the local guide to offer me another hunt at cost to make up for this fiasco, but I nix it. What could I expect next time, a Russian firing squad?

Trophies eventually fade into the wall, but what you have left lasts forever—the stories and memories.

My first sheep hunt in 1982 in one of Montana's open areas ended without a ram, but it wasn't a bust. I solo-ed through three glorious backpack expeditions in the Absaroka-Beartooth Wilderness—a total of five weeks—trekking, fishing, hunting deer, elk and bighorns, and couldn't have a better time though I never got the crosshairs on a sheep. I blame that expedition, along with Jack O'Connor's sheep stories in the old *Outdoor Life*, for turning me into a sheep hunter rabid enough to hock his house for one last ram hunt. About that time, I moved to the Yukon River wilds. I made ten or so white sheep hunts, trekking the bush alone for a month or so, bagging a ram, and then floating out and back to civilization, if you call the Yukon River civilization. Put a double Scotch in my hand, and I'll regale absolute strangers with tales of those golden Yukon years and the grizzly charges, wolves in camp, avalanches, swimming glacial rivers to fetch a shot caribou that jumped in, casting smoke-colored dry flies at two pound grayling, and jump-shooting ptarmigan. I'll have those recollections 'til I die, with any luck, in one last sheep pasture.

I can't forget the California bighorn hunt along British Columbia's Fraser River, either. My guide Ken Olynyk, wrangler Bill and I "camped" in an ancient miner cabin dug into the slope. At night, a packrat danced across my face, tipped over cans and pots, and generally raised rodent hell. What really pissed me off, though, was the guys didn't stir. The bags under my eyes became satchels, when I decided enough was too much. That night, I slipped Ken's Colt .22 revolver out of its holster, grabbed a flashlight, and propped myself against the wall. On cue, that nocturnal quadruped pogo-ed onto my shin. I couldn't shoot unless I could spare a toe or knee-cap. When he catapulted onto the plank table, I thumbed back the hammer, froze him in the flashlight beam, and plugged a jug of Log Cabin syrup. The guys didn't stir while syrup oozed onto the table. The rat dove under Olynyk's bunk, I dropped to knees, got the bugger in the beam and opened fire. Clean misses, and the guys didn't even slow their snoring. The rat missiled under Bill's bunk. I beamed him, shot and missed, and the beast disappeared. Moments later, I got him in the beam on my bed, but if I shot I'd ruin a $300 down sleeping bag. I waited a moment, then five, and the rat stared me down. My shooting eye began watering, my pistol hand trembling. That damned rat. He hopped onto a shelf and I blasted as fast as I could thumb the hammer, and on a Lourdes-type miracle, shot him through the eye. He flopped onto my sleeping bag and bled all over it. Nobody stirred. I placed the varmint on the table eye-level with the wrangler when he awoke, and never slept better. Oh yeah, I bagged a ram, too.

I'd written about my December 2000 Marco Polo hunt in east Tajikistan along the China border before, and about the ram of a lifetime I bagged, but that was just the beginning. After shooting that ram close enough to 63" to call it that and a magnum ibex, everyone pulled out of the Lake Karakul camp; mine was the last hunt of the season. Pamiri Guide Toktomat lived at Karakul, so he stayed. Tajik guide Dovelat beelined for the city lights of Dushanbe, and outfitter and guide Yuri Matison, skinner Andrei and *major domo* Boris, Cheri and I made our way toward Moscow. First, we skidded the Russian Uaz vans out through blizzards, three-foot drifts and 20-below temps toward Osh in Kyrgyzstan. We passed overturned trucks and frozen bodies, too, and the journey remains one of those inexplicable miracles of life, because we lived through it. Boris knew it was my birthday, and in Osh the partying started, complete with bar hopping and a Kyrgyz rock band that sang "Happy Birthday." The vodka bottles and food cramming our tables never ended. Cheri danced with local Russian expatriates and Andrei became the unofficial teetotaler and babysitter, all the way to Moscow. Without him, we'd never have made it. Boris and Yuri washed down breakfast with more vodka, kept at it all day until our flight to Biskek, continued through Biskek by falling on tables and rolling on the floor, until we boarded a flight on a converted Badger bomber to Moscow. Boris at six feet plus and 250 lbs owned an unlimited capacity for vodka. They hauled bottles of vodka aboard and lost consciousness half way to Moscow, while Andrei navigated all of us through the formalities of the flight. That party remains my wildest birthday ever, and whenever I gaze at my life-size Marco Polo ram mount, I remember that bachanal. Whew!

*****

I recall the urial hunt in late 2004 in Turkmenistan, just before the country closed its hunting. And three snow sheep hunts in the Russian Far East. On one, the helicopter stopped to drop off supplies to trappers and outfitter Sergei jumped out for a quick pee. The giant Soviet-era 'copter took off without him and nobody knew he'd gone until we got back to the village of Nelkan. On another, thunderstorms forced down the fixed-winged plane flying us north from Khabarovsk at the mining camp in Ayan; the gold miners treated us like royalty and we feasted on crab, salmon, caviar and their best vodka, and until the weather cleared, we had the time of our lives. I got two grand rams that time, too. I remember a Mongolian argali that took two hunts to put in the salt, and it gave me a pickup load of angst, but I wouldn't change a thing about that hunt.

Like I said, you forget the inches and scores and the certificates and plaques. What you have left are recollections. To my ram collection, I can say, "Thanks for the memories."

TIMBERLINE CAMPFIRES

*Courts and camps are the only places to learn the
world in.* Earl of Chesterfield, 1747

Once, the perfect blizzard caught me solo field-butchering a
bull elk in a 10,000-foot Montana basin off Buffalo Plateau.
One moment I owned a pleasant south wind and sleeves
rolled to elbows, and three shakes and a yawn later temps dropped
30 degrees and banshee horizontal snow obliterated the Douglas firs
a long spit down-slope. The comfy tent camp hunkered in lodgepole
pines two miles south, and no way I'd find it in the sudden white-out
maelstrom. I scavenged caribou moss and fir twigs for kindling and
within moments thawed fingers over a crackling fire under protective boughs of two big pines and a deadfall windbreak. I short-tied
the packhorse in forest cover and prayed a widow-maker wouldn't
drop on her, and gathered deadfall before it disappeared under what
became 26-inches of snow. That elk hide cinched to fir branches at
the corners made a handy shelter from the snow melting off boughs
from the heat of the fire. Skewered elk chops kept my belt snug,
too. I slept the night curled around pine coals, finished the butchery
and made it to the camp next afternoon, and continued to hunt
bighorns. Lessons relearned? Always carry matches and a dry means
of kindling fires, and never panic. And heck, have fun. Bivouacs like
that one make good stories later on.

Another time a high country blizzard caught me out, so I piled
dried lichen and spruce twigs in a tiny cave mouth, kindled them,

added heavy deadfall and crawled in and slept warm and snug in my hunting togs. I made it back to camp dry and rested that night.

While backpacking for Utah desert rams, we camped in sandstone alcoves to avoid lightning immolation, and in one cave I snored in the company of a rattler and score of scorpions, I learned next dawn. Lesson here? Pick your roommates, but use what's available, if you must. The rattler was more upset about sleeping arrangements than I.

Alright. Most of us won't choose those kinds of bivouacs, but if you're afield long enough the Red Gods will catch you, so prep yourself mentally (don't panic, and have fun) and physically (always keep dry kindling and matches).

When I think of mountain camping, though, I think of cheery and planned camps, not those The Fates thrust upon us. The wildest, most isolated camps are best. My favorite campsite rests in an unnamed glacial valley a hundred miles north of the Arctic Circle, and maybe 300 miles from the nearest pavement, this in those now surreal days before cell phones, GPS and perpetual contact with civilization. The absolute isolation made for most of the camp's mystique. I've never camped anywhere in North America where you'd see more game, and this made the place magical, too. On any day, you'd ogle Dall sheep, caribou, moose, wolves and grizzly (we had enough near misses with the bears to write a book, but that explains some of the camp's cachet), often within a few yards of the tent. We'd spot gyr and peregrine falcons, the odd snowy owl, and a golden eagle nearly scored a Dall lamb on a blade ridge. I added a handful of species to my bird life list. Wolves serenaded us most nights. Once we roasted ram haunch for our next day's trek. I wrapped it in something, and forgot it. As I wormed from the tent at dawn, a wolf grabbed the roast two yards away and galloped off into the dwarf birch followed by her three pups. Sure, I had a rifle, but I'd have starved before taking aim. Beside, Cheri would shoot me if I orphaned those pups. That camp owned what it took—isolation, myriad wildlife, and its unique brand of comfort. I've seldom slept more comfortable in any camp, and I'm not talking cushy comfort. And I've never slept better in a Hyatt or Ritz, either.

A goat camp in the Cariboo country of British Columbia had its own mystique. I'd made the solo drive from Utah and high school in my tender teens and planned on stalking mountain goats on money I'd slaved for all year. My parents weren't hunters, but the Old Man lent me his Oldsmobile and Mom gave her blessings with crossed fingers, because a rattlesnake bit me on my last solo wilderness foray.

First, we hurrahed a string of perverse gear-laden nags that took glee in unbalancing loads against every spruce tree we passed. Five hours from a logging road in 15-inches of November Chinook snow later, we made camp for my first mountain game hunt. Tangy spruce boughs carpeted the wall-tent floor, and a half 50-gallon oil drum stove glowed in one end. Shuswap guides Charlie and Herbie and I tossed bedrolls on the spruce boughs and slept as near or far from the stove as we wanted. I got lost one night on a short jaunt from camp and why I didn't freeze in the sub-zero temps remains a mystery. A horse rolled over me, too, but all I got was a bloody nose. We cooked on that stove, and it got so smoky I often shoved my head through the flaps to breathe. We scored grand goats, too. The hunting aside, I recall the camp with fondness because it became a heck of an adventure. Exactly what a wannabe mountain man teenager needed.

Wilderness float-hunts are favorites, because you can pack luxuries like coffee pots, champagne, and clean socks. I've float-hunted the Sheenjek, Colleen, Porcupine and Yukon Rivers, and the drill was cache gear, including the inflatable boat, in steel drums brought for such purposes to keep out the grizzlies, and trek into the heights for one week or three to hunt rams. On those floats we found favorite campsites we stayed at year after year. Ptarmigan Camp across from Lobo Lake became a favorite because we'd been out of meat that first time, Cheri was a Michigan urban transplant on her first Far North wilderness expedition (and frankly, she didn't trust me yet) and if she wasn't yet panicky, she oozed angst about the dismal grub situation. One dawn I clawed up from a dream about my cousins' farm, to clucking. I pushed open the tent flap with the shotgun to a dozen ptarmigan scratching for gravel through the camp, scored half of them with the single bore 12 gauge, and we had our meat.

Remember, this was not sport hunting. After that, we pitched tents at Ptarmigan Camp every one of the seven or so float expeditions.

We had other favorite camps, and we named them. Surprise Camp because of the moose right in camp, the lone caribou that bee-lined straight at us from two miles, wolves chasing a caribou through the camp, and other surprising events. Bluff Camp because of the big esker across the river; we always spotted game from it. And we camped on the Big Island in the Yukon, and usually at the mouth of Charley River.

Describing all the best mountain camps I've snored at is impossible in less than 2000 words, but British Columbia owns some of the planet's top game animals and mind-numbing scenery, so logically it owns stunning camps, too. I've already mentioned one, but another favorite was the Toad River geography and the pack trip into it where I put my first Stone's ram in the salt with guide Ralph Kitchen and the Folding Mountain outfit back in the 1980s.

Another favorite was the Dzhugdzhur snow sheep hunting camp in the Russian Far East, because of the tough hunt, the stunning geography, and I scored my first Asian rams. And though we didn't speak the same language, the Russian guides and I got along famously.

We pitched a spike camp at over 10,000 feet in Azerbaijan's East Caucasus, and I bagged two grand tur, one of them close enough (if 1 cm., or 2/5 of an inch, is close enough) to 40-inches to call it that. From camp, you gazed into Russia, and Arif, the local guide and outfitter and his four sons were the best of company and ran a tight outfit. Professional hunter Erdogan Avci made the shebang purr, too.

Mongolia is my favorite hunting destination. When I dream of Mongolia, I don't first envision the grand argali and the other four magnum trophies I bagged there. I see the ger camps. A ger is a Mongol yurt. Nomads live in the circular felt shelters full time, they're cushy with a dung-fired stove in the center, beds and other furniture about the circular wall, and it's tough to think of them as camps. But if locale means anything, they squat like behemoth ice cream scoops in remote game terrain. Still, they're too comfortable, in 80-degree temps or 26-below-zero banshee sandstorms, to think of them on the same terms as Arctic trekking camps or Canadian wall tent camps. We've "camped" in maybe ten ger camps, and the most remote and my favorite squatted between May snowfields in the south Altai Range near the Chinese border at 11,000 feet; we scored a 14-year-old Altai ibex there, too. Gers are little changed in millennia, unless you count the odd solar panel or midget wind generator, so I get a sense of history sleeping in them. I'm anticipating my next Gobi expedition largely because of the ger camps. I'm not adverse to camping luxury now and then.

A snug camp offers other amenities. Few things get as intense as stud poker for matchsticks when you're weathered in a sheep camp. You don't mind if the guy sitting across from you hasn't shaved in a week and stinks of goat, either. (You do mind the clean-shaven fellow that reeks aftershave and sports a pressed safari outfit, because he makes you want to tuck in your shirt and clean your fingernails.) It's healthy to have a handy ear to brag up your ram or commiserate about the one that got away, too.

The hunting "camps" I hate? A room at the Family Inn with hamburger steak and mash potatoes thrown it.

Give me a trekking tent in an Arctic basin or a ger in the remote Gobi any day. I've learned everything I'll need in a hunting camp, and I expect I'll learn more in that graduate school of life.

Pure Adrenaline

"Yer free now, Hombre," Sarge Brown said as I swung onto the pale buckskin gelding. Two hours earlier I'd sprinted through the Buena Vista school doors and piled into Sarge's battered Willy's pickup for three weeks of Xmas vacation pack trip in the Sierra Madre. Two days trailing pack mules and hounds across northern Mexico desert later, we rode up a sycamore-lined creek to the headwaters of the Rio Sonora.

"Best damn camp in the Sierra," Sarge said as we unsaddled and hobbled the stock and the half-dozen lion hounds lapped clear water. Sarge had camped in the same meadow half a century earlier while chasing Apaches that jumped the reservation.

Sarge quit the cavalry when the army phased out horses, and he'd lived in a stone house in the Huachuca Mountains a long spit from the Mexican border ever since.

In the next weeks we chased lions and killed a big tom, bagged Coues whitetail bucks so fat rain water puddled on their backs, shot turkeys, quail and javelina, and I had the best time I'd ever have.

"Time t' git ya back fer school," Sarge said one evening as he tossed blackjack oak deadfall onto the fire, "or yer old man the Major'll pelt us both." We packed the outfit one dawn and trailed north across the mesquite desert. Sometimes we road abreast with Sarge telling of the old cavalry days and when the trail narrowed I rode behind hazing the pack mules along. I followed when a *Slap!* plumed dust from the canvas pannier on the mule ahead. A split-second later we heard the rifle shot. Sarge pivoted in the saddle and yanked the Model '94 from the saddle boot and yelled "Git!" I kicked the two-inch Mexican rowels into the buckskin and whipped the mule and galloped into the arroyo.

"Where'd thet come from?" Sarge yelled. "Seed tracks a while back—two horses an' two loaded-down mules trailin' north like us. Wonder if they's some of them dope runners. Mebbe thought we was followin'." Sarge took the binocular and climbed the arroyo bluff and glassed then slid back down. "Dust a mile northwest. If that's them, they're rippin' fer cover. Ya can put that thing away now," he said, nodding at the .30/30 I held. "We ain't havin' a shootout jest yet."

We trailed up the arroyo, Sarge riding to the rim every so often and glassing, then crossed the double-strand barbed wire that marked the international boundary, and made Sarge's Bear Creek corrals and cabin just as the sun speared itself on a volcano out toward Nogales.

When we'd unpacked, Sarge held up the soot-blackened coffee pot. A neat hole drilled its center, the edges silver where the porcelain had splintered off. We found the spent slug in the pannier bottom.

"Kinda fun, warn't it?" Sarge said. "'Minds me o' the ol' days."

As we lay in bunks that night and listened to coyote wails and then lion hounds answering, Sarge said, "Best not to tell yer ol' man the Major, neither." At the time I was young enough to believe I was bullet proof, so it was all a great adventure. I'd been back to the country a dozen times since, and desperados still trail narcotics and humans across the trails into the American Huachucas. It's spooky carrying a deer rifle you might have to use against a two-legged beast.

After my voice solved its adolescent squawk, I'd backpacked into a north Utah gorge to scout for the upcoming deer season. By that time the Old Man had retired from the army and moved us north, and Sarge Brown had died of cancer—the result of a life of heavy smoking.

I was always catching one beast or another. I'd pinned the rattler with my boot and grasped it just behind the head. No big deal—I'd done it plenty before. I stood in a rockslide and as I shifted the snake to my right hand for a better grip, a rock rolled. As I stumbled for balance, I loosened the grip and the snake sunk both fangs into my index finger. To make a long story short, I lay with my hand in the creek at my camp for days as sick as it is possible to be and live, before

I got enough strength to climb out of the gorge to my jeep on a ridge miles above.

I've had other snake encounters—once I bellied up a bluff on a Red Desert pronghorn and came face-to-face with a coiled prairie rattler. I revved back before the snake struck, and the buck sprinted for Colorado. Then the siwash camp on a desert bighorn hunt in southern Utah when I awoke in the dawn with a rattlesnake coiled comfortable six-inches from my nose.

Once in the South Africa, Piet Cloete and I had waited for a calf-killing leopard in a burlap and thatch blind. Hours into the night, I shifted my foot and put it down on something that gave under the weight. It tapped my boot, and when I figured it out I yanked my foot up so hard I nearly tipped the lawn chair over. Piet flicked on the "torch" in time to see a black, scaly tail disappear under the thatch and a wet smear on my boot.

"*Naja*," Piet said, "cobra to you and me." We abandoned the blind.

Other reptiles offered spooky moments, too. In the Okavango a crocodile crawled into the camp after PH Willie Phillips's chained dogs. The cook had trouble discouraging the beast, too. Or that time at the Bubye River camp in Zimbabwe; the staff took down the outhouse for repairs, so Cheri walked out of camp to answer nature's call.

"WALT!" yanked me out of a nap faster than a bucket of ice water. I grabbed the nearest rifle and sprinted through the tent flaps. Cheri squatted with britches dropped.

"Snake?" she quavered. A big, black-and-white beaded head slid out of the grass six-inches behind her. I thought of python, but when an eye blinked, I recognized the Nile monitor, a four-foot lizard that could, if so inclined, make hamburger out of an exposed half-moon.

I'd hunted Cape buffalo throughout Africa, and the normal drill is a stalk, the bull profiling just ahead, and a slug through the lights. The bull whirls and gallops off and you put one or two more aft if you have time, and when you spoor up the buff is anchored or dead. That had always been my experience, until that Tanzanian July.

On an extended safari, you're allowed three buffalo. We'd stalked a big herd along the Msima River. When the herd scented us and galloped for cover, I put a 300-grain A-frame through a bull's heart and collected my first Tanzanian buff.

Another afternoon we'd followed a herd into riverine bush. The herd kept whirling and stampeding off and we'd follow, and they'd do it again. In the late sun, a bull fat enough to have learned dinner habits from a hippo refused to run farther, pivoted and faced us. The .375 slug slammed the chest where I'd aimed and the bull galloped off into thick bush before I could shoot again. I expected the usual—following lung-blood spoor and finding the dead bull a hundred yards on. We found blood, alright, but it was dark muscle blood, not the pink, frothy gore you'd find with a lung hit. We trailed into dreadlock riverine tangles, but we gave it up when the equatorial night dropped like a rock. We drove out of camp the next dawn toward where we'd last seen the buff. Half-way there, the Maasai tracker Gabreli hissed, "M'bogo!"

I spotted the dried, blackened blood, and Richards said, "That's your bull." I hammered it in the chest as it charged. The bull staggered sideways, and I hit it again and again until it collapsed. The first bullet in, the one that counts, had hit the point of the shoulder but instead of drilling straight into heart and lungs, deflected outward along the outer plain of the shoulder blade. I'll always wonder if the bull, angry and vindictive from a night of pain, blood-hounded toward the camp with mayhem on its mind. After all, he'd halved the distance and was still coming.

Hundreds of miles farther east on the Maasai Steppe, we faced a second charge. We'd motored toward camp after a day searching for fringe-eared oryx. A young Maasai herder panted down the path; a buffalo had chased him from the water and scattered his cows. When we approached the water, the buff charged the Toyota. Richards ground into gear and roared off. When things quieted, the tracker, a Maasai elder and the government game scout decided we should settle the buff before it murdered someone.

We drove back. The buff charged the Toyota, Richards skidded to a stop, and when I fired the .577, the buff dove into the dust with a shattered spine. When it raised its head and tried to lunge to its feet, I put 750-grains of metal through its skull. The buff was a cow with a 40-inch spread. Pus oozed from lion claw wounds. Charge number two.

I still wanted a buff with a mid-forties spread. We motored into a fever tree thicket miles long, then stalked a big buffalo herd. As we neared, a hundred buff rumbled off in the choking volcanic dust, and we'd follow. Finally, Richards said, "That's forty-five," as he glassed a bull in the rear. The bull broadsided and I double-lunged it. It whirled and galloped off and I hit it in the hips. We trailed the frothy pink lung blood in the dust. I spotted our bull waiting in ambush. Blood ringed the bull's nostrils—a lung hit, all right. The bull galloped off when it realized we'd spotted it. We followed. Our bull waited in ambush again, silhouetted against the open plain beyond. We halved the distance and halved it again.

The bull's stance told us it would run no more. I kneeled, held low on the shoulder and pressed the trigger. The .375 flattened the bull so suddenly no one had any doubt it was dead. Richards broke open his .577 double and handed it to Gabreli. I thought of jacking out the one up the throat of my .375, but didn't. As we back-slapped from mere feet, the bull lunged up and rushed faster than a singed impala. Out of the corners of my eyes the trackers and PH disappeared into bush. I fired the .375 from the hip as I leaped aside. Heck, I might have fired in mid-air, I don't know. To my astonishment, the bull collapsed in the dust three paces from my toes with shattered neck vertebrae. I was as surprised as anyone, but acted like I did it all the time. That safari, three buffalo charged us.

I've faced elephant charges, and on one Zimbabwe safari with a neophyte PH, we were lucky to live, but I believe buffalo are more apt to charge than any African game. Some of those charges are unprovoked, too; if you doubt it, ask outfitter Bob Fontana's widow, or PH John Wambach how he lost his Mozambique tracker.

While buff may charge with little cause, the grizzly is more likely to charge without provocation than any beast. It was in the '80s, that season of grizzlies. For whatever reason, the bears were oddly aggressive. Maybe I'd gotten careless, too. I'd trekked grizzly-thick Denali

National Park each summer photographing wildlife without problems; we'd kept to ourselves, the bears and me. I'd been within fifty yards of grizzlies hundreds of times, of course unarmed. After the Denali trek, the usual drill was a bush flight into the wildest geography on the continent, eastern Arctic Alaska. Then we'd trek the high country, return to our cache on the upper Sheejek River weeks later and spend another six weeks float-hunting out to the bush village of Ft. Yukon, then Cessna upriver to our cabin on the Yukon from there.

One morning Cheri and I started from our tent to look over a band of rams. A quarter-mile downwind, we spotted a bear lying on a talus slope. I shouted, normally good bear medicine. It wasn't fazed. We shouted ourselves hoarse, but the grizzly just watched us. I fired the 7mm/08 over its head, then powdered a rock three feet in front of it. Nothing. Though I'd seen maybe a thousand grizz in the wilds, I'd never had one act like this. No question it was downwind of the camp, and it could smell us.

We returned to camp to await developments. We couldn't risk the loss of the camp, because we'd have a tough time surviving without it seven weeks out from civilization. Two minutes after we got into camp, the bear trotted onto the bench and stared, then grazed soapberries. The bear acted cute, since it had no interest in the berries. No matter how clean your camp, you can't banish all odors— food, bug dope, medicine, leather, soap, boot treatments. Something smelled better than berries to the bear, and it was going to find out what. The bear grazed but edged closer. "Start packing," I told Cheri. While she broke camp and shoved gear into the packs, the bear sidled closer. I banged pots together. Nothing. I shouted. Grizz paid no attention. I fired over the bear's head. Still nothing. The bear edged closer. I picked a boulder 10 yards from camp. I wouldn't let the bear get nearer.

Grizz got cheekier, then sauntered straight at me. I shot at that boulder and splintered limestone fragments in its face. It grunted, staggered backward, then shuffled off the bench. It returned minutes later. We shouldered packs and trekked upcanyon. If we stayed, we'd have to kill the bear.

An hour later we climbed onto a high bench and glassed below. The bear blood-hounded after us. My hair stood and scalp prickled. I was too used to being the hunter to have something hunting me.

We trekked another eight miles, and each time we glassed we spotted the bear below, and it halved the distance. Finally, we crossed a col into another drainage. The bear turned back. Possibly we'd wandered into another bear's home range.

Down on the river weeks later, we found more bear trouble. We'd killed a moose and caribou and floated down the Sheenjek toward its confluence with the Porcupine River. One evening we paddled the raft into a big eddy, and I climbed the bluff to check for a campsite, without the gun, as always. I paced off potential tent sites, when brush shattered behind me. I guessed a surprised moose, but when I pivoted a grizzly missiled through dreadlock jackspruce and its canines neoned in the shadowy gloom.

I was unarmed and as helpless as I've ever felt. Everything seemed to slow and I crouched and my chest tightened as I waited for the impact and ripping teeth. I was as sure as I've ever been of anything that I'd get mauled, as certain as the falling rock climber is of hitting rocks below. The inevitable calmed me and I thought beyond to Cheri in the raft, all this in nanoseconds. "Get the gun!" I half-croaked. Cheri might make it to Fort Yukon alone, if the bear didn't get her, too.

Cheri shouted something back and the confused bear skidded to a stop three yards away. I lunged three steps and dove off the bluff onto the raft, and nearly bounced out again. "ROW!" I hissed. A moment later we were into the current and a moment after that the bear searched the bluff for us. I was giddy with the unexpected reprieve, astonished to be alive and in one piece.

From there downriver I rigged aluminum pans around the camp so if bears came I'd know about it. I half-slept with a round up the throat and the .270 beside me.

We hauled out early one afternoon and Cheri handed me a pail and said, "Pick." She meant blueberries. I picked my way slowly over the hill when something moved below.

"Not again," I hissed aloud as blood pooled behind my eyes. By then, I carried the rifle everywhere. The bear saw me and stood on hind legs and weaved to keep balance. I threw the bolt and shoved a cartridge in the chamber. Grizz dropped to all fours and rushed like a steam engine in a silent movie. Glossy fur filled the riflescope as I shot down on the bear, it was that close. It hung at the shot, almost in surprise, before sagging into the crimson dwarf birch. I tried to spit away the brassy taste, but I had no spit. Lucky—I had a bear tag that season.

With enough time, portfolios become meaningless and trophies fade into the wall. What you have left are stories, and with luck, some are pure adrenaline.

Gold-Grade Mountain Guides

W hen you plunk your nickels down for a hunt, they beeline to the broker, then the outfitter, and finally trickle to the guide. No surprise. The chap that first digs his fingers into your shekels is farthest from the action—the way of the world. But you'll share leaky tents in timberline basins, finger-and-toe scarps, and commiserate about weather and life with the guide. He'll round up the nags that strayed into the next basin in the night, sweat a ram off a peak, and yank on soaked duds in a freon dawn for one more day incinerating 5000 calories to get you your trophy. While the outfitter and broker get the glory, gold, and pics in brochures, the guide goes back to goat herding in the Caucasus or strumming a guitar in a backwoods Canadian honky-tonk. Here's a salute to the unknown guys that get your trophy on the wall.

Like dentists and mechanics, you'll find good and not-so-good guides. My first mountain guide, Herbie, was a short and stalky middle-aged Shuswap Indian decades back when I was a teenager on a mountain goat hunt on the Cariboo Plateau of British Columbia.

Thawing November Chinook winds swooped in from the Pacific, and each night avalanches rumbled and rattled the rickety log cabin base camp on Crooked Lake.

"Worth a man's life to hunt goats in that," outfitter Cliff Eagle *tsked* each dawn as we forked flapjacks and boiled moose-nose, so we hunted deer and moose in the spruce and willow bogs and waited for the freeze that wouldn't come.

"Let's go," Herbie said one pre-dawn and poked a flapjack-laden fork at the hissing lantern and the looming plateau beyond the cabin window. Cliff raised eyebrows as we swung onto horses and the dark faded. We sat creaky-cold saddle leather to the end of the lake, cinched the horses to spruce deadfall and spread them a bucket of grain, then waded soggy, thigh-deep snow up a blade ridge. Goat trails criss-crossed new snow thousands of feet above. As we trudged, avalanches rumbled loose as the snow thawed in the scarps. "Wouldn't make a half mile up thet crick bottom," Herbie said. He was dead right. Emphasize "dead." An avalanche terminus dammed the creek into a small lake below. "Don't git downstream of thet when it lets loose."

To shorten a book's worth of adventure, we cut fresh billy tracks on top of the plateau, and tracked them along the rim and jumped them.

They all looked big. I settled the crosshairs of the 7mm magnum behind the last goat's shoulder blades as he scaled a limestone bluff, and touched off. I came out of the dancing stars and the blood dripping off the end of my schnozz as the billy staggered over the rim. We tracked the goat miles. I was young and tough and as I wallowed over a bluff, a goat ghosted into timber just below, and the trail led right to him. I made sure this time and broke both shoulders. It was a grand old goat, too, but the trail led beyond him and into an avalanche chute and up cliffs on the otherside. And there stood my billy. In those days, you could hunt two goats, and a good thing. I killed him, too, and he tumbled into the chute and didn't stop for two thousand feet. The first goat taped ten-inches, and the second a hair shorter.

We staggered to the horses late that night after dodging an avalanche and plunging waist-deep through creek ice and surviving hypothermia. The nags didn't plod into base camp until dawn. Good mountain horses always know the way home.

I had other gold-grade guides in BC. Ken Olynyk and I bagged a bighorn above the Fraser River gorge. Olynyk felled big timber in the off-season. I gave him my pet .270 after the hunt to replace the battered antique he carried. Years later, he bagged a grand ram with it, too. Ralph Kitchen and I collected a photo-perfect dark Stone ram in Toad River geography in far north BC, too. Kitchen went off to the university to chase down an engineering degree, last word. Canada holds a handful of other little-known, unheralded guides

I've hunted with, too. I hope they're thriving, and once in a while, remember our hunts together.

I hunted four times with Russian Far East guide Vladimir Plaschenko. We'd bagged snow sheep rams, including a 40-incher, passed up others, and hunted bear. During the off-season, Vladimir trapped fur and fished the salmon runs, and sometimes panned for gold—a true *taigachik*. The first time we hunted together, in the early '90s, we chased snow sheep far to the west of Okhotsk Village. Plaschenko was a meat hunter, had no experience with trophy hunters, but what he lacked in finesse, he made up for in tough. Once he figured out I wouldn't shoot any but a King Kong ram, that you shouldn't skyline on a ridge, and that I could trek with anyone, we got along fine. Six days into the hunt, we spotted a band of rams a mile off on a piney ridge. We made a two-mile circuit to get downwind, and cat-walked a mile down the ridge toward where we hoped the rams still bedded in pine scrub. Vladimir motioned me on without him; one always stalks quieter than two. After an hour of snaking from snag to pine tree, I spotted horns above the pine scrub. Then another set, and another. One sent my pulse off like a conga drum. I still couldn't see a hair, so I slinked closer, and closer still, until I edged to a snag 25 yards away. I put a 7mm/08 slug behind the shoulder and had my best of a handful of trophy snow sheep trophies. We quartered and caped the ram, then clawed through larch and pine tangles into the gorge then finger-and-toed up the other side to camp. Half way down, Vladimir emptied his rubber boot, no laces, into the creek when he thought I wasn't looking. It turned the creek bloody. The next morning, I suggested he kick back and let his feet mend. When Olga Parfenova, our translator echoed it, he turned crimson and swore he'd rather be boiled in bear grease, to be polite. One tough guy. I could go on about our exploits, but I already have in at least one of my books and several magazine articles.

Talk about tough. In winter 2009, I booked a hunt with Orhan Konakci's Safari Tours. I'd hunted with Orhan's outfit before and had bagged three trophies, two of them top-ten class (though I've yet to list them). Orhan fixed me up with veteran guide Hasan and we hunted Bezoar ibex in the Aladaglar Range of central Anatolia. To shorten the story, Hasan and I stalked while my better half Cheri and the park ranger watched through binocs. One shot killed a 48-inch ibex, but the story gets better. That ibex dropped on a wind-blown south-facing slope that plummeted a thousand feet to the snowy bottoms. One misstep, and you wouldn't pull up until you splashed into the creek a lump of raw hamburger.

Now, I'd done some mountain hunting in my decades, but it wouldn't occur to me to do what Hasan did. He tied the billy's legs on one side together, did the same to the other side, slipped his arms through the "straps" the legs made, and hefted the ibex on his back, guts and all. He grunted the goat all the way to the bottoms. If he'd slipped once, he wouldn't have quit bouncing until the creek. Then we dragged the ibex four miles to the Nissan mired in mud and snow.

In Tajikistan, Yuri Matison outfits and guides. He's famous, too (just check the record books). But I've got to mention him and his guys anyway, because they helped me score my favorite mountain trophy—a 62 ½ by 17-inch Marco Polo argali in the gales of December. We hunted in twenty-below temps and winds that would scalp a yak. Old-timer Pamiri guide Toktomat trekked 16,000 foot cols with Yuri, our second guide Dovelat, Cheri and me. We bagged a grand ibex, too, whether of the Himalayan variety or the mid-Asian is open to question, since we bagged him where the two boundaries met. Given the complicated and primitive logistics, the late season and extreme weather, the hunt couldn't have gone better.

In much of Asia, a translator/professional hunter keeps the hunt purring like a Porsche. That's the idea, anyway. Erdogan Avci accompanied my party of three hunters and two observers from Istanbul to Baku, Azerbaijan, and from there deep into the eastern Caucasus. We hunted with local goat farmer Arif and his four sons. The Soviets tagged a price on the rebel Arif's head during their regime, and to further irk the communists, he became a famed poacher. We all collected Dagestan tur, and Erdogan taped my largest a millimeter off 40-inches. Arif, at 65, scaled the steepest geography on the planet with the best of us, and despite living as a good Muslim, toasted us at his humble abode with cold beer on our way out. As the village elder, he farms, makes life hell if his sons get out of line, and advises the locals during the off-season. Check the record books for Erdogan's achievements, and he books his own hunts when he's not out chasing down the planet's top trophies, too. Orhan Konakci arranged this hunt, though.

Turkoman guide Jumaa led us to a handful of the biggest kind of Trans-Caspian urial. We hunted the winter of 2004-2005. Our hunt was one of the last, if not the last, for the species before Turkmenistan stopped hunting. We closed on four magnum rams the first morning, but I try never to shoot on the first day, to drag the hunt out. One looked near 38-inches, but by the time I'd thought it over, he was out of range anyway. I spent a sleepless night staring out the shack window at the Badkhyz stars.

Jumaa led us to a herd of 65 sheep the next dawn containing three trophy rams. One had a close curling, full-curl set of horns I had to collect, whatever they measured. Jumaa did the math, tested the wind swirling out of Afghanistan, and we circled to head them off. As planned, they crossed the ridge bleating and belching, and I shot the ram at 60-yards. Jumaa was a real gentleman, soft-spoken, modest, and when he said something, you believed him. I wonder what he does now. To give credit, Vance Corrigan's Hunting Consultants arranged and Vladimir Treshchov outfitted this hunt. I could mention a score of other fine Asian guides, too, but space forbids it.

When home-bound, my favorite thing, bar none, is to retreat to my own clean, well-lighted place and ogle my trophies. Each trophy mount jogs memories, but I don't remember the guy that grabbed my check, or the outfitter that fielded question-laden emails and letters, though they're part of it, too. Instead, I see Herbie bobbing in that way that told you he was fast asleep astride his saddle nag plodding toward camp while moonlight danced on Crooked Lake. I glance at that 40-inch tur and remember Arif, his hospitality and acceptance, and that cold beer after a week in wilting August Caspian Sea winds. I recall Yuri, Taktamat and Dovelat posing with my grand Marco Polo ram in gales cold and fierce enough to freeze ears in minutes, and I envision Luya and Zorig on two Mongolian expeditions that netted 5 different trophies. Here's to all those little-known, unheralded guides that helped put the fur on the ground.

Printed in the USA
CPSIA information can be obtained
at www.ICGtesting.com
LVHW050850110124
768548LV00049B/1432/J